ISAIAH DECODED

ISAIAH DECODED

Ascending the
Ladder to Heaven

AVRAHAM GILEADI

Hebraeus Press

Isaiah Decoded: Ascending the Ladder to Heaven

© Copyright 2002, 2013 by Hebraeus Press

www.IsaiahExplained.com

All rights Reserved

Published in the United States of America

Second Edition, Second Printing, 2018

Softcover ISBN 978-0-910511-06-3

E-Book ISBN 978-0-910511-21-7

Remembering all who have perished
through the oppression of others, for whom
"there was no *man*," for whom "there was no *intercessor*"
—Isaiah 59:16; emphasis added.

Contents

FIGURES

PREFACE

People have long wondered why this best-known prophecy in the Bible seems so obscure or what relevance, if any, it has for them. Could the Book of Isaiah have meaning for today? If so, why its puzzling language and jumping from one context to another without any apparent time frame? Was the prophet lacking in literary skills or was there a hidden method in this madness? A document comparable in structure is the Copper Scroll among the Dead Sea Scrolls, whose parts appear so scrambled that many scholars dismiss it as nonsensical. Shouldn't a revealed Word of God like the Book of Isaiah be more intelligible than that? Shouldn't it make things clearer and synchronize with other inspired writings?

By giving the ancients the benefit of the doubt, however, we may yet find treasures in their writings that we had no idea existed. I would like to suggest that the Book of Isaiah is a far more sophisticated document than we could have supposed, that the difficulties we encounter are the very things that hold the key to understanding it once we figure out the mechanics of its composition. Getting into the Hebrew mindset and unveiling some of the book's mysteries may indeed turn the key that opens our understanding to *all* scriptures, before and after Isaiah.

A problem many scholars face is that they spend years researching and publishing things nobody sees except the academic community among which they publish. My life's work in scriptural analysis, for example—*The Literary Message of Isaiah*—although considered by leading American scholars to be a major breakthrough and at the cutting edge of Bible studies, is published in a scholarly style that is sometimes difficult for the lay person to wade through.

This book—*Isaiah Decoded*—while for the most part based on literary evidence set forth in *The Literary Message of Isaiah*, thus attempts to put into plain terms a complex but amazing message by a prophet-poet of extraordinary talent. I believe no one else comes close to Isaiah in conveying a message so relevant to the times in which we live and to our divine destiny as children of God.

Avraham Gileadi, 2002

The interval of eleven years that has elapsed between the first and second editions of *Isaiah Decoded* have seen worldwide changes that make it even more imperative to understand Isaiah's message if we would not be swept away by forces beyond our control. As people's confidence wanes, world economies collapse, natural disasters increase, wars threaten, hostile world powers make a comeback, and covert factions seek to overthrow the freedom of all lands, the prophet Isaiah stands out as the most lucid descriptor of our time. We may therefore do well to pay the small price of learning Isaiah's encoded message as he reveals God's word that has been held in reserve to come forth in this very day and age.

Avraham Gileadi, 2013

INTRODUCTION

When Pilate asked Jesus "What is truth?" (John 18:38), he didn't wait for an answer. As with many people then and probably most people now, truth wasn't central to Pilate's thoughts although it still affected everything he did. In that moment, if he had possessed the power to discern the truth and had not condemned Jesus, the course of history could have been changed.

Like Jesus, a lot of prophets were put to death for testifying of the truth. What is it about the truth that so provokes a society that it starts killing people? My answer is that a *particular* truth caused this violent reaction—for Jesus and the prophets alike. It wasn't just the everyday little truths that teach you to be good. Rather, the truth of which Jesus and the prophets testified ran completely counter to the teachings of the day—religious teachings, that is.

People get fanatical over religion. When evils in society cause the lights to go out, religion inevitably changes into a skewed version of the truth it once promoted. Its perception of God becomes virtually that of a false god, and people unaware of this mutation are offended by the real thing.

It intrigues me—after thirty years as a layman and thirty as a Bible scholar—how differently believers in God respond to the same truth. What makes some reject it altogether, while others assume salvation is theirs, although their idea of the truth may be mistaken or incomplete? What makes the great religions of

Judaism, Christianity, and Islam view the same Word of God through different lenses, dividing the world into sects?

And if the truth is, in fact, being taught today, why isn't anyone killing prophets for it now? As a literary analyst of the Hebrew Bible, I am sure I don't have all the answers to such questions. However, some things I have discovered may add a fresh perspective.

I confess it was only after I looked *outside* of centuries-old traditions that I obtained new insights into the truth about God, which I quickly realized were actually old insights waiting to be rediscovered. Not that I didn't give traditional religion my best effort or that it didn't teach me valuable lessons. But when I unlearned limiting my viewpoint to a fixed set of beliefs, when I opened my mind to all the possibilities the Word of God could contain, then scriptural insights came so fast I had to completely reevaluate what I had learned before. As I discovered literary devices the prophets were using, I realized they had hidden secrets in their writings that demand such a rethinking from all of us.

I also realized it wasn't so much that people read the same Word of God differently, but that many weren't reading it at all—not the scripture itself—at least not in a manner that allowed them to fit every piece of it into one cohesive panorama of the truth. Instead, people were reading materials their religions published for study. Often these were selective—preserving some threads of the truth while excluding others—so that the *total* picture was so incomplete it constituted a distortion.

I found, too, that the more truth you discover, the more your knowledge of the truth keeps widening exponentially. That can be scary. As what I had started to learn turned many of my former beliefs upside down, I was tempted to call off my quest to learn more and to stay on a comfortable level with its own limited understanding, realizing that people and institutions alike had become satisfied with doing just that.

But I also knew the danger of saying "enough." I had seen such self-sufficiency acted out in the lives of people who practice a kind of religion that lacks substance. Instead, my viewpoint became the opposite of one who thinks he knows all there is to know about religion, that there is nothing more to interest him because he has it all figured out. What I have written here, therefore, is open to the continued unfolding of the truth and, if necessary, to correction.

We may sometimes lay aside ancient prophets' writings because modern technology, with its instant access to information, persuades us we are so much more advanced than they. But there is a danger in that, as our "advanced" knowledge of earthly things can be the very thing that clouds our knowledge of heavenly things. Our focus on the physical may blind us to what is spiritual—not that the two are mutually exclusive, not at all. Isaiah, for instance, speaks of the earth's "sphere" and of an expanding cosmos, although not long ago people still believed that the earth was flat.

Another problem is that the truth isn't easily discovered, forcing us to exert ourselves to find it. Consider how long it takes the scientific world to make a breakthrough in human health, while diseases continue to destroy countless lives. Can we suppose that isn't the rule for *all* truth? We must exercise care, because if we presume to know something then that in itself can prevent us from knowing more—lesser truths can become a trap.

Also, to believe something isn't the same thing as knowing it. We may *believe* whatever we want, whether it is true or false. But we can't *know* something unless it is true. Because each of us has the God-given ability to determine truth from error, we have a personal responsibility to do so. We speak of the "light of truth" because it has the capacity to guide and enlighten us until we know for ourselves whether something is true.

As this learning process is built into our very existence, that teaches us an important thing about ourselves: for each of us life is a personal journey in which we can advance at whatever pace we want toward a more intelligent condition than we started from. And if we become more intelligent, then we become more useful, influential, and powerful in the service of the very truth that makes us so. Because life is so configured that we grow from processing through truth and error, that means life itself is a test of how far we can advance.

When Jesus said "The truth will make you free," he implied that the more truth is in us, the more we are our own agents. By living the truth—by living the laws of God that are grounded in the truth—we become increasingly independent. The opposite is also true: the more we live a lie, the more we are bound by lies and become less free. Because God is the source of truth, he is also the source of freedom—not the freedom to do as we want but to live the truth, which makes us free. We thus become acquainted with the "power of truth."

For most of us, our spiritual side has barely been tapped. We haven't asked the right questions but have simply assumed that things are so. We haven't lived the truth we could have lived and so we are still less than what we can be. Our lives are very much a "work in progress," as we learn by trial and error to "get it right."

When it is over, our time here on earth will undoubtedly seem more like an incubation than a full-fledged flight. And when we reach the end, we will surely find it is only a rest stop on a much longer journey than we could have anticipated. But my guess is, it won't be long before we will want to continue on to the next phase as we view the prospect of even greater growth. Instead of languishing endlessly in some static state we call heaven, we will want to rise higher on the "wings of truth."

What I present in this book, therefore—which I have arrived at using different methods of analysis that converge on the same truth—is one level of understanding a single work of prophecy: the Book of Isaiah. Although I am sharing these insights with you, I will understand if you treat them as fiction. Compared to today's well-worn interpretations, some of these views may seem radical indeed. But I have found them easier to support with hard textual evidence. Governing structures, literary patterns, ministructures, typologies, word links, codenames, key words, and so forth uncover levels of meaning you may not have heard from a rabbi, preacher, or college professor, although they are true.

While my approach has been academic, the truths I present here for the layperson, which are distilled from analyzing the writings of Isaiah, are far from academic—I consider them life giving. I invite you, the reader, to put them to the test, to see if they aren't enlightening, empowering, and freeing to your spirit for that flight to heaven which God has invited every one of us to make.

1

THE LADDER TO HEAVEN

Jewish tradition has it that God revealed the law to Moses in a stream of consecutive letters, which Moses then dissected into words. When he found the people of Israel worshiping a golden calf, Moses broke the stone tablets that contained God's "higher law." In its place Israel received a "lesser law." During their centuries-long sojourn in the pagan culture of Egypt, the Israelites had lost touch with the God who had created the heavens and the earth, the God of their ancestors, Abraham, Isaac, and Jacob. Like the heathen nations, they mistook the true character of God. So God gave Israel an *interim law* or stepping-stone to the higher law. By keeping the one they could prepare to receive the other.

Yet, the image of Moses at Mount Sinai breaking the tablets written by the finger of God was deeply imprinted in the national memory. The lesser law, known as the Law of Moses, didn't satisfy some people. They believed the higher law somehow still existed in the writings of Moses. They reasoned that the words we read from Genesis through Deuteronomy were hiding another message beneath the surface, although it wasn't clear how. To obtain the higher law, some surmised, all they had to do was discover the key to deciphering what was already hidden there. If they could find it, keeping the higher law would then bring them greater blessings or powers from God similar to those of Moses.

The problem was that no one could figure out how to unlock these hidden features of Moses' writings. For centuries, Jewish kabbalists—people who study the secrets of Hebrew law—tried to decode Moses' writings to retrieve the "original." By running the letters back together again and then redissecting them, kabbalists hoped to recover the higher law. By substituting some letters for others, they sought to hit upon the key to a kind of mystical formula. They never succeeded. They nonetheless discovered geometric patterns in Moses' books that contained clues to the existence of encrypted data. Whether such encryptions will ultimately lead to the discovery of the "higher law" remains in dispute.

Today, using high-tech computers, proponents of the "Bible Code" have deciphered subliminal content encoded throughout the Old Testament. But even these modern-day "kabbalists" haven't come up with anything resembling a higher law. What they have found are individual Hebrew words made up of letters that occur at exact numbers of digits apart. For instance, the name "Jesus" (ישוע, "Yeshua") appears encrypted in passages that seem to confirm Jesus' role of Savior. In the following examples, encryptions of his name intersect with depictions of (1) the bronze serpent Moses made as a Messiah symbol, and (2) Jehovah's role as the Savior of his people Israel who look to him (see Figure 1).

Many Christians would point to the New Testament as the answer to the higher law: Jesus "fulfilled the Law of Moses" so it may seem that accepting him as one's Savior is all that is necessary. But is such a simple interpretation of Jesus' teachings really a higher law? How does it differ, for example, from a Jew accepting Jehovah or a Moslem accepting Allah, each looking to God as the source of salvation, especially if they are the *same* God? Reducing the New Testament to a single idea doesn't do justice to its total message. There is a danger in making an incomplete idea into the whole. Looking at things realistically, does accepting Jesus make the difference, or is it also living his teachings?

Figure 1 Encryptions of the Name of Jesus in the Old Testament

ויעש משה נחש נחשת וישמהו על-הנס

והיה אם-נשך הנחש את-איש

והיט אל-נח**ש** הנחשת ו**חי**

ויס**עו** כני ישראל ויחנו כאכת

So Moses made a bronze serpent and put it on a pole.
And it happened that when a serpent bit anyone,
if he looked at the bronze serpent, he lived.
So the Israelites traveled on and camped at Oboth.

(Numbers 21:9–10)

(The encrypted name ישוע, "Yeshua," appears in the italicized lines six digits apart.)

אנכי אנכי יהוה ואין מבלעדי מושיע

אני הגדת**י** והו**ש**עתי וה**ש**מ**ע**תי

ואין בכם זר

ואתם עדי נאם-יהוה ואני-אל

I myself am Jehovah; apart from me there is no savior.
It is I who foretold and wrought salvation, making it known
when there was no strange [god] among you. "You are my witnesses," says Jehovah, "that I am God."

(Isaiah 43:11–12)

(The encrypted name ישוע, "Yeshua," appears in the italicized line four digits apart.)

As we take Jesus' words to the lawyer seriously, we must assume that the *whole* law of God—the higher and the lesser— is contained in the two commandments, "You will love the Lord your God with all your heart, and with all your soul, and with all your mind. . . . You will love your neighbor as yourself" (Matthew 22:37, 39). Still, putting that law into practice differs dramatically from the lesser to the higher. Much of the Law of Moses, for example, deals with what *not* to do, with repenting of wrongdoing and with rituals that symbolically represent God's redemption of his people. Jesus, on the other hand, adds a new dimension to the word "love," showing us how to love God and neighbor.

Living a Higher Law Leads into God's Presence

The prophet Malachi identifies "righteous" people in God's Day of Judgment not as those who profess a particular creed or repeat religious slogans but as those who "serve God," while the "wicked" are those who "don't serve him" (Malachi 3:18). Noah wasn't *born* "a righteous man, perfect in his generation," but he became this by loving and serving God (Genesis 6:9). God directed Abraham to attain the same perfection (Genesis 17:1). Those who knew God anciently didn't know him all at once, but God revealed himself to them to the degree that they sought him. As it was in the past so it is in the future: "You will seek me and find [me] when you seek me with all your heart" (Jeremiah 29:13).

Living a higher law, then, may not mean just more or greater blessings from God. It could be the path that literally brings us into God's presence, enabling us to interact directly with God. We see in the Bible that specifics of this higher law were the privilege of prophets and others to whom God appeared and gave instructions. It makes sense that much of the time such a law would follow a personalized script, not written down but rather revealed by God through his holy Spirit. Thus, Abraham didn't see God until he had acted on faith and followed God's word to him personally (Genesis 12:1–7). Moses didn't see God until he had valiantly defended the rights of the oppressed (Exodus 2:11–3:6).

We often pass by the *Old* Testament as if it doesn't relate to us, as if its "sacred history" is no longer sacred. And yet, who today can match the spiritual heights those ancients attained? The law they kept went beyond not sinning. Their lives were models of love and service. In comparison to the higher law, the lesser law centers around becoming clean of sin and spiritually pure. The higher law puts us on a path to attaining perfection by loving others as God loves us, so that we can enjoy the company of God and angels (see Figure 2). Those who loved God and neighbor so as to attain this perfection also truly loved themselves, as we do justice to ourselves only when we love God first and foremost.

Figure 2   **Difference between the Higher and Lesser Law**

The Higher Law—Attaining Perfection

The Lesser Law—Overcoming Sin

The fact that Israel's God Jehovah met with people anciently shows that a higher law existed *before* New Testament times. Keeping that law led to the extraordinary blessings those persons received, as God called them to be patriarchs, prophets, and kings to his people. Some of those "men of God" wrote down the things God revealed in words and visions, which became the Bible. Like Moses, they may have hidden in their writings things they considered sacred or ahead of their time—knowing that people exposed to the higher law who rejected it would come under condemnation. But to their disciples, and to all willing to search their writings for deeper meanings, they left a profound spiritual legacy.

We should not be fooled by the fact that the individuality of illustrious Old Testament figures and their diverse personalities have been succeeded by today's *group psyche*. Our different religious and cultural denominations cultivate stereotypes that tell us we must believe and perform the same sorts of things. Clearly, those personalities from millennia past were beloved of God and were privileged to see and know more about God and angels than many of us can comprehend. That isn't because we are inferior but because we consider ourselves superior, though we have little to show for ourselves by comparison. If we allow those men of God to speak to us there might be a lot we can learn.

One who thus instructs us is the prophet Isaiah, although it wasn't until the 1950s when the Dead Sea Scrolls came to light that his scroll seemed unlike others. This profound book of prophecy had puzzled scholars. They were stumped over its passages, disputing who wrote the words and what they meant. Because it contained different kinds of writing, covering several time periods (see Figure 3), scholars concluded one author could not have written the entire book. Although some had seen poetic patterns such as Coronation Hymns, Messenger Speeches, and Songs of Salvation, they hadn't discerned its structuring into one integrated whole; nor had they perceived what that might mean.

Figure 3   **Composition of the Book of Isaiah**

Oracles and Narratives   Written Discourses

(chapters 1–39)   (chapters 40–66)

Yet, the Book of Isaiah may fulfill the deepest expectations of those who seek the higher law. Whether in the future people will "crack the code" of the Law of Moses or whether it actually contains an encrypted higher law remain big questions. But the idea of deciphering messages hidden beneath a surface reading of a prophet's words, of living a lesser law in order to receive a higher one, and of determining what that higher law is—these are all things we indeed find in the Book of Isaiah. Kabbalists were right in assuming that the writings of the prophets contain more than just the lesser law. But would its discovery really depend on modern computers or was that looking beyond the mark?

From God's past dealings with peoples and with individuals, there seems no need to resort to extremes to discover deeper truths. The ancients had no high-tech instruments, yet they saw God, conversed with him, and were blessed. On the other hand, can we possibly assume that a higher law would be easier to keep than a lesser one—that all God requires of us is to accept a prescribed set of beliefs and attend religious services on the Sabbath? Was that how the ancients came to know God and receive promises of land and posterity, thrones and dominions, and divine protection at the threat of death? Of course, seeking was essential to finding, but would it be *that* simple, or could it be *that* complex?

The mystery Isaiah conceals and reveals is the knowledge of God.

As Isaiah teaches it, the higher law is nothing but an expression of God's love in its purest form, revealing God's design and desire to lift us up. Isaiah's message involves far more than salvation from sin, from the effects of evil, or from death itself, although that is a key theme in his book. At the center of Isaiah's prophecy, for all who have "eyes to see and ears to hear," we discover God's eternal plan to *exalt* his children. The whole purpose of life—of the creation, of our dwelling on this earth, and of God's covenant with the people of Israel—revolves around Isaiah's theme of exaltation. However, he has us search for his message by decoding not encryptions but the literary devices of his day.

Christians may appreciate that Isaiah anticipates the teachings of Jesus, presenting us with a preview of the "good news" that places the New Testament in a new light. Although he lived 700 years before Jesus, sometimes we forget that he and others of his day were *prophets* who knew things only God could disclose, including the higher law. In defining a connection between the Book of Isaiah and the New Testament, we might say that one is a second witness of the other. Perhaps, to our surprise, Isaiah maps out a kind of spiritual genetic code, a blueprint of a perfect son or daughter of God to whom heaven is "home." The mystery he conceals and reveals in his book is the knowledge of God.

As if to prove that point, Isaiah also predicts a future world scenario whose fulfillment will be evidence to all that God is real and that he revealed the truth to Isaiah. That scenario, sooner or later, will involve everyone then living on the earth. When we see his prophecies come to pass, it will be a sign that *all* of Isaiah's teachings—his message of the future and the higher law—are true. God will validate Isaiah's words, fulfilling what Isaiah has prophesied to the end of time (Isaiah 44:26; 45:21; 46:10; 55:10–11). Isaiah interweaves predictions of the end of the world with teachings of the higher law, giving both a special meaning in an endtime context: at that time, both will be realized together.

The Dead Sea Scroll of Isaiah Contains a Clue

I became fascinated thirty-five years ago by Professor William Brownlee's exploration of peculiarities in the Dead Sea Scroll of Isaiah. Brownlee discovered a seven-part division of the book in two parallel blocks of chapters (see Figure 4). Aligning the chapters in this way revealed information no one had guessed at. In Brownlee's day scholars had barely determined that biblical books even had literary structures. By "literary structure" I mean the way a book divides into parts, each reflecting an idea or set of ideas that the writer develops, tying in to other ideas in other parts of his book. As literary analysis was in its infancy, the significance of Brownlee's discovery was mostly passed over.

Figure 4   **The Seven-Part Division of the Book of Isaiah**

Isaiah 1–33   Isaiah 34–66

1a—2a—3a—4a—5a—6a—7a   1b—2b—3b—4b—5b—6b—7b

My mentor, Professor Roland K. Harrison, a colleague of Brownlee's, suggested I examine this seven-part division of Isaiah's scroll for my doctoral thesis. Although Brownlee discovered its existence, he left it up to others to analyze. Some believed it was merely a mechanical way of organizing the material, not realizing that a literary structure could convey a prophetic message all its own. When I investigated this structure, Isaiah's scroll seemed suddenly not just an antique document describing obscure events in Israel's remote past, which is what many people think when reading the Bible, but it also detailed an entirely modern chapter of history, one that could easily come to pass in our day.

Although Isaiah's writings were ancient, they appeared to express thoughts that were somehow modern and familiar. The chasm of human history separating our day from Isaiah's was also a "chiasm," mirroring two time periods that parallel each other, two separate scenarios that strangely resemble each other (see Figure 5). Thus, what appears to be old is also new, and what appears to be new is also old. Whether then or now, the actors perform their parts according to archetypal patterns. From the way Isaiah presents these patterns we can learn how to interact with God. Isaiah shows how God enables a person to attain perfection, to align one's life with God's timeless code—to attain heaven itself.

Figure 5   **A Chiasm of Human History**

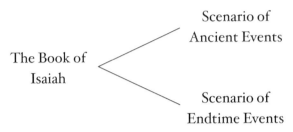

It became apparent that the Book of Isaiah was a highly organized literary creation; each piece of its puzzle served a purpose essential to the whole. I found that the Seven-Part Structure was only one of several layered structures in the book, though I consider it the most significant. By unscrambling these literary devices, one could decipher Isaiah's encoded message of a higher law and of the earth's future destiny. That message was just as real and compelling as what we read on the surface. In other words, Isaiah revealed some things through words and other things through structures. These different elements were so closely interwoven, however, that his message could be unraveled only as a whole.

It may be a stretch for most moderns to believe a person living so long ago could predict the future in such detail. Those who have known time travel in a Near-Death Experience may have a better idea of this than the rest of us. Yet, God showed Isaiah many things about this earth, by no means all of them local events. That is the only way Isaiah could have spelled out the end from the beginning, writing it down ahead of time. Clearly, God has a purpose for his creation and knows how everything will turn out, even given the variables of everyone exercising free will. That being so, is it strange that a loving God would give those who were willing to receive it a perfect pattern of life from the start?

But let's begin at the beginning. Do you remember Jacob's "ladder" reaching from earth to heaven on which angels ministered up and down? Jacob called it the "gate of heaven," with Jehovah visible at the top (Genesis 28:12–17). Around that idea, Isaiah builds a *theology*—a way we define humanity's relationship to God. In other words, what is God's role toward us and ours toward him? Isaiah's theology embraces all people born on the earth, no matter how good or evil they turn out to be. In the process, Isaiah describes different ways of living that people choose for themselves, some drawing them nearer to God, others distancing them from him. Each *way* has a place on the ladder to heaven.

Where we find ourselves in this divine scheme depends on us, on what law we live—a higher or lesser law. When we discern the different levels represented on the ladder, we can learn a great deal about ourselves by asking, How does my life fit with this picture? Probably most of us would like to know more about where we stand with God. We have questions such as, How did I get where I am, and where am I going? Or, more to the point, Where do I *want* to go? In addressing such questions, Isaiah eliminates the need for a lot of speculation about ourselves. He shows us the ladder to heaven and we answer our own questions. Most importantly, Isaiah teaches us how to get through heaven's "gate."

Humanity Divides into Seven Spiritual Categories

I found that Isaiah's Seven-Part Structure contains seven pairs of themes, each theme with its opposite, which express ways we interact with God. They are (1) "ruin" and "rebirth"; (2) "rebellion" and "compliance"; (3) "punishment" and "deliverance"; (4) "humiliation" and "exaltation"; (5) "suffering" and "salvation"; (6) "disloyalty" and "loyalty"; (7) "disinheritance" and "inheritance." Isaiah develops his theology by organizing his writings around these seven pairs of themes. Isaiah thus uses New Testament themes, such as "salvation" and "exaltation" (or "glory"), but not as isolated ideas. He presents them within a holistic framework (see Figure 6) that develops the idea of a ladder to heaven.

Figure 6   **Isaiah's Seven-Part Structure**

Ruin and Rebirth
(Isaiah 1–5; 34–35)

Rebellion and Compliance
(Isaiah 6–8; 36–40)

Punishment and Deliverance
(Isaiah 9–12; 41–46)

Humiliation and *Exaltation*
(Isaiah 13–23; 47)

Suffering and *Salvation*
(Isaiah 24–27; 48–54)

Disloyalty and Loyalty
(Isaiah 28–31; 55–59)

Disinheritance and Inheritance
(Isaiah 32–33; 60–66)

You will notice, in parenthesis, that the seven pairs of opposite themes prominent in Isaiah 1–33 are also the themes of Isaiah 34–66—the book's two halves parallel each other. The only difference between them is that Isaiah develops ideas from the first half to the second. For example, Isaiah 1–5 establishes the concepts of "ruin" and "rebirth," which are developed further in Isaiah 34–35. They, in turn, become a starting point for Isaiah 6–8, which, *in addition*, establishes its own concepts of "rebellion" and "compliance" that are developed further in Isaiah 36–40; and so forth, until all ends in Isaiah 60–66 (see Figure 7). Through such means Isaiah reveals a plethora of mysteries or hidden truths.

Figure 7   **A Seven-Part Development of Ideas**

1a—1b, 2a—2b, 3a—3b, 4a—4b, 5a—5b, 6a—6b, 7a—7b

By organizing his writings into this arrangement, Isaiah initiates us into many prophetic and theological wonders—into the higher law of God. On a basic level, we learn that "salvation" means deliverance from evil. However, we observe differences in spiritual growth as some people experience salvation while others don't. Some make covenants with God while others don't. Many are blessed while others are cursed. Many live to see God and have their hopes fulfilled, while others know "suffering" and die in torment. Things aren't simplistic so that everyone fits in just two categories. There are distinctions within each set of choices: some people are *more* blessed, or *more* cursed, than others.

A ladder to heaven appears when we recognize these categories of people as an ascending order, from the lowest or farthest from God to the highest or most like him. The different rungs on the ladder represent spiritual levels on which persons operate. Isaiah identifies seven of these, including God's level at the top. Isaiah's themes express the conditions God has prescribed under which people ascend or descend from one level to the next. Lower rungs on the ladder represent inferior or disagreeable conditions from which one may be saved. Although all categories are fixed or permanent, people can move up or down through them as they decide—when they do what is required to ascend or descend.

Every person fits somewhere in this divine scheme of things. We ourselves determine our place before God by what choices we make—by what spiritual law we live or fail to live. Isaiah's themes deal with what happens when people ascend or descend the ladder. His concept of "salvation," for example, is by nature both spiritual and physical, not just one or the other. A person qualifies for *physical* "deliverance" by fulfilling *spiritual* requirements. "Exaltation," on the other hand, pertains to the highest rungs on the ladder. We qualify for heaven when we enter God's presence. Some people attain that state in this life; while still living on the earth, they see God. Others fail to do so even after death.

> By its very nature, "salvation" is both spiritual and physical.

Before exploring Isaiah's ladder further, we should note that, in spite of parallels with the "corporate ladder" of the business world, in reality the two are worlds apart. In many ways one is a warped imitation of the other, giving the sense of upward mobility that comes with ascent on the ladder, but not itself leading to God. Rather, the corporate ladder may consume us to the same degree the spiritual ladder does but leave us instead with a substitute "heaven" that in time evaporates, robbing us of the heaven of eternity we were born to inherit. A big part of life's test lies in what we love and worship—God or idols like success and money. The bottom line is, are we self-serving or do we serve God?

Whether we finally reach the goal of seeing God depends largely on us, on our desire and determination. Isaiah knew Israel's religion wasn't limited to a few privileged groups such as the Hebrew patriarchs Abraham, Isaac, and Jacob; Moses and the ancient Israelites; or King Hezekiah and the Jews of his day—many of whom saw God. Anyone can inherit Abraham's blessings by being loyal to God as Abraham was. God can call other prophets to do what Moses did if their commitment to God equals that of Moses. Others besides Hezekiah can cause

God to deliver his people when their lives are threatened if they pay the price Hezekiah paid. Isaiah develops these ideas in his Seven-Part Structure.

In short, Isaiah's message is that true religion—the higher law—encourages us to strive for the same blessings God gave to those who came before. On Isaiah's ladder, persons who served God's people in the past become role models who show the rest of us how to attain greater levels of blessedness. When Isaiah mentions anyone by name, such as Abraham, Moses, or Hezekiah, it is because that person is an example of something we can learn to live up to (see Figure 8). Events repeat themselves in the lives of individuals just as they do in the lives of God's people. We may ask if being a member of a church, synagogue, or mosque alone will lead to our meeting God. Or does God ask more of us?

Figure 8   **Some Persons Named as Role Models**

Abraham—Obeyed God in All Things

Moses—Delivered His People from Bondage

Hezekiah—Interceded for His People's Deliverance

As God is the same yesterday, today, and forever and is "no respecter of persons," he does not favor any one of us above another. Only as we love him above all else—when we do what he desires and become like him—do we finally see God. And what does God want of us? The very things that will get us up the ladder, that lead to *our* eternal happiness. According to Isaiah, we can trust implicitly in that idea as a universal principle because God backs it up. In the very act of giving up our own will in order to do God's will, we achieve our highest goal. There exists no other way to attain heaven. Like a real-life fairytale, to "live happily ever after" is what our lives on this earth are all about.

In the sublime plan that Isaiah reveals, when we please God we help ourselves at the same time. God designs our circumstances in life to facilitate our climb up the ladder. When we align our lives with God, we take full advantage of what life offers us, including the hard things. Every person Isaiah describes, himself included, experiences just that—a personal set of circumstances and challenges. During the whole process, God reveals himself as a willing friend to aid us along life's path. People on low spiritual levels may forget him but he never forgets them. There is no pressure: we ourselves decide whether we will ascend or descend. As the old proverb says, "God will force no one to heaven."

Isaiah Presents Models on Each Level of the Ladder

The Book of Isaiah portrays many kinds of people who performed various political and religious roles in antiquity. From the lives of these biblical personalities—from recognizing what law they kept—we learn how to ascend the ladder. Isaiah describes people in his book for the very purpose of illustrating higher and lower spiritual categories. Seeing what they do gives us an idea of what people on each level do. Even the worst persons have something to teach us: how to avoid making the mistakes they made—what *not* to do. Isaiah's ladder accommodates every class of character, from the noblest to the basest. Everyone fulfills a part that is necessary for the process of ascent on the ladder to work.

As on Jacob's ladder, Jehovah, the God of Israel—the creator of heaven and earth—stands at the top. But he is not an aloof God who disregards those beneath him. Instead, he serves those below as Savior and Exemplar. He is wholly committed to furthering and facilitating our eternal happiness. Directly below him are those whom he lifts or exalts above others. Although all of us at some point start on the same footing, because of their greater "loyalty" to God and "compliance" with his will (two key themes of Isaiah) some grow more like him than others. Having moved beyond living the lesser law, they serve others as God has served them. Thus, the more godlike we become, the higher we ascend.

The only way to attain heaven—to experience "salvation" *and* "exaltation"—is to meet these requirements. Money cannot buy it, nor can worldly influence decide it. God puts people in relationships with each other so they can grow and attain their full stature. God never abandons us; when we feel he has, we may not be seeing how human relationships are gifts from God to help bring us to him. On the other hand, if we think we have made it, it is a sure sign we are losing our way. God asks each of us to love and be loved, to give and receive, to reach out and be reached. Isaiah's ladder to heaven is a ministering model that embraces everyone, in which each of us discovers he or she is important.

As on Jacob's ladder, God calls those above to minister to those below. At the same time, they themselves are ministered to by someone above them; and so forth up and down the ladder. In this divine game plan everyone performs. For example, Jehovah ministers to Isaiah, and Isaiah ministers to King Hezekiah. Hezekiah ministers to his servants, and the servants minister to the people. Because heaven and earth overlap spiritually, the same pattern applies to both. Those who occupy upper levels on the ladder fulfill angelic functions—as Isaiah himself does in the latter part of his life. The higher that people ascend, and the more effective their ministry, the more like "angels" they become (see Figure 9).

At the base of the ladder is the king of Assyria/Babylon. Isaiah depicts him as an archtyrant who conquers and destroys much of the ancient world. When most of the earth's inhabitants—including many of God's people—transgress against God's law and word, God raises up this enemy of humanity to destroy the wicked who won't repent. People on the lowest rungs of the ladder follow the archtyrant's example of despotism. The more we resemble this evil ruler, the lower we descend. At any time, all of us without exception are moving up or down the ladder. Just as Jehovah serves as a model of righteousness at the top, so the king of Assyria/Babylon is a model of wickedness at the bottom.

Figure 9   **Isaiah's Ladder to Heaven**

Jehovah—God of Israel

Seraphim—Angelic Emissaries

Sons and Daughters—Servants of God

Zion/Jerusalem—God's Covenant People

Jacob/Israel—Believers in a Creator-God

Babylon—the Wicked of the World

The King of Assyria/Babylon—Perdition

Like the archtyrant, people in the Babylon or next lowest category are in a descending mode. They include the liars, oppressors, and idolaters of the world who *choose* evil. The Jacob/Israel category consists of people who believe in God but don't venture far beyond that. They don't live God's law, not even the lesser law. People in the Zion/Jerusalem or middle category, on the other hand, live the lesser law. They enjoy a special relationship with God and are blessed by him. Sons and daughters and seraphim live the higher law. They assume many of God's character traits and attain advanced degrees of perfection. Jehovah ministers to them in person and appoints them to minister to his people.

Isaiah provides a yardstick by which we can measure ourselves. If we want to know what level we are on, we can compare ourselves with the people on Isaiah's ladder. We don't need to wait until we are dead to discover how far we have ascended or descended. Knowing exactly where we stand puts to rest any false notions of grandeur we may have about ourselves. On the other hand, it may surprise us to learn we are not as low down the ladder as we might have thought. We can discern a lot about our standing with God from how we match up with the heroes or villains in Israel's history. On whatever spiritual level we find ourselves, our challenge is to advance from there all the way to God.

The Past Provides a Sure Pattern of the Future

By knowing about ourselves we can get a good idea of where we fit into the scheme of things were the end of the world to occur in our day. According to Isaiah, our place on the ladder has a crucial impact on what becomes of us. Many events in the beginning of Israel's history repeat themselves at the end, so that events at the end won't come as a surprise to those familiar with the scripture. Just as the Bible teaches that "what has been shall be again" (Ecclesiastes 1:9), so Isaiah predicts new versions of ancient events. That is how he prophesies—foretelling the future by basing it on the past. He limits himself to that method of prophesying so that we may understand the future in terms of the past.

Realizing this—that the method Isaiah uses to prophesy is based on things in Israel's past—caused me to look at the Old Testament in an entirely new light. I found that Isaiah predicts new versions of more than thirty ancient events: a new decline into wickedness, a new Sodom-and-Gomorrah type of destruction, a new "Assyrian" world conquest, a new exodus of God's people out of bondage, a new inheritance of promised lands, a new building of the temple, a new descent of Jehovah on the mount, and so forth. I began to see the Bible as a template for what is still to come. History is going to repeat itself in a big way. Major events of antiquity await a second fulfillment at the end of the world.

Major events of antiquity await a second fulfillment.

In referring to the end of the world, I don't mean the annihilation of the earth or even the end of life on earth but rather of civilization as we know it. In prophesying the end from the beginning, Isaiah doesn't use the popular expression "end of the world," although it is appropriate for what he predicts. He sees the end of an essential *phase* in the earth's existence involving a worldwide destruction of the wicked—all who don't repent of evil but who instead harden their hearts even when offered a hope of salvation. God's determination to rid the world of wickedness is further tied to his desire to deliver the righteous and to usher in a civilization based on his standard of righteousness (see Figure 10).

How do we know Isaiah could be speaking about this happening in our day and not later on? You can be the judge as you familiarize yourself with what he predicts for the future. There are too many things in today's world resembling Isaiah's endtime scenario for it all to be coincidence. Of course, people in the past thought the end of the world would occur in their day. But in their day the players Isaiah describes were not yet in place, and parts of the drama had not already been rehearsed. I am certain that as you examine Isaiah's writings you will see virtually every prop is set up ready to begin the final act. In the light of Isaiah's message the world really does appear poised for what he predicts.

Figure 10   **The "End of the World"**

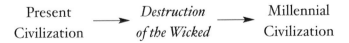

| Present Civilization | → | *Destruction of the Wicked* | → | Millennial Civilization |

Isaiah also shows that the way people acted in the events of old is how they will act again when the events roll around a second time. And how God dealt with people in the past—in delivering the righteous and punishing the wicked—is how he will deal with them in the future. Times may have changed—they may be radically different—but God hasn't changed. That keeps things on the same footing they have always been on. In Isaiah's endtime scenario the future is a mirror of the past, both in the events themselves and in the way God acts in history. I find that idea comforting because it affords us incredible hindsight. We can turn such hindsight into foresight as the end of the world draws near.

It is too easy to focus on mistakes people made in the past. We reassure ourselves we would never have made such mistakes. Isaiah gives us a chance to see how we will respond in similar circumstances. The beauty of Isaiah's writings is that they open our minds to the possibility that we might participate in many prophetic events of the kind that occurred anciently. By their very nature, Isaiah's writings can prepare us for that. We can decide ahead of time what we would do in a given situation. How we act reflects what spiritual level we are on. We may aspire to higher things but we can attain them only after we obtain a clear idea of what God requires of us as we work our way up the ladder.

Isaiah Predicts Two Separate and Distinct Scenarios

Using his own day as a jumping-off point, Isaiah predicts a future world conquest and destruction involving a new king of Assyria/Babylon whom God empowers for the job. That king will resemble the ancient kings of Assyria and Babylon who conquered and destroyed much of the old world. Isaiah predicts this endtime scenario using a simple but effective technique: he organizes his writings using two entirely different kinds of literary structures simultaneously. The way the individual parts of these structures interrelate conveys its own prophetic message over and above what we read on the surface. That way of prophesying is more sophisticated than most, concealing multiple levels of meaning.

First, Isaiah uses several layered *linear* structures that follow a timeline—one that begins in Isaiah's day and ends in a millennial age of peace. In linear structures history appears as one long continuum covering centuries of time (see Figure 11). Most Bible scholars have understood the writings of Isaiah in that way. But Isaiah doesn't invent these linear structures. Instead, he takes the archetypal patterns of all ancient Near Eastern literatures—Egyptian, Ugaritic, Babylonian, and so forth—and adapts them for his own prophetic purpose. His vision embraces the whole world, inviting other cultures to relate to his writings. The message is Hebrew, but it is far-reaching and universal in its perspective.

Figure 11 · **Example of a Linear Structure**

Israel in the Promised Land (Isaiah 1–39)	→	Israel Exiled Abroad (Isaiah 40–54)	→	Israel Returned from Exile (Isaiah 55–66)

The second kind of structure—like Isaiah's Seven-Part Structure that I analyzed—is *synchronous*. In synchronous structures the events of the past that Isaiah describes no longer relate just to the past but also to the future. In other words, the things Isaiah mentions concerning his day will happen again in one form or another though not necessarily in the same order. Instead of a series of historical events that occur over long periods of time, as in antiquity, Isaiah depicts a scenario of similar events that occur *all at once* within a few years. The advantage of synchronous structures is that history serves a double purpose: (1) in depicting ancient events; and (2) in presenting an allegory of future events.

Synchronous structures differ from linear ones in that all the events mentioned comprise a *single* scenario, in which everything that happens is interconnected. Ancient events that were separated in time by perhaps hundreds of years now come alive again as essential parts of a new sequence of events. Those events occur synchronously or "in sync" with each other (see Figure 12). The literary structures Isaiah uses that depict these synchronous events are superimposed upon the linear structures that depict these same events chronologically. While through linear structures Isaiah describes one thing—perhaps events of his own day—in synchronous structures he describes another: events still to come.

Figure 12   **Illustration of a Synchronous Structure**

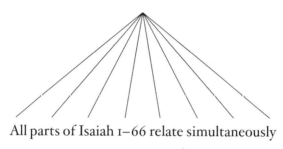

All parts of Isaiah 1–66 relate simultaneously

Synchronous structures make Isaiah's writings multi-dimensional, enabling the prophet to predict events on several levels, relating to more than one time frame. In the light of the Seven-Part Structure William Brownlee discovered, for example, Isaiah's entire prophecy describes a single chain of events. Through that structure's interconnections Isaiah identifies the time frame of those events as the "last days" or end of the world, a transitional phase that ushers in a millennial age of peace (see Figure 13). The "last days" thus consist of an *endtime* scenario that covers the entire Book of Isaiah. Yet, it takes nothing away from the *historical* scenario that Isaiah's linear structures depict—both apply.

One synchronous structure that doesn't cover the entire Book of Isaiah, discussed in the next chapter, contrasts the king of Babylon verse by verse in one part of the book with the King of Zion in another. This means that we can learn more about each king by studying them together, not separately. Yet another literary device Isaiah uses connects different events to each other domino fashion. In the "last days," for example, many "nations" or "Gentiles" (Hebrew *gôyîm*) "flow" to Zion (Isaiah 2:2–3), though it isn't clear under what circumstances. Other instances of "nations" or "Gentiles" (*gôyîm*) "flowing" to Zion, however, identify that event as Israel's return from exile (Isaiah 60:3–5; 66:12).

Figure 13   **The "Last Days" or End of the World**

Some people suggest that Israel's *physical* return from exile (which exile occurred in Isaiah's day) depicts our *spiritual* return from sin—that its prediction is figurative, not literal. In fact, many predictions *are* figurative but they are first of all literal. In Hebrew prophecy almost everything a prophet describes has a literal meaning, besides additional levels of meaning it may have. Using the domino principle, for example, Isaiah may describe several physical events in a short sequence somewhere in his book, connecting them in a particular order. But he will then take each event and describe it again in other combinations in other parts of his book, thereby linking it to still other physical events.

For example, God calls Moses as a "shepherd" to "lead" his people as a "flock" at their exodus out of Egypt through the "deep" (Isaiah 63:11–14). A new "shepherd," however, "leads" them as a "flock" before Jehovah comes to reign on the earth

(Isaiah 40:10–11). God's "shepherd" announces the rebuilding of the temple in Jerusalem when God again dries up the "deep" (Isaiah 44:27–28). In the new exodus through the "deep," God's people return to "Zion," a place that transforms into a new Paradise (Isaiah 51:3, 9–11). Jehovah comes to reign in "Zion" when his people return in the new exodus (Isaiah 52:7–12). Their exodus to "Zion" is from throughout the earth (Isaiah 11:11–12:6). And so forth.

Although word links accompany Isaiah's interconnecting of events in these examples, they aren't essential. What is important is that Isaiah ties all events in his book together into *one* sequence (see Figure 14). That sequence is itself a synchronous structure whose individual parts form an organic whole. In their light we may apply the entire Book of Isaiah to our own day and read it as a soon-to-be-fulfilled endtime scenario. Even the parts of his writings that are biographical in nature—that mention persons, places, and incidents of his day—foreshadow something that occurs in the future. Isaiah's writings, in effect, are an *apocalyptic* prophecy, one that predicts what happens at the end of time.

Figure 14   **Sequence of New Events Linked Domino Fashion**

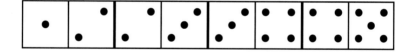

In sum, by using two kinds of literary structures, linear and synchronous, superimposing them one upon the other, Isaiah predicts two separate time periods simultaneously. That method of prophesying—for both his own day *and* the "last days"—may take a bit of getting used to. In rabbinical school I learned that it has been a teaching of Judaism down the centuries that the Hebrew prophets prophesy on these two distinct levels at the same time. The rabbis, however, base that intriguing idea on oral tradition, not on any apparent literary evidence. I discovered the evidence later for myself as I analyzed Isaiah's structures. I saw that Isaiah was as much a literary genius as he was a prophet of God.

Ancient Names Are Codenames of Endtime Powers

So while Isaiah is talking about a king of Assyria/Babylon who fulfilled his role anciently, he is also talking about a new king of Assyria/Babylon. In Isaiah's day and shortly thereafter, such a king, or several kings, conquered and destroyed much of the known world. But because the events of Isaiah's day repeat themselves at the end of the world, we will see the same scenario again. In other words, a new king who conquers and destroys the world will become a major player on the world stage in the "last days." He will do the kinds of earth-shaking things his ancient counterparts did but on a larger scale. Today's known world is a much bigger place, so what he does will impact billions of people.

> Any precedent set in the past can serve as a "type" of the future.

In that endtime setting the names Assyria, Babylon, and others function as *codenames* of endtime entities. Isaiah uses ancient names to depict future world powers based on the prophetic idea of "types," a literary term that describes a thing in the past that resembles something in the future. Anciently the militaristic kings of Assyria, who came from the North, were the first to conquer the known world; by so doing they set a *precedent*. For that kind of thing, therefore, they became a *type*. Kings of Babylon, on the other hand, set a precedent of world rulers promoting an idolatrous ideology, a belief system all its citizens were compelled to accept. For that kind of thing they became a *type*.

According to Isaiah's method of prophesying, any precedent set in the past may serve as a *type* of the future because in the prophetic worldview God orchestrates human history so that what happened before occurs again at end of the world. But things aren't quite so simple. A prominent person or nation in the past may have set a single precedent Isaiah can draw on to depict a similar person or nation in the future, whereas the future entity may be a blend of several precedents from the past. The future person or nation, in other words, may follow more than one precedent or type. In that case, Isaiah depicts the future entity as a *composite* of ancient types, combining a number of traits in one.

At some point, for example, there will arise a tyrannical ruler from the North, ambitious and militaristic, who will conquer and destroy much of our present world—in the same manner that the kings of Assyria conquered the ancient world. That is one idea we can read into Isaiah's prophecies about a "king of Assyria." But that same ruler will also attempt to make himself into the god of the world he conquers, commanding all peoples everywhere to worship him. He will promote his false and idolatrous ideology following the pattern of the kings of ancient Babylon. Isaiah thus blends several *types* from the past—the kings of Assyria and Babylon—to describe a single future world ruler (see Figure 15).

Figure 15   **The Endtime Archtyrant—A Composite of Types**

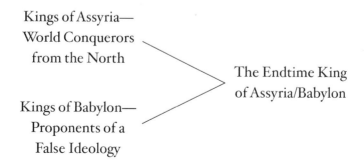

Kings of Assyria—
World Conquerors
from the North

Kings of Babylon—
Proponents of a
False Ideology

The Endtime King
of Assyria/Babylon

We Determine Our Own Level on the Ladder

According to Isaiah's scenario, when that archtyrant performs his role on the world stage, all those living will be caught up in the events one way or another whether they like it or not. World conditions will suddenly have become unstable, as if the bottom had fallen out of life. What we do in that situation will profoundly determine how high we will ascend the ladder, or how low we will descend. According to Isaiah, those times will be so compelling that no one will be able to stand still. We will either be actively involved in overcoming evil, or the evils of those times will overcome us. Such circumstances will require us all to take a course of action that will lift us higher on the ladder or drop us down.

Even though those events will directly fulfill prophecy, I believe they will still seem familiar, as if we had seen them before. Like Hitler, in Germany, the king of Assyria/Babylon will have plenty of helpers who will brutally carry out his bizarre policies. Others, out of fear for their lives, will give lip service to the archtyrant or commit atrocities so that they themselves may escape free. Yet others will seek to hide away from it all, eking out a miserable and uncertain existence as they seek to avoid reality. Isaiah depicts the entire spectrum of human weaknesses: rejection of God, ruthless tyranny, betrayal of friends, submission to terror, predatory behavior, desertion of dependents, escape to hideouts.

So where will we stand in that fateful day? Will we behave badly and end up lower on the ladder, or will we accept the challenges of those times and rise higher? We will either succumb to fear or exercise faith in God and perform nobly. Our beliefs alone won't save us, nor will the props of the past support us. Isaiah's scenario teaches that people ascend the ladder by meeting hardships head on—by passing tests of "loyalty" to God and "compliance" with his will. God permits these adverse circumstances for us to utilize as stepping-stones in our climb upward. World conditions in that day will provide a unique means for us to obtain "salvation" and "exaltation" and every blessing God has promised.

Our choices have an eternal, not just temporary impact.

Our choices, moreover, will have an eternal, not just temporary impact. Time and eternity merge in Isaiah's theology, one being a continuation of the other in a different dimension. How we act in the moment of crisis and where we arrive when it is over is largely determined by how we act as a rule—whether we are self-willed or do God's will—because what occurs spiritually manifests itself physically, and vice versa. The time of trouble can actually help, not hinder, ascent on the ladder as our difficulties bear down on us. Those who qualify for *spiritual* deliverance from sin in that day will also qualify for *physical* deliverance from mortal danger. In Isaiah's theology the two go hand in hand.

When we die, the level we end up on becomes our starting point in the next life. Isaiah teaches that loyalty to God through the midst of trials helps us ascend, in life or in death. In Isaiah's day, King Hezekiah's faithful suffering "unto death" during an apparent mortal illness lifted the king to the next highest level. Ultimately, it didn't matter if he lived or died; his spiritual state would be the same. He passed the test of loyalty his God had set up for him, in that very hour. In his case God also chose to deliver him physically, but that was less important than his spiritual victory. What we lose or sacrifice in this life in the course of complying with God's will, God always restores—with added blessings.

Isaiah Sees a Glorious New Era for God's People

Isaiah foretells a glorious future for God's people. Ancient prophets looked forward to that golden age we now call the

"Millennium." To them, that was a major purpose of the earth's creation from the beginning. In the "last days"—in the brief period before the millennial age—many attain the highest levels on the ladder as they prove faithful to God under all conditions. Many will accept momentary trials cheerfully, knowing that such trials are a part of God's plan. While some will do anything to avoid suffering, rejection, persecution, or death, many will accept these things, if necessary, as "more par for the course," as doors to divinity, as opportunities for ascent—until they see God.

God never abandons those who trust in him. While he hands over into the power of the tyrant those who are determined to descend, to teach them the consequences of their actions, God protects those who ascend. As he has done in times past, God helps his people at the end of the world by raising up a righteous leader to lead them (see Figure 16). God's "servant" comes on the scene at a critical moment in history. Like Moses in Egypt, the servant delivers God's people from forces seeking to take them over and enslave them. God empowers his servant and others in the category of seraphim to gather his people from the four directions of the earth and lead them in a new exodus to the Promised Land.

Figure 16   **Two Principal Actors in Isaiah's Endtime Drama**

The Archtyrant—	God's Servant—
a Destroyer	a Deliverer

That physical exodus occurs for all who qualify spiritually—for all who live God's law. The new exodus will by no means be limited to the Jews or the land of Israel. Isaiah predicts that God's people—all who recognize the hand of God in his servant—will gather from among all nations in response to the servant's mission. Many new versions of ancient events will occur in which God will deliver his people from catastrophe. In the end, after all who refuse to repent have passed away, the whole world becomes Jehovah's, his kingdom on earth. Israel's God will grant lands of inheritance to those who ascend the ladder, and they and their descendants will live through the entire millennium of peace.

Under God's terms, however, simply saying you follow him doesn't qualify you for salvation. In fact, that can mark you as a hypocrite if you don't practice what you preach. Many people today wait for a "rapture" that for them will never happen. If people are going to be "caught up into heaven" it will occur on the same principle as when persons in the past were caught up. As everything that happens at the end of the world has a *type* in antiquity, we can know how such things work. If we want to learn the conditions under which people physically ascend into heaven, Enoch, Elijah, and others provide the type. To ascend as they did, we must attain a degree of righteousness resembling theirs.

Everything at the end of the world has a *type* in antiquity.

God will not establish a new set of rules to accommodate the moment. Nor will he grant "favored-nation status" to his people or placate a "vocal minority." He will do things the way he has always done them—according to the law they live. The circumstances for someone to be "translated" or caught up into heaven are simple, though not easy. They must ascend the ladder step by step, becoming more like God until they attain the level of seraphim. Isaiah provides a pattern of the way it is done: those who "hope in God" through hard times "will be renewed in strength. They will *ascend* as on eagles' wings; they will run without wearying and walk and not faint" (Isaiah 40:31; emphasis added).

Many besides these exalted individuals will enjoy the millennial age, as not all become seraphs. Isaiah predicts that Jehovah himself will come to reign on the earth as King of Zion to govern *all* who are loyal to him, great and small, whom he will deliver from the king of Assyria/Babylon. As ascent to heaven is a personal journey, not everyone who lives God's law advances at precisely the same rate. The purpose of a ladder is to make provision for persons of every kind, to whom God may minister directly or indirectly, each on his own level. Then, when many ascend to higher levels and qualify to see God, Jehovah cannot refuse to come and dwell among them, ushering in the millennial age.

Postscript: Today, it seems, many more books are published than people are born on the earth. Yet, the Bible remains the world's all-time bestseller. And at the heart of the Bible is the Book of Isaiah. That book encapsulates the message of both the Old and New Testaments. Isaiah's writings contain elaborate prophecies about the end of the world and an all-inclusive theology of "salvation" and "exaltation." According to Isaiah, for people to be born on the earth is but a part of life's equation. Ascending the ladder to heaven completes the process.

It is therefore a comforting thing to know that God accommodates everyone born on the earth, equipping each of us with a script that is individualized according to our needs and desires. That way, we aren't in competition with anyone but may work out our salvation at the pace we choose. As God comes from a position of infinite love, he knows that the circumstances into which we are thrown in life are the best for us personally, that from them we are able to gain the most growth. Ask those who have "gone through it" and they will tell you it is so.

2

THE ARCHTYRANT,
CANDIDATE FOR PERDITION

*An endtime "king of Assyria/Babylon," who represents the lowest
level on the spiritual ladder, heralds the end of the world. Chaos
precedes a new creation. Ascent on the ladder follows a temporary
descent. America fulfills a dual role in Isaiah's endtime prophecy.
The tyrant possesses the opposite character traits of a servant
whom God raises up.*

Because people follow more or less what they see by example,
for good or for evil, Isaiah uses real individuals in his book to
teach us patterns of right and wrong. Just as Jehovah is the
model for the highest levels on the ladder, so the king of Assyria/
Babylon is for the lowest. Jehovah and his endtime servant show
us the good: the closer we get to the top of the ladder, the more
we resemble them. The tyrannical king of Assyria/Babylon
demonstrates evil: the nearer we get to the bottom, the more
we resemble him. People's behavior shows precisely who they

are loyal to, whether they realize it or not. Whom they think they are loyal to has little to do with it—"actions speak louder than words."

Isaiah defines the king of Assyria/Babylon's character traits as the opposite of Jehovah's, so by identifying Jehovah's characters traits we gain a clearer idea of what kind of person the archtyrant is. As Jehovah is the Savior of his people and seeks to deliver them, so the archtyrant is their Destroyer and seeks to slay them. As Jehovah deals justly and mercifully with his people, so the archtyrant deals unjustly and unmercifully with them. As Jehovah is wise understanding in ministering to his people, so the archtyrant mindlessly and senselessly tyrannizes them. By setting himself in opposition to God, the king of Assyria/Babylon follows a pattern of hate instead of love, of darkness instead of light.

From the writings of the Hebrew prophets kabbalists have drawn up a model of a "Tree of Life" that depicts God's attributes such as wisdom, justice, mercy, and understanding. It represents an attempt to depict the nature of God and our relationship to him. According to the kabbalist model, God created our physical selves four levels below his own. We progress up through these levels to the extent that we assimilate God's character traits pertaining to each level. Unlike the kabbalist model, however, Isaiah shows *how* we follow God and become like him; and, conversely, how those who follow the archtyrant adopt attributes opposite to God's and experience an opposite fate (see Figure 17).

A key character trait kabbalists attribute to God—"crown"— parallels Isaiah's key theme of "exaltation," expressing God's essential nature and humanity's divine potential. On Isaiah's ladder we begin earth's journey four levels below God's as Jacob/Israel. By keeping the lesser law—by repenting of sins and purifying our lives—we ascend to Zion/Jerusalem. From there, as we live God's higher law, we ascend and become sons/

servants; and, beyond that, seraphs. Isaiah's themes of "rebirth," "deliverance," "salvation," "exaltation," and "inheritance" to a greater or lesser degree characterize ascent on every level of the ladder. Those who attain the highest levels are crowned kings and queens.

Figure 17   **Opposite Dispositions of the Righteous and the Wicked**

All who follow this divine model become *like* Jehovah, the God of Israel. They assume increasingly important roles in ministering to others of God's people, which, in turn, aids their ascent further up the ladder. The king of Assyria/Babylon, on the other hand, heads in the opposite direction, moving down the ladder. Instead of reaching his divine potential, he descends to damnation and loses his crown. He and those like him follow a reverse kabbalist model, a "Tree of Death" ending in "ruin," "punishment," "suffering," "humiliation," and "disinheritance." They are damned souls "whose worms do not die and whose fire will not be extinguished: they will be a horror to all flesh" (Isaiah 66:24).

Although God gives everyone the chance to choose life or death, joy or misery, beauty or ignominy, at some point time runs out for the world. God's foreordained plan includes closure, and humanity's temporal history comes to an end. Our mortal existence wasn't meant to last forever. Instead, it prepares us for a better life ahead. As the end of the world draws near, things get more intense: evil grows stronger, but so does good. Under such circumstances many ascend the ladder, while many others descend. Isaiah's Seven-Part Structure shows the world polarizing into two camps in the "last days," one aligned with God and one against him. The conflict between them decides each side's fate.

> At some point, time is going to run out for the world.

In that endtime scenario the king of Assyria/Babylon is a key player. When he arrives on the scene we will know the end is near. Because his appearance is one of the first things to occur among Isaiah's new versions of ancient events, he heralds the end of an era for humanity but also the beginning of a new one. In his days political evil escalates more than ever before, much as happened with Hitler in Germany prior to World War II. In response, many people either go over to him or renew their commitment to God. Things come to a head as people realize that the world's days are numbered, that they face a point of no return. The world will never be the same again after the archtyrant appears.

The king of Assyria/Babylon will be a direct cause in the disappearance from the earth of the three lowest levels on the ladder—all who are determined to do evil, who refuse to heed God's warning to repent. They can't remain on the earth because in that day the earth itself ascends a level on the ladder also. It goes through "ruin" and "rebirth" and becomes a new Paradise—a new version of the old. The earth's physical condition responds to the spiritual state of its inhabitants. A complete cleansing of the earth marks the beginning of the millennial age of peace. Only those who ascend to Zion/Jerusalem and levels higher remain on the earth after the catastrophes of the "last days" (see Figure 18).

Figure 18 **Millennial Residents on the Earth**

The God of Israel—King of Zion

Seraphim—Angelic Emissaries

Sons and Daughters—Servants of God

Zion/Jerusalem—God's Covenant People

Non-Millennial Residents on the Earth

Jacob/Israel—Believers in a Creator-God

Babylon—the Wicked of the World

The King of Assyria/Babylon—Perdition

In the end, those who choose evil—though they may believe in God—exit the earth before the millennial age begins. God sends against them the king of Assyria/Babylon, who commits wholesale genocide in the course of conquering the world. Persons who repent, on the other hand, God protects both directly and indirectly. Although the archtyrant may seem to wield all power, his influence won't be the strongest force in the world. Jehovah and his servant, whom he sends to minister to his people, provide a powerful counterforce to which all who keep God's law may look for deliverance. Persons on the highest spiritual levels will labor with the servant to prepare the way for Jehovah's coming.

A Return to Chaos Is the Prelude to a New Creation

Before God's new creation of the earth it temporarily reverts to chaos. As there was chaos in the beginning, before the first creation (*tohû wabohû*, Genesis 1:2), so chaos will envelop the earth once again. As darkness ruled before the light appeared, so the world will experience a brief but real "dark age." The king of Assyria/Babylon and his military machine will bring upon

43

the world this physical consequence of humanity's spiritual decline. They will cause destruction on a scale unknown since the Flood. Their large and formidable armies will conquer and lay waste all countries and lands before they themselves are destroyed. Whatever they do to others, the same is ultimately done to them.

According to Isaiah, God orchestrates these events, using people's actions to further his own purpose. The archtyrant and his evil alliance form a part of God's plan to erase the wicked from the earth. In other words, God uses the wicked to destroy the wicked. But for every evil that exists he also provides the remedy. So when the king of Assyria/Babylon causes "ruin" in the earth, God empowers his servant to put him down after the tyrant has served God's design of eliminating evildoers. Because the servant and the tyrant are at opposite ends on the ladder, they are perfectly suited to dealing with each other. Like David and Goliath, each has the other to contend with as they fulfill God's plan.

As their destinies are so closely connected (what the one does affects the other), we should note some roles of God's endtime servant when discussing the king of Assyria/Babylon. Because the servant is a counterforce to the destruction the archtyrant causes, we must remember that while one is "doing his thing" so is the other. Although they are contemporaries, they have opposite agendas. We shouldn't get the idea that the end of the world is "all gloom and doom." Isaiah characterizes the archtyrant as a power of chaos or evil in the world, but the servant is a power of creation on the side of God (see Figure 19). God didn't create the earth to remain in a state of chaos but to experience "rebirth."

Thus, David's victory over Goliath is just one *type* of how the servant interacts with the king of Assyria/Babylon. Isaiah identifies other types as well. Like the archtyrant, the servant is a *composite* of ancient types. Like Moses, he leads God's people in a new exodus to the Promised Land, this time not to escape the plagues of Egypt but the worldwide catastrophe engineered by the archtyrant. Those who choose God and renew their allegiance to him come out of all nations on the eve of the nations' destruction. As the angels of God took Lot out of the fiery destruction of Sodom and Gomorrah, so God's servant and his associates gather up God's people to escape the desolation of the wicked.

Figure 19   **Opposite Forces in the "Last Days"**

The King of Assyria/Babylon	God's Servant	Israel's God
←	→	→

Thankfully things don't end there. God brings a new creation out of the chaos the archtyrant leaves behind, restoring a peaceful and happy life to his people. God's servant and all who escape destruction begin a new, millennial civilization on the earth in which all who ascend the ladder participate. Like Cyrus, the Persian emperor, the servant reconquers the world from its evil overlords and reestablishes God's people in promised lands. Like Joshua—when Israel seized the Land of Canaan from its corrupt occupants—the servant assigns God's people permanent inheritances. Like Solomon, he builds the temple to which Jehovah comes to reign as King, with which event the millennial age begins.

God brings a new creation out of chaos.

In contrast to the king of Assyria/Babylon, the servant takes on several saving roles on behalf of God's people, each of which has a type in the past. Just as many ancient events repeat themselves in a single endtime scenario, so various roles of God's ancient servants repeat themselves in a single

45

endtime individual (see Figure 20). That individual is the enemy of the tyrannical king of Assyria/Babylon and the forerunner of Israel's God. As Moses tried valiantly to do but failed, the servant prepares God's people to meet their Maker when he comes to reign as King. That entire replay of ancient events—in which God's servant and the archtyrant perform leading roles—constitutes the "last days."

In each of his roles, the servant counters the king of Assyria/Babylon's power in the world. In the past, if God hadn't sent his servants to deliver his people, they would have remained in bondage in Egypt, or been wiped out by the Philistines, or stayed in Babylon, never to rebuild the temple. However hard the archtyrant tries to prevent Israel's God from delivering his people, he can't thwart the work of his servants, just as Pharaoh couldn't prevent Moses. When we stand in awe of the desolation the archtyrant causes among the nations, and perhaps even see it come to pass, we should remember that God gives the evil ruler power only over the wicked. God's deliverance of his elect will be complete.

Figure 20   **God's Servant—A Composite of Types**

Moses—Leading the Israelites'
Exodus out of Egypt

Moses—Preparing God's People
to Meet their God

Joshua—Assigning Inheritances
in the Promised Land

David—Leading Israel's Victories
over Her Enemies

Solomn—Building Jehovah's
Temple in Jerusalem

Cyrus—Conquering the World
from the Babylonians

Jehovah's
Endtime
Servant

The Tyrant and the Servant Are Our Role Models

So that those times won't catch people off guard, they will have a perfect example of righteousness and a perfect one of wickedness—God's servant and the king of Assyria/Babylon. God will provide a stark contrast between good and evil. No one will participate in those events blindfold. As contrary as it may sound, people will *choose* "rebirth," "inheritance," "deliverance," "salvation," and "exaltation," or "ruin," "disinheritance," "punishment," "suffering," and "humiliation." If they miss out on God's blessings it will be because they decide it. And yet, paradoxically—because self-deception opens the door for deception by others—the archtyrant will easily beguile a self-deceived world.

To illustrate the distinction between good and evil, Isaiah has encoded a prophetic message in a mini-structure I call the Servant–Tyrant Parallelism. That synchronous structure consists of twenty-one pairs of antithetical verses that compare characteristics of the archtyrant with those of Jehovah and his servant. It gives the clearest definition of opposite ideologies in the Book of Isaiah and perhaps in the entire Bible. That mini-structure contrasts the King or kings of Zion in one set of consecutive verses with the king of Babylon in another. Without going into detail on their verse-by-verse comparison (which appears in my book *The Literary Message of Isaiah*), I here present a summary (see Figure 21).

Not only do we learn more about the character traits of the archtyrant by comparing him with Jehovah and his servant, we also learn more about those of Jehovah and his servant by comparing them with the archtyrant. For example, Jehovah is willing to let the "king of Babylon" (and, by extension, other human rulers) rule first in the world, before he himself comes as King. He doesn't simply assert that he should be the one to reign on the earth. He comes to reign only after others have made a mess of things, which culminates in the chaotic rule of the Tyrant. Jehovah agrees to take a backseat, if that is what his people want, and even to suffer and be humiliated by them before being exalted as King.

Figure 21 **The Servant—Tyrant Parallelism**

Isaiah 14:4–23	Isaiah 52:7–53:12
The Tyrant strikes the nations.	The nations feel God's saving *arm*.
The Tyrant subjugates the nations.	The Servant purifies the nations.
The Tyrant causes havoc and destruction.	The Servant causes peace and healing.
The Tyrant keeps people in bondage.	The Servant releases people from bondage.
The Tyrant aspires to be like God on high.	The Servant is as the lowliest of men.
The Tyrant enjoys prominence.	The Servant endures ignominy.
The Tyrant "ascends" in the heavens.	The Servant "ascends" out of the earth.
The Tyrant is deposed as king.	The Servant returns as King.
The Tyrant's reign of tyranny ends.	The Servant's reign of peace begins.
The Tyrant is exiled to Sheol (Hell).	The Servant's people return from exile.
The Tyrant is utterly humiliated.	The Servant is highly exalted.
The Tyrant is slain for his own crimes.	The servant is slain for others' crimes.

God's servant follows Jehovah's example, as he too is subjected to ridicule and hostility before God vindicates him. All who ascend to the highest spiritual levels encounter defiance from those who oppose them, just as Jehovah does. The higher we ascend, the greater the degree of opposition. Because pretenders and impostors arrive before the real thing, by the time what is genuine and of God appears, people have been desensitized. The king of Assyria/Babylon is one such false Christ. He leads away many people—his followers—who persecute the followers of Jehovah. God's servant, on the other hand, does for God's people as God does for him, delivering them from the power of their enemies.

It may seem odd that Isaiah blends the attributes of Jehovah and his servant, changing the subject back and forth between the two. In this mini-structure I identify both as the Servant, although each "serves" on his own level. Why does Isaiah include *both* in this parallelism? First, when the servant attains the seraph level he acts as a model of righteousness in preparing God's people for the coming of their King. The servant *personifies* righteousness, and Isaiah often refers to him *as* "Righteousness" because he keeps the terms of the covenants God makes with his people on the highest human level possible. We see a similar thing in the New Testament, where Jesus personifies the law and word of God.

Second, Jehovah takes upon himself the form of a servant when redeeming his people from their sins. (See Chapter 8, which discusses Jehovah's role as a Savior who suffers on behalf of his people.) Without actually calling him a "servant," Isaiah's mini-structure shows Jehovah fulfilling the *role* of a servant. Scholars refer to him as the "Suffering Servant," which may cause confusion, as Isaiah calls only Jehovah's forerunner his "servant." Isaiah's mini-structure, moreover, identifies the suffering figure as Jehovah, the King of Zion. In effect, because he pays the price of his people's salvation by taking their transgressions upon himself, Jehovah, in a sense, *personifies* salvation (see Figure 22).

Figure 22 **Twin Representations of Jehovah and His Servant**

Jehovah—*Salvation*   God's Servant—*Righteousness*

The Dead Sea Scrolls show that the Qumran community understood these twin personifications of *righteousness* and *salvation*. Isaiah depicts the oneness of Jehovah and his servant many times, not only as *righteousness* and *salvation* but as powers of creation and co-workers in redeeming God's people. They are a perfect example of how a person ascends the ladder and becomes one with God. Jesus prayed that his disciples would be one. But we can't truly enjoy oneness with each other until we have oneness with God. The more we become *like* God—by becoming godlike in our thoughts and actions—the more we are one *with* God and one another. We do this by becoming "servants" of God.

> The more we become *like* God, the more we are one *with* God.

The Servant–Tyrant Parallelism shows how the king of Babylon exalts himself above all but ends up humiliated below all. And its opposite: the King of Zion is humiliated below all before being exalted above all. These reversals establish the pattern of "humiliation" before "exaltation" for every level of the ladder in between. Jehovah's servant, for example, follows the pattern of Jehovah but on a lower level. In delivering God's people from evil—spiritually on the one hand and physically on the other—Jehovah and his servant experience "suffering" and "humiliation" as precursors to "salvation" and "exaltation." In the same way they experience these things, so do we, to a degree, as we ascend.

Humiliation Is Essential for Attaining Exaltation

What, then, do we learn from the Servant–Tyrant Parallelism? That "exaltation"—ascent to the highest levels—is possible only on God's terms, on conditions that never change. Jehovah and his servant show the way, each on his own level. The archtyrant, on the other hand, seeks exaltation in a way that is counterfeit and opposite to Jehovah's. He shows there is no shortcut to heaven. That doesn't mean we can't attain heaven, only that the archtyrant goes about it the wrong way. We learn this from the interrelationships of persons who appear in the structure, from the bottom of the ladder to the top. They reveal that exaltation is possible for all who model themselves on Jehovah and his servant.

Although Jehovah and his servant suffer evils, there exists a "redeeming factor" in their adversity: good things happen that let us know all turns out right in the end. Two parallel verses in the Servant–Tyrant Parallelism, for example, show that the suffering Savior receives an honorable burial, which is a covenant blessing, whereas the archtyrant receives no burial, which is a covenant curse (Isaiah 14:20; 53:9). The next parallel verses show that the suffering Savior has offspring, also a covenant blessing, whereas the archtyrant has no offspring, a covenant curse (Isaiah 14:21; 53:10). So it is with us. Although we meet with evil, when we follow Israel's God there is always a "redeeming factor."

As all relationships with God that are acceptable to him are *covenant* relationships, Isaiah's Seven-Part Structure develops the idea that "loyalty" to God and "compliance" with his will are preconditions for "rebirth," "inheritance," "deliverance," "salvation," and "exaltation." A covenant, moreover, is a formal contract between two parties, in this case God and his people. Such a relationship benefits the lesser party—God's people—as God blesses them when they keep the terms of the agreement. God's law and word, which are universal and eternal, constitute the terms of any covenant God makes; whether a covenant is with his people collectively or with individuals, it is the same (see Figure 23).

Covenants are also made between equals, as between a husband and wife. In that case the covenant benefits both parties as well as their dependents, creating trust and stability. The optimum course in life is faithfulness to one's marriage covenant alongside, and as an integral part of, God's covenant. How we relate to one another is a measure of how we relate to God. People express their "loyalty" to God and their "compliance" with his will by keeping the terms of all divinely instituted covenants, thereby qualifying for his blessings. Because the archtyrant has no covenant relationship with God, and is ignorant of or breaks covenant terms, he *descends* the ladder in his very attempt to ascend.

Figure 23 **God's Relationship with His Children**

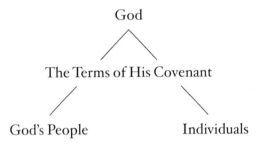

By complying with God's law and word, on the other hand, we *ascend* the ladder, the terms of his covenant being the pathway that leads to heaven. Another way won't work. As each level on the ladder is governed by its own covenant, each possesses a different set of terms. The loftier the level, the higher the law of its covenant. Thus, God's "higher law" pertains to a higher covenant while a "lesser law" pertains to a lower one. God requires more from those who have come further up the ladder than from those further down. As we ascend toward heaven— as we grow spiritually more refined and godlike—God's word becomes more exacting and his requirement for covenantal loyalty greater.

According to this pattern we must temporarily descend into "humiliation" before we ascend. That descent is part of God's test of loyalty for all who ascend (see Figure 24). God proves the measure of our covenant relationship with him, adapting the test to our individual circumstances, gaging the level of our commitment. The higher the ascent, the lower the temporary descent or the greater the test that precedes it. Both Jehovah and his servant submit to such trials, providing a pattern for all. One is "led like a lamb to the slaughter" as he "makes his life an offering for guilt" (Isaiah 53:7–10). The other is "marred beyond human likeness" before God heals and empowers him (Isaiah 52:13–15).

Figure 24   **God's Pattern of Humiliation and Exaltation**

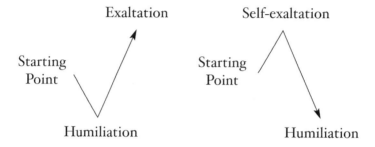

We see a type or precedent of such humiliation before exaltation in the life of Jacob, ancestor of God's people. You may recall that Jacob paid tribute to his brother Esau, even kowtowing before him before God established Jacob permanently in the Promised Land. Job provides another example, when his friends scolded him in his tragedy before God "blessed the latter part of Job['s life] more than the first" (Job 42:12). This humbling at the hands of others isn't meant to instill a victim mentality or generate a persecution complex or make us wallow in "suffering" and "humiliation," no matter how much we bear. Instead, it is a chance to exercise faith in God—that God *will*, in fact, deliver us.

Conversely, the king of Assyria/Babylon and people like him are unwilling to follow God's pattern of ascent. They lord it over others and promote themselves shamelessly, with devastating results. But theirs are the kinds of behavior that enable God's people to rise to new heights—if they endure their humbling well. The polarization of peoples that thus occurs forms a key theme of Isaiah. People's actions towards each other determine where they end up, whether they ascend or descend. Those who are humbled are exalted and those who exalt themselves are humbled. God's servant and the king of Assyria/Babylon, respectively, set this standard for a final showdown between good and evil.

God's People Are the Object of Assyria's Aggression

Just as with ancient Assyria and Babylon, so endtime "Assyria" rises to power in the world as God's people decline into a state of spiritual decay. That correlation works as predictably as a mathematical equation. You recall that Moses outlined the blessings and the curses of the Sinai Covenant, telling God's people that if they proved loyal they would receive certain blessings. But if they were disloyal they would be cursed or plagued (Deuteronomy 28). One such blessing was that God's people would become the "head of the nations"—in other words, the leading nation in the world. And its opposite: if cursed, they would be the "tail"—foreign nations would dominate and oppress them.

Under David and Solomon Israel became the "head of the nations." That was Israel's Golden Age and the type of a future millennial age of peace. Later, when his people rejected him, God allowed the Assyrians, Babylonians, Romans, and others to destroy them and take them captive. From that time forth—through many centuries—the ethnic lineages of Israel have been the "tail" of the nations. Isaiah, however, predicts that at the end of the world they will see spiritual and political "rebirth," which will usher in the millennial age. When they again prove loyal to him, God reconstitutes the nation of his people and they again receive the blessings of the covenant that he made with them at Sinai.

America's prosperity relates to God's covenant with his people.

Meanwhile, today, America is the "head of the nations." It has always received God's covenant blessings—the very ones God promised his people Israel. The founding fathers established "one nation under God" in a modern fulfillment of God's promise. They built their political dream on the foundation of their religious beliefs, a system that acknowledges people's God-given rights, that protects the free expression of religion. We may not recognize the real reason we have had such a prosperous and blessed life. We can't imagine our extraordinary successes could have come from anything but our own efforts. America's prosperity, however, clearly relates to God's covenant with his people.

After ancient Israel was exiled from its land, God scattered his people among all nations. Many mingled with other groups and lost their identity as Israelites (see Figure 25). But Israel's assimilation into the nations opened up new possibilities: *all* peoples of the world could now receive Israel's covenant blessings because of their Israelite lineage. Otherwise, God could not bless them with the blessings of Israel. According to his promise, God reserved those blessings for his own people based on his covenant relationship with them. Wherever those blessings have been in evidence in the world, therefore, is where we most find the descendants of Israel who kept the terms of God's covenant.

Figure 25   **Israel's Evolvement into Two Subgroups**

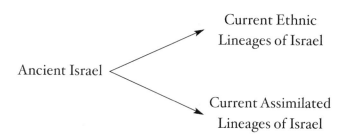

Isaiah's Seven-Part Structure identifies many ancient names as codenames for peoples who participate in an endtime scenario, not just Assyria and Babylon. In that future context, "Israel" is itself a codename. How does this relate to America? America was established as a "people of God" from the beginning. Starting with the Pilgrims, who sought religious freedom in a free land, America has led the world in upholding humanity's right to worship God according to the dictates of one's conscience, creating a constitutional framework that protects this. In an endtime or prophetic sense, therefore, when Isaiah refers to "Israel," we can just as easily read "America." America, too, is God's people.

The Sinai Covenant, through which God established a special relationship between himself and his people, was broken anciently but was never annulled. It remains as valid today as it was then, based on God's word revealed through his prophets. To receive the blessings of the covenant, all his people have to do is keep its terms. Isaiah pleads with them to again observe this perpetual law, in the "last days" as well as his own day. What are the terms of the covenant exactly? That is not difficult to discover: the Ten Commandments provide a basis of God's law and word to his people. Over many generations, people in America lived by that moral code. Only in modern times have we turned from it.

In fact, the same kind of wickedness that brought calamity on God's people in the past prevails in America at present. We see every kind of social disorder and moral perversion in American society, and when we live that way we will also see the result. What happened to God's people anciently will happen to us: God will bring the curses of the covenant on the nation that rejects him, just as Isaiah says. Even as we have enjoyed the blessings—based on past observance of God's commandments—so we must endure the curses if we don't change. We can know what is coming because Isaiah spells out its specifics. He warns us as individuals even when it is too late to prevent trouble as a nation.

The Sinai Covenant was broken anciently but was never annulled.

America, more than any other nation on the earth, qualifies as the modern counterpart of ancient Israel. Today's Jews don't fit the description of a people of God caught in a spiritual downturn. Nor have the Jews been the "head of the nations" in modern times. And the State of Israel in the Middle East hasn't been the focus of hostility from a militaristic superpower from the North. Only America fits these descriptions, as Israel did in Isaiah's day. Looking at it this way, we can discern such preliminaries—"the beginning of the end"—already happening. As Isaiah portrays it, the nation of America is a perfect reflection of God's blessings, and upcoming curses, according to God's unchanging law.

When reading the Old Testament we may be used to thinking of Israel as the Jews, especially the Jews in their homeland. It may be hard to imagine those who are not Jews as "Israel." However, Isaiah does this all the time, using codenames to refer to endtime nations and peoples. Because we can relate the entire Book of Isaiah to two time frames—Isaiah's day and the "last days"—we may need to rethink the situation today. By now, Israel has existed about 3,270 years (see Figure 26). The biggest part of that—2,600 years—has been *after* it was exiled from the Promised Land. Two kinds of Israelites live in the world today—ethnic and assimilated—both of whom God says he will reckon with.

Aren't the Jews God's chosen people then? Have they lost their inheritance? Not at all. Isaiah predicts that they and other ethnic lineages of Israel, such as the lost Ten Tribes, will all ultimately return from dispersion. The prophets talk about the *whole* nation of God's people, both ethnic and assimilated, when predicting the end of the world. Indeed, God accounts for his children everywhere, giving all an equal opportunity to come into his covenant. That is the only way we can hope to escape calamity, the only way we can ascend the ladder high enough to qualify for "deliverance." As Isaiah teaches it, God's plan provides for everyone who desires it to escape the "punishment" of the wicked.

Figure 26   **A Timeline of Israel's History**

Birth of Nation after Exodus from Egypt, circa 1260 B.C.	Exile to Assyria and Babylon, 722–587 B.C.	The "Last Days" 21st Century A.D.

Endtime "Assyria" Conquers and Destroys the World

As mentioned, the declining spiritual condition of an endtime "Israel" brings about the rise of an endtime "Assyria." Just as occurred anciently, God's people turning their backs on God brings about Assyria's world conquest. Otherwise, the king of Assyria/Babylon could have no power over them. According to Isaiah and other prophets, the fall of Israel spiritually causes its fall physically. Thus, Israel's God says, speaking of the archtyrant: "I will commission him against a godless nation, appoint him over the people [deserving] of my vengeance, to pillage for plunder, to spoliate for spoil, to tread underfoot like mud in the streets" (Isaiah 10:6). God strengthens him against his own people!

Meanwhile, the king of Assyria/Babylon wants much more than to subdue and destroy God's people, although that is a chief goal. His desire for power is insatiable—it knows no bounds. The archtyrant wants to rule the whole world, not simply bring people to justice or humble them. Although God appoints him to punish the wicked, "it will not seem so to him; that will not be what he has in mind. His purpose will be to annihilate and to exterminate nations not a few" (Isaiah 10:7). As they set out to conquer the world, the king of Assyria/Babylon and his alliance of nations commit murder on a scale never before seen. The horror of their rape of the earth will surpass all that has gone before.

The archtyrant doesn't know God permits him to do all he does. He thinks he achieves it all by himself, unaware he is only a part of a larger purpose. He boasts (here, the pronoun *I* appears seven times): "I have done it by my own ability and shrewdness, for I am ingenious. I have done away with the borders of nations, I have ravaged their reserves, I have vastly reduced the inhabitants. I have impounded the wealth of peoples like a nest, and I have gathered up the whole world as one gathers abandoned eggs; not one flapped its wings, or opened its mouth to utter a peep" (Isaiah 10:13–14). For the moment, this tyrant of tyrants appears all-powerful and the whole world writhes in fear of him.

The fall of God's people spiritually causes their fall physically.

So devastating is the work of this mass murderer that Isaiah likens his global destruction to a new "Flood" overflowing the land. In other words, the Flood that wiped out the earth's inhabitants in the days of Noah will see a horrific new version at the end of the world. Isaiah calls the king of Assyria/Babylon by the names "Sea" and "River." He and his military alliance are as the "Sea" in commotion heaving itself beyond its bounds, or like a "River" in flood sweeping everything before it, destroying all in its path. The names "Sea" and "River" identify him with an ancient Near Eastern power of chaos. They belong to a Canaanite god who, like him, seeks to usurp God's authority and rule supreme.

The archtyrant and his multi-national coalition have a common, unrelenting hatred for God's people: "He will be stirred up against them in that day even as the *Sea* is stirred up. And should one look to the land, there [too] will be a distressing gloom, for the daylight will be darkened by an overhanging mist" (Isaiah 5:30; emphasis added); "Woe to the many nations in an uproar, who rage like the raging of the seas—tumultuous nations, in commotion like the turbulence of many waters!" (Isaiah 17:12); "Jehovah has in store one mighty and strong: as a ravaging hailstorm sweeping down, or like an inundating deluge of mighty waters, he will hurl them to the ground by his hand" (Isaiah 28:2).

"My Lord will cause to come up over them the great and mighty waters of the *River*—the king of Assyria in all his glory. He will rise up over all his channels and overflow all his banks. He will sweep into Judea [like] a flood and, passing through, reach the very neck; his outspread wings will span the breadth of your land, O Immanuel" (Isaiah 8:7–8; emphasis added). The archtyrant's reaching the "neck" leaves the head, which represents God's righteous people who come under siege in the days of "Immanuel," a codename Isaiah uses for God's servant. A *type* of these events were the people of King Hezekiah, whom God miraculously delivered from Assyria's siege of Jerusalem in Isaiah's day.

By means of such sweeping devastation, the archtyrant tries to make endtime Assyria, not "Israel," the head of the nations. As in the past, God allows that to happen when it serves his purpose to purify his people. Being vehemently "stirred up" against the God of Israel, the king of Assyria/Babylon mocks and rails against God's people (Isaiah 37:23, 28). However, while he gains power over those on the lowest levels of the ladder, he never fully achieves his objective of ruling the entire world. Although he thinks he is doing just what he wants, he is doing only what God wills. Through it all, God preserves alive those on the highest levels, for whom a glorious peace dawns after the archtyrant's fall.

America Has a Double Role in Isaiah's Prophecy

Isaiah uses yet another type from the past to predict the future. Just as the king of Assyria attacks God's people "Israel," so he attacks "Egypt." In Isaiah's endtime scenario the name Egypt too is a codename; it doesn't refer to present-day Egypt at all. Historically, the nation Isaiah addresses as Egypt no longer exists. Isaiah's Seven-Part Structure, on the other hand, identifies "Egypt" and "Assyria" as two endtime superpowers— as *political* opposites—just as elsewhere it identifies "Zion" and "Babylon" as two *spiritual* opposites (see Figure 27). As ancient Assyria invaded Egypt, so endtime "Assyria" invades "Egypt." A world war resembling the one in Isaiah's day occurs in the "last days."

Isaiah's use of Egypt and Assyria as codenames for endtime world powers follows a pattern used by the Hebrew prophets. Zechariah, for example, speaks of "Egypt" and "Assyria" as world powers God subdues in a future day of destruction (Zechariah 10:11). Yet, in Zechariah's day those nations were no longer a force to be reckoned with. Similarly, Daniel sees a vision of a great war involving "Persia" and "Greece," both world powers in his day (Daniel 11–12). Yet, Daniel's vision is about the end of the world, not his own day (Daniel 11:40; 12:4, 9). Although there may be a current Persia (Iran) or Greece, these nations resemble the old only in name; they aren't the world powers Daniel saw.

Figure 27   **Opposite Political and Spiritual Powers Today**

"Egypt"   ⟵——⟶   "Assyria"

"Zion"   ⟵——⟶   "Babylon"

Egypt anciently had a reputation as the most powerful nation in the world, though it dwelt geographically apart. It was religious, had a stable political system, and was highly productive in industry and agriculture. But by Isaiah's time, when ruled by a black pharaoh, it perilously declined, growing so corrupt and weakened that a spirit of anarchy took over and the land turned to ruin: "I will stir up the Egyptians against the Egyptians; they will fight brother against brother and neighbor against neighbor, city against city and state against state. Egypt's spirit will be drained from within; I will frustrate their plans, and they will resort to the idols and to spiritists, to mediums and witchcraft" (Isaiah 19:2–3).

In Isaiah's day Egypt's corrupt heads of state consider themselves as astute and enlightened as Egypt's founding fathers: "The ministers of Zoan are utter fools; the wisest of Pharaoh's advisers give absurd counsel. How can you say to Pharaoh, 'We ourselves are as wise as the first rulers?' Where are your wise men indeed? Let them please tell you, if they can discern it, what Jehovah of Hosts has in mind for Egypt! The ministers of Zoan have been foolish, the officials of Noph deluded; the heads of state have led Egypt astray. Jehovah has permeated them with a spirit of confusion; they have misled Egypt in all that she does, causing her to stagger like a drunkard into his vomit" (Isaiah 19:11–15).

When Assyria suddenly becomes a world threat, other nations still look to Egypt's immense military might to defend them, trusting in human alliances for protection: "Woe to those who go down to Egypt for help, relying on horses, putting their trust in immense numbers of chariots and vast forces of horsemen, but who do not look to the Holy One of Israel, nor inquire of Jehovah! . . . The Egyptians are human, not divine; their horses are flesh, not spirit: when Jehovah stretches out his hand, those who help them will stumble and those helped will fall; both will come to an end together. . . . Pharaoh's protection will turn to your shame, shelter in Egypt's shadow to embarrassment (Isaiah 30:3; 31:1, 3).

At the time Assyria's aggression seems inevitable, the Egyptians become "as women, fearful and afraid at the brandishing hand Jehovah of Hosts wields over them" (Isaiah 19:16). In an actual confrontation Assyria ravishes Egypt. The nations that depend on Egypt are desolated together with it, ending up embarrassed at Egypt's weakness. Relying on an "arm of flesh" instead of on God, they lament "See what has become of those we looked up to, on whom we relied for help and deliverance from the king of Assyria! How shall we ourselves escape?" (Isaiah 20:6). Egypt was the greatest military power in the world, but that was no guarantee of God's protection when the nation turned to evil.

Isaiah uses that ancient scenario as a *type* of the future. The only nation today, however, that fits Isaiah's description of "Egypt" is America. So to see how Isaiah's literary patterns work we may apply both names—"Israel" and "Egypt"—to America. In that sense America is a *composite* entity (see Figure 28) as are other endtime entities. In a future rerun of past events we may expect to see a scenario like that in Isaiah's day: when Egypt's inhabitants do evil, choosing idols and becoming spiritually estranged, Egypt's economy crashes and civil war sweeps the land; when Egypt's politicians take matters into their own hands and mislead the nation, God empowers the king of Assyria against them.

Figure 28   **America—A Composite of Types**

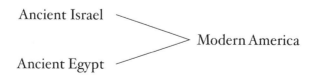

A worldwide dread of Assyria occurs as it encroaches upon the surrounding nations and assimilates them into its empire. Then, for a time, Assyria reigns in its aggression and feigns peace. When he arises, the archtyrant consolidates his power and readies his weapons of mass destruction. Just as the nations begin to believe he is willing to make permanent peace, however, he turns on them like a traitor and destroys them. After a flurry of diplomatic efforts to avoid disaster—as world leaders grow nervous about Assyria's aggressive goals—Assyria invades Egypt. For a brief, dismal interval of time Assyria conquers and annihilates the nations and compels all in its power to bend to its iron will:

"Although nations form pacts, they will be routed. Give heed, all you distant lands! You may take courage in one another, but will be in fear; you may arm yourselves, but will be terrorized. Though you hold consultations, they will come to nought; though you make proposals, they will not prove firm" (Isaiah 8:9–10). As people fail to repent of their wicked ways, "Jehovah of Hosts will carry out the utter destruction decreed upon the whole earth" (Isaiah 10:23): "See, their stalwarts sob in public; the champions of peace weep bitterly. The highways are desolate, travel is at an end. The treaties have been violated, their signatories held in contempt; mankind is disregarded" (Isaiah 33:7–8).

The people who survive are Zion/Jerusalem and levels higher.

Because many countries depend on endtime "Egypt" to defend them against "Assyria," they are appalled when Egypt is smitten. In spite of military alliances, Egypt is no help. People had looked up to Egypt and held it in awe. Now they look down on it, as all countries, including Egypt, fall prey to Assyria's treachery. The archtyrant destroys the nations and their lands by fire and the sword and annexes them into his world empire.

Ultimately, in Isaiah's scenario, the only people who survive are Zion/Jerusalem and levels higher on the ladder. When the archtyrant tries to attack Zion, thinking to deal the deathblow to God's people, he himself is destroyed and his invincible armies are wiped out:

"Jehovah of Hosts made an oath, saying, 'As I foresaw it, so will it happen; as I planned it, so will it be: I will break Assyria in my own land, trample them underfoot on my mountains.' . . . These are things determined on the whole earth; this is the hand upraised over all nations" (Isaiah 14:24–26); "Jehovah will cause his voice to resound, and make visible his arm descending in furious rage, with flashes of devouring fire, explosive discharges and pounding hail. At the voice of Jehovah the Assyrians will be terror-stricken, they who used to strike with the rod. At every sweep of the staff of authority, when Jehovah lowers it upon them, they will be fought in mortal combat" (Isaiah 30:30–33).

Even for Egypt all is not lost, as those in the Zion/Jerusalem category and above live in Egypt also. A type of God's people dwelling in Egypt are the twelve tribes' ancestors, whom Joseph brought there to escape a famine in the Land of Canaan. God's only purpose is to cause his people to return to him: "Jehovah will smite Egypt, and by smiting heal: they will turn back to Jehovah, and he will respond to their pleas and heal them" (Isaiah 19:22). Isaiah goes so far as to say that "Jehovah will make himself known to the Egyptians, and the Egyptians will *know* Jehovah in that day. They will worship by sacrifice and offerings, and make vows to Jehovah and fulfill them" (Isaiah 19:21; emphasis added).

The King of Assyria/Babylon Seeks to Displace God

As in the ancient version of these events, when the archtyrant turns against Zion—and thus against Zion's God—he seals his own doom. As he does with the wicked of the world, he attempts to vaunt his power over God's people, railing and raging against God with boasts and blasphemies. He won't stop his aggression until he succeeds in exalting himself over those whom he regards as rivals. He is so angry with them, he tries his utmost to exterminate them. He even claims God's own attributes and credits himself with divine power. In short, the king of Assyria/Babylon wants to rule supreme both on earth and in heaven. As his life shows, however, all who fight against God end up perishing:

"Whom have you mocked and ridiculed? Against whom have you raised your voice, lifting your eyes to high heaven? Against the Holy One of Israel! By your servants you have blasphemed Jehovah. You thought, 'On account of my vast chariotry I have conquered the highest mountains, the farthest reaches of Lebanon. I have felled its tallest cedars, its choicest cypresses. I have reached its loftiest summit, its finest forest. I have dug wells and drunk of foreign waters. With the soles of my feet I have dried up all Egypt's rivers!'" (Isaiah 37:23–25). Isaiah's use of *trees, forests,* and *mountains* as metaphors for people, cities, and nations, respectively, means he is describing a world conquest.

All who fight against God end up perishing.

Isaiah uses the imagery of a wild horse and bull to depict the archtyrant's rage against God and his elect people: "I know where you dwell, and your comings and goings, and how stirred up you are against me. And because of your snortings and bellowings against me, which have mounted up to my ears, I will put my ring in your nose and my bit in your mouth and turn you back by the way you came" (Isaiah 37:28–29); "Thus says Jehovah concerning the king of Assyria: 'He will not enter this city or shoot an arrow here. He will not advance against it with armor, nor erect siegeworks against it. By the way he came he will return; he will not enter this city,' says Jehovah" (Isaiah 37:33–34).

Although "whole nations have been burned like lime, mown down like thorns and set ablaze" by the archtyrant, he himself suffers the same: "Woe to you despoiler, who yourself was not despoiled; O treacherous one, with whom none have been treacherous: when you have done with devastating, you will be devastated; when you are through betraying, they will betray you!" (Isaiah 33:1, 12). Even the wicked won't be as badly off as their destroyers: "Was [Israel] smitten as were his smiters? Or was he slain as were those who slew him? You have dealt with them by utterly banishing them [O Jehovah]. By his fierce blasts they were flung away in the day of the burning east wind" (Isaiah 27:7–8).

Isaiah uses an Assyrian myth to paint a picture of the archtyrant as an impostor who seeks to reach the highest heaven to displace the God of Gods: "You said in your heart, 'I will *ascend* in the heavens and set my throne above the stars of God; I will seat myself in the Mount of Assembly [of the gods], in the utmost heights of the North. I will rise above the altitude of the clouds; I will make myself like the Most High [God]'" (Isaiah 14:13–14; emphasis added). Although Isaiah uses mythology, he lets us know he is describing "a man," not a myth (Isaiah 14:16). That man matches Habakkuk's prophecy of a wicked one who "sets his nest on high" to escape calamity on the earth (Habakkuk 2:9).

Only with today's technology could someone pull this off.

Only with today's technology could someone pull this off—to mimic God by going up into "heaven." For the first time in history, a person could possibly rule the world from a space station or "cosmograd" in a real-life version of *Star Wars*. But after his brief tenure as a demigod, the archtyrant pathetically perishes. His spirit is "cast down to Hell, to the utmost depths of the Pit" (Isaiah 14:15). His corpse lies disfigured and unburied on the ground, devoured by maggots. His forces are massacred—"lest they rise up again and take possession of the world" (Isaiah 14:11, 19–21). The whole earth rejoices to see the last of him, knowing the time of tyranny is past. The war to end all wars is over.

People mourn the archtyrant in a mocking funeral song: "How the tyrant has met his end and tyranny ceased! Jehovah has broken the staff of the wicked, the rod of those who ruled—him who with unerring blows struck down the nations in anger, who subdued peoples in his wrath by relentless oppression. . . . How you have fallen from the heavens, O morning star, son of the dawn! You who commanded the nations have been hewn down to earth! . . . Those who catch sight of you stare at you, wondering, 'Is this the man who made the earth shake and kingdoms quake, who turned the world into a wilderness, demolishing its cities, permitting not his captives to return home?'" (Isaiah 14:4–6, 12, 16–17).

John, in the New Testament, calls this archtyrant the "Antichrist" (1 John 2:18), which term refers to two things: (1) a person who rises up at the end of the world; and (2) the atheistic spirit that then prevails. Anti-Christ means anti-Messiah—opposed to God and his servant and all that they represent (see Figure 29). Echoing these prophecies, Daniel predicts that at the end of the world the "king of the North" will "exalt and magnify himself above every god and say astonishing things against the God of Gods" (Daniel 11:36). Daniel foresees that the archtyrant's forces will "devour the whole earth." He will "wage war against the saints" of the Most High God and then meet his end (Daniel 7:21–26).

Other prophets, speaking of their own day or the end of the world, describe additional antichrist types. Ezekiel depicts a "king of Tyre" whose "heart is lifted up," who says, "I am a god;

I sit on the throne of God in the midst of the seas" (Ezekiel 28:2). And yet, egotist is "a man, and no god," as is evident when he dies (Ezekiel 28:9). The king of Tyre, who denies the God who created him, is simply another type of an endtime archtyrant. Although not the same as Isaiah's king of Assyria/Babylon, he is like him, with him occupying the bottom rung on the ladder. Both seek to take upon themselves God's power and authority and are bedfellows of Perdition—inhabitants of the deepest Pit.

Figure 29   **Parallel Depictions of the Endtime Archtyrant**

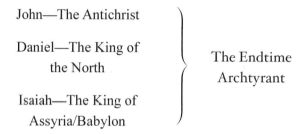

John—The Antichrist

Daniel—The King of the North

Isaiah—The King of Assyria/Babylon

The Endtime Archtyrant

From the days of the Hebrew prophets, a long line of anti-God tyrants has made an appearance as "bad guys" on the world stage. Every age has produced villains who attempt with their might to thwart God's plan for his children. Their atrocities make them ready candidates for Isaiah's lowest category. Although few descend to that depth, they labor as hard for evil as those on the highest levels labor for good. Perhaps each in his own way also qualifies as a type of the endtime Antichrist, who seems to possess all their character traits rolled into one. This tyrant of tyrants will accomplish more evil and destruction in the earth than anyone has before, at which point God destroys him and his kind forever.

Speaking of such candidates for Perdition, Isaiah says "They are dead, to live no more, spirits who will not resurrect; you have appointed them to destruction, wiping out all recollection of them" (Isaiah 26:14). With the archtyrant's passing the whole earth is "at rest and at peace"—it resounds with "jubilant celebration" (Isaiah 14:7). The inhabitants of Zion "shout and sing for joy" (Isaiah 12:6). God "comforts Zion and brings solace to all her ruins. . . . Joyful rejoicing takes place there, thanksgiving and the sound of music" (Isaiah 51:3). Those who trust in Israel's God, who wait for him to come, then "joyfully celebrate his salvation" (Isaiah 25:9). At last, the millennial age of peace begins.

Postscript: Chapter Two, and I ask, "Who can comprehend this?" I know Isaiah's message will go over the heads of some in spite of how well it is explained or how fully the evidence supports it. Many people react and turn off at the very mention of the "last days." The symptoms in every case of spiritual regression include a lack of recognition of the illness: "Doctor, please don't tell me the worst." Well, in response I say, "I am giving the bad news first and then I give the good news." Isaiah himself does that.

The "good news," of course, is *the* message of Isaiah. But he has us wade through the bad before we get to the good in case we assume too much about ourselves. After 2,700 years Isaiah still makes more sense than syndicated talk shows. Unfortunately, his voice is barely audible— a mere whisper out of the dust—so many louder voices have so much to say. Still, there exist a few spiritual antennas able to pick up sensitive signals. I know one doesn't need a Near-Death Experience to learn from the dead.

3

Babylon, Rebels
and Worshipers of Idols

*By choosing evil rather than good, Babylon descends the spiritual
ladder. Ancient Zion and Babylon form types of endtime
Zion and Babylon, representing two spiritual opposites. John's
"Babylon the Great" resembles Isaiah's Greater Babylon. A false
socio-economic system sustains Babylon's production of idols. The
rebellious of God's people join Babylon.*

The next-to-the-lowest level on the ladder, just above the
archtyrant and others in the Perdition category, is Babylon.
People of Babylon resemble the archtyrant, but they don't go
all out to persecute others as he does. They are the laborers
and technicians of evil rather than its architects and engineers.
Knowingly or unknowingly, they serve the despots who actually
call the shots. They don't design evil on the world, as the king of
Assyria/Babylon does; they just carry out his orders. Along with
those in Perdition, they perish from the earth just before the

dawning of the millennial age. As makers of chaos, they can't participate in God's glorious new creation. Given the chance, they reject salvation.

Babylon is not in an ascending but descending mode, unwilling to observe even common standards of decency. No one is born on this level; people get there by making wrong choices—forsaking God and willfully transgressing his law. Babylon is a catch-all for spiritual "losers" who refuse to admit or make up for their mistakes. They give themselves over to evil, seeking immediate pleasure instead of everlasting joy. Babylon consists of those who outright rebel against God, including every ilk of evildoer. Babylon's sins are injustice and idolatry—in other words, oppression of others and setting one's heart on the things of this world. As a category of wickedness, Babylon is a spiritual dead end.

We can tell that people don't originate in the Babylon category when we compare it with the next highest—Jacob/Israel—which functions as a pivot point, a crossroads all must pass. From Jacob/Israel, those who come into the world either ascend to Zion/Jerusalem or descend to Babylon; they don't remain where they are (see Figure 30). In short, as God's children we are born on a level higher than Babylon but may descend to it by the choices we make. Because no one originates as Babylon or Perdition, those who descend elect to not live up to their divine potential. Consequently, they act unnaturally or display spiritual deviations or moral depravity, oftentimes behaving less than human.

While the Babylon category defines people in a descending mode, ones higher than Jacob/Israel are in an ascending mode, rising above the basic human level. The Zion/Jerusalem category, for example, is heading in an opposite direction to Babylon. It is no wonder, then, that tensions arise between these ascending and descending categories who may live side by side in the same world but who adhere to entirely different philosophies in life. Babylon deals with that disparity by tormenting and persecuting those higher than itself, attempting to justify itself in the face of its own inherent failings. In that way it momentarily alleviates feelings of guilt and paranoia that are common to lower levels.

Figure 30   **Jacob/Israel—A Spiritual Crossroads**

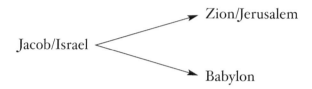

An ancient book, "The Ascension of Isaiah," depicts Isaiah's ascent to the "seventh heaven," from which he sees the end of the world. As he ascends through the different levels or "heavens" of God's creation, he can see what happens on all the levels below him but not those above until he gets there. So it is with people on different levels on the earth. Those who ascend the ladder can discern what lower rungs do because often they themselves have "been there and done that." Babylon, however, can't see anything above itself. People on that level may sense something higher, but because they have chosen evil they attribute little value to it. Yet, they may feel the loss of what they once had.

Babylon's descent on the ladder, on the other hand, shouldn't be confused with the temporary descent Jacob/Israel experiences before it ascends to Zion/Jerusalem. All ascending categories go through a *descent phase* while passing tests of "loyalty" to God and "compliance" with his will. Before their "rebirth" on a higher level, they may suffer "ruin" on a lower one. Before receiving an "inheritance" in the millennial age, they may see "disinheritance." Before realizing "salvation," they may endure "suffering." Babylon, on the contrary, always attempts to get the upper hand in the world. Its false "salvation" ends in "suffering." Its momentary "deliverance" leads to prolonged "punishment."

Ancient Zion and Babylon Are Types for Today

Both Isaiah's Seven-Part Structure and the Servant–Tyrant Parallelism contrast Babylon with Zion, portraying one as the opposite of the other. As codenames, "Zion" and "Babylon" represent two spiritual entities that coexist in the "last days," one ascending, the other descending; one righteous, the other wicked. From the way Isaiah contrasts them—juxtaposing Zion and Babylon within different literary patterns—we may best learn about them by comparing the two. In other words, we can't get a clear idea of the one without also examining the other because their very differences define who they are. As we did with the servant and the tyrant, therefore, we will look at both at the same time.

We don't find such an explicit contrast between Zion and Babylon as Isaiah's from merely reading the Bible. The Old Testament simply identifies Zion as a place connected to or synonymous with Jerusalem. Zion is an idealized locale linked with God's highest blessings. In Zion people worship God unaffected by the idolatrous practices surrounding them. The very name "Zion" (Hebrew ṣîyyôn, meaning "marked spot" or "designated place") alludes to something exclusive. Zion is where Jehovah dwells, as seen by the pillar of cloud by day and fire by night that rests on the temple. Israel's God protects Zion because its people are righteous; he is bound to deliver them when they prove loyal to him.

The very name "Zion" alludes to something exclusive.

Babylon, on the other hand, was historically the seat of the Mesopotamian empire that extended to much of the ancient world. The prophets associate Babylon with the worship of *idols*—false gods men make for themselves—which God condemns. Idols entice us away from the true God to a counterfeit, making it impossible to attain lasting happiness. Instead of experiencing "salvation" and "exaltation," people in the Babylon category incur "suffering" and "humiliation" as their final state, with dwindling hope of redemption. Babylon may wield power in the world, but the prophets remind us not to be taken in by it. Its power is transitory—like a passing parade of idols that fades from view.

Through literary devices, Isaiah develops further definitions of Zion and Babylon whose comparison, as noted, helps identify the attributes of each. Without losing the traditional connotations associated with their names, Zion and Babylon assume apocalyptic and prophetic importance (see Figure 31). They represent peoples or institutions we can identify in the world today. They also represent rungs on the ladder, revealing modes of behavior benevolent or malevolent toward humanity. Zion and Babylon illustrate our ever-present choice between ascent and descent. At the end of the world that choice makes the difference between life and death, though it equally impacts life after death as well.

Figure 31   **Zion and Babylon—Codenames for Endtime Entities**

Ancient Zion   ⟶   Modern "Zion"

Ancient Babylon   ⟶   Modern "Babylon"

Zion and Babylon Are Two Peoples and Places

A surface reading of Isaiah's writings alone provides a contrast between Zion and Babylon. In one definition, for example, Isaiah characterizes Zion as those of Jacob/Israel who repent of transgression (Isaiah 1:27; 59:20). In other words, if we belonged to Jacob/Israel and were willing to give up old ways in order to embrace God's ways, we could ascend to the next level by renewing the covenant with God and keeping its terms. Such proves to be a motivating experience, moreover, because when we live God's law we see its fruits blossom in our lives. As a spiritual category, Zion thus grows out of Jacob/Israel. It defines a people *within* a people of God—those who repent—not all Israel.

Elsewhere, Isaiah defines Zion as the place to which God's people return from among all nations at the end of the world (Isaiah 35:10; 51:11). On that occasion Israel's exiles gather to Zion from the four directions of the earth in an exodus like Israel's exodus out of Egypt. In Zion, they receive lands of inheritance after the wicked of the world pass away. Zion is a safe place for God's people when the archtyrant desolates the earth and cleanses it of wickedness. God's cloud of glory protects Zion as it protected his people from the armies of Pharaoh. The land of Zion becomes a new Paradise when the returning exiles inherit it. Only those who *are* Zion—not God's people in general—live *in* Zion.

Understanding this narrow definition of Zion helps to see who belongs to it. "Zion" is both a *people* and a *place*: those of God's people who repent and the place to which they return—a place of refuge in God's Day of Judgment (see Figure 32). The Hebrew verb "repent" (*šwb*) is the same as the verb "return" (*šwb*). That implies that those who return from exile are the same as those who repent. And its opposite: those who don't repent don't return but are destroyed together with the nations. In short, Zion is a select group within God's people; but it is also a new, more glorious version of the Promised Land. God blesses the people Zion and their land because they keep his law and word.

Figure 32   **Zion as a People and a Place**

A surface reading of Isaiah's writings identifies Babylon, too, as both a people and a place (see Figure 33). Isaiah 13 defines Babylon by context as the "sinners," "wicked," "insolent men" and "tyrants" of "the earth" and "the world"—all that God destroys as he anciently destroyed Sodom and Gomorrah (Isaiah 13:1, 9, 11, 19). God brings a harsh judgment on Babylon as he did on the cities of Sodom and Gomorrah that were leveled by a hail of fire and brimstone until nothing of them was left. Their residents were guilty of injustice, tyranny, murder, exploitation, and sodomy. The very names Sodom and Gomorrah came to mean everything evil in humanity and how God cursed those who condoned it.

Figure 33   **Babylon as a People and a Place**

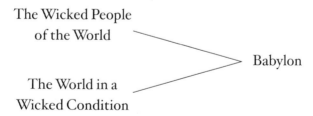

In effect, "Babylon" refers not to a single city or even an empire but to a broad, corrupt category of people and the place where they reside. Babylon comprises the world in general and its wicked inhabitants, all who are under condemnation for transgressing God's word. With such a wide definition of Babylon we begin to see its contrast with Zion. Babylon is Zion's opposite. At the end of the world the righteousness of one group offsets the wickedness of the other. Zion consists of those who repent, Babylon of those who don't repent. God blesses Zion for keeping the law of his covenant, but he curses Babylon for breaking it. Zion miraculously survives destruction, but Babylon utterly passes away.

In those terms Isaiah could be speaking of a Sodom-and-Gomorrah type of destruction literally repeating itself at the end of the world. A shower of gigantic meteors could cause the kind of worldwide devastation Isaiah predicts. If that happened, however, all people on the earth might perish, not just Babylon. Instead, Isaiah uses the escape of Lot and his daughters from Sodom anciently as the type of those whom God saves alive. And, to be realistic, the likelihood of an entire planet being desolated by meteoric collision is considered practically nil. Although Isaiah predicts that a "hail" will fell forests and level cities, he links that destruction to the king of Assyria/Babylon, not to natural phenomena.

Such an immense devastation is possible with today's technology.

Instead of fire and brimstone, a global conflict wipes out many of the world's wicked. Isaiah sees that "an army marshaled for war" carries out this massacre of humanity. That formidable army consists of an alliance of nations from "beyond the horizon" which "causes destruction throughout the earth." God's judgment of Babylon comes "as a violent blow from the Almighty. . . . as a cruel outburst of anger and wrath to make the earth a desolation, that sinners may be annihilated from it. . . . Whoever is found will be thrust through; all who are caught will fall by the sword. . . . They will show no mercy to the newborn; their eye will not look with compassion on children" (Isaiah 13:4–6, 9, 15, 18).

God has "decreed calamity for the world, punishment for the wicked." He will "put an end to the arrogance of insolent men and humble the pride of tyrants." The elements will be in commotion, causing "disturbance in the heavens when the earth is jolted out of place by the anger of Jehovah of Hosts in the day of his blazing wrath." A pall of darkness will hang over the earth: "The stars and constellation of the heavens will not shine. When the sun rises, it will be obscured; nor will the moon give its light." In the end, the human population is vastly reduced. Men become "scarcer than fine gold"—gold denoting God's elect—and but a small percentage of the earth's inhabitants survives (Isaiah 13:10–13).

Such an immense devastation is of course possible with today's technology. Weapons of mass destruction exist that could resemble a fiery hail falling from the sky. In fact, word links and other literary devices identify the Assyrian archtyrant as the perpetrator of that worldwide holocaust. His military machine, Isaiah predicts, will conduct a merciless war of annihilation. The endtime Sodom-and-Gomorrah destruction, therefore, is humanly engineered, besides whatever natural phenomena are involved. It leads us to wonder if a nuclear strike and its aftereffects could cause such a horrendous scenario of human genocide. How else can we explain an all-out world war of cosmic proportions?

Babylon Is the Antithesis and Adversary of Zion

To fully understand what Babylon is, however, we must search deeper. Synchronous structures in the Book of Isaiah require that we "change the rules" for interpreting it, signaling that traditional methods of explaining its message are insufficient. Thus, Babylon is not merely the antithesis of Zion but also its sworn enemy. Whatever Zion does, Babylon fundamentally opposes it. Whatever God does for Zion, he does the reverse to Babylon. God deals with each according to how it deals with others, conforming with Jesus' teachings in the New Testament. In Zion and Babylon we see the inevitable consequences of righteousness and wickedness played out as Zion ascends and Babylon descends.

The opposition between Zion and Babylon in Isaiah's Seven-Part Structure resembles that between the King of Zion and the king of Babylon in the Servant–Tyrant Parallelism. Just as the archtyrant fights against God, so do those who follow him. Such opposition, however, serves God's people by creating an opportunity for the righteous to ascend. Evils committed by those on the lowest levels may turn to the advantage of those on higher ones. As victims of injustice, God's people suffer, but without responding like victims. Rather, Isaiah encourages them to endure adversity well, assuring them that their afflictions will have a happy ending—God delivers those who pass his test of their loyalty.

We need opposition to ascend because that is how we grow—with God's help. We ascend the ladder in stages in direct proportion to God's fortifying us against evil (see Figure 34). God empowers all who comply with his will so that they can overcome their troubles. He allows us to experience adversity, often letting it run its course so we can learn to rise above it. In fact, God makes us equal to each challenge—to whatever opposition we receive—so long as we stay loyal to him by keeping his law and word. Unless we again transgress against him, his empowering us is cumulative. In other words, God's grace remains with us from that time forth, increasing our capacity to manage adversity.

It is important, therefore, to perceive the true nature of Zion and Babylon as everyone potentially belongs to one or the other. As the end of the world approaches we may find ourselves preferring one above its opposite. Both multiply enormously at that time, especially Babylon. Isaiah draws such a stark contrast between Zion and Babylon to inform us of the consequences of our choices. By measuring one against the other we get an idea of which one we want to be a part of. Isaiah's structures contrast their two opposite ideologies, one inviting a person up the ladder, the other down. In addition, as a further literary device, Isaiah layers the opposite attributes of Zion and Babylon throughout his book.

Figure 34 **Opposition Is Necessary for Ascent**

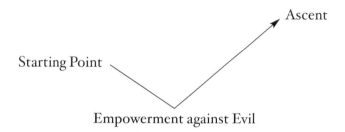

For example, Zion gathers up God's people who were outcasts from society; but Babylon shows them no mercy, yoking young and old in hard bondage. Zion's residents wait patiently through trials for God to deliver them; but Babylon's residents forget God and turn aside to idols. God forgives Zion's inhabitants their transgressions; but he doesn't forgive Babylon's inhabitants until they die. God empowers Zion against adversity; but in one day he renders Babylon powerless. God clothes Zion in robes of glory; but he strips Babylon naked. God ransoms Zion from catastrophe; but Babylon, unable to ransom herself, he visits with disaster. Zion lives through the devouring fire; but Babylon burns up.

Zion lives through the devouring fire, but Babylon burns up.

God redeems Zion; but he condemns Babylon. Zion, forsaken, God espouses anew; but Babylon, favored and espoused, he widows and bereaves. Zion's children gather safely home; but Babylon's children scatter and die. Zion enjoys peace and an absence of fear; but fear and terror overtake Babylon. God comforts Zion; but he discomfits Babylon. God lays in Zion a sure foundation; but Babylon's foundation he shakes loose. Zion sings with joy; but Babylon weeps and laments. Zion's land gloriously regenerates; but Babylon's land decays and dries up. Zion, jubilant, spreads abroad and inherits nations; but Babylon, speechless, rules nations no more. God glorifies Zion; but he disgraces Babylon.

Coinciding with this layered contrast of Zion and Babylon, Isaiah's Seven-Part Structure links its seven pairs of opposite themes with one category or the other (see Figure 35). Babylon consists of those disloyal, who rebel against their Creator, while Zion comprises God's loyal people who comply with his law. Babylon ultimately descends from her throne and goes into the dust as she who exalted herself incurs final "suffering" and "humiliation." At the same time, Zion rises from the dust to sit on her throne, her involuntary humiliation leading to her final "salvation" and "exaltation." Zion and Babylon thus form archetypes of good and evil, with little room, in that day, for maneuvering between the two.

Figure 35	Babylon's Seven Themes	Zion's Seven Themes
	Ruin	Rebirth
	Rebellion	Compliance
	Punishment	Deliverance
	Humiliation	Exaltation
	Suffering	Salvation
	Disloyalty	Loyalty
	Disinheritance	Inheritance

One typically finds these distinctions between opposite entities such as Zion and Babylon in apocalyptic writings, which deal with worldwide events. Apocalypses predict the end of the world and teach the doctrine of the "two ways" or two ideologies. In that literature, Babylon epitomizes evil, and Zion, good. Using literary patterns to define "Zion" and "Babylon," however, Isaiah teaches the doctrine of the two ways precisely as apocalyptic writings define it. Isaiah also shows where each *way* leads: up or down the ladder. In a literary sense, therefore, Isaiah's prophecy *is* an apocalyptic prophecy—it deals with both the "last days" and theological concepts such as ascent on a ladder to heaven.

A Worldwide Conglomerate Asserts Itself over All

Isaiah's Seven-Part Structure defines Babylon as a *composite* entity made up of individual entities of various kinds (Isaiah 13–23; 47). These consist of the nations of the world, aggressive world powers (like Assyria and its alliance), tyrants and oppressors, rulers and men of power, enemies and adversaries, proud kindred peoples, and the wicked of God's people (see Figure 36). Each of these groups possesses one or more types in the past, and all exist at the end of the world. The global cartel they make up shares a universal and multi-national consciousness, as its participants hang together in a kind of codependency. Underlying Babylon's ideology are an unrestrained arrogance and utter godlessness.

Types from the past of this Greater Babylon include the old Babylonian empire, the alliance of nations ancient Babylon sought to bring against Assyria, and the Neo-Babylonian empire of King Nebuchadnezzar. Individual entities comprising Isaiah's Greater Babylon, such as Tyre and Moab, depict different character traits of the whole. But all have one thing in common: self-exaltation—lifting oneself above others. Isaiah's Babylon consists of every biblical reprobate whose modern counterpart is involved in an endtime showdown with Zion. Babylon is thus not merely a composite entity but one that is antagonistic; Babylon ultimately fights against Zion. So long as Zion exists, Babylon can't rest.

Figure 36   **Babylon—A Composite Entity**

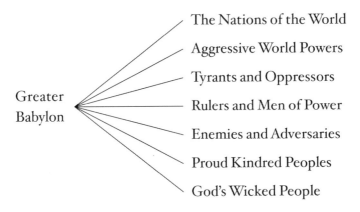

John's concept of Babylon the Great in the Book of Revelation parallels Isaiah's concept of this Greater Babylon. In fact, when you compare the two it becomes clear that John depends on Isaiah for much of his apocalyptic version of Babylon. In the light of Isaiah's Seven-Part Structure, John's New Testament idea is seen as an Old Testament idea also. The kinds of imagery John uses similarly have their roots in the writings of the Hebrew prophets. Of course, John received his own vision of the end of the world, but he also followed the age-old pattern of building on what former prophets had spoken or written. God sends more than one witness to testify of the same truths that lead to salvation.

John's Babylon the Great parallels Isaiah's Greater Babylon.

For example, John describes a great "city," a "whore" or harlot—Babylon the Great—with whom the rulers of the world have committed fornication. All peoples come under her intoxicating spell. She makes the inhabitants of the earth drunk with the wine of her adulteries. She sits on a red beast that has seven heads and ten horns. Its horns are ten rulers who will rise to positions of power at the end of the world. They burn Babylon with fire (Revelation 17:1–18; 18:3). Because John's symbolic imagery—the whore, beast, heads, horns, dragon, false prophet, etc.—appears in previous prophetic writings, we can draw on those to understand what it stands for, besides what John tells us directly about it.

In John's vision, Babylon's sins, like Sodom's and Gomorrah's, have reached up to heaven. Because she corrupts the world, John calls her the Mother of Harlots and the mother of all abominations in the earth. In just "one day" she is utterly incinerated and exists no more. Billowing pillars of smoke from her burning cause those who indulged in her luxuries to stand afar off, afraid of her torment. They lament because in "one hour" her immense wealth has come to naught (Revelation 17:5; 18:5–10, 17). Using such allegory, John predicts that an affluent worldwide establishment—which deceives all nations into participating with it—will be laid waste in a Sodom-and-Gomorrah type of destruction.

Trade and merchandising feature in John's characterization of Babylon. Her socio-economic structure collapses when people can't buy her goods any more. John depicts her commodities in terms familiar to our modern economy: gold, silver, precious stones, pearls, fine linen, silks, ivory, wood, brass, iron, marble, spices, perfumes, oils, frankincense, fruits, delicacies, wines, flour, wheat, beasts, cattle, horses, chariots, slaves, and human souls (Revelation 17:4; 18:11–16). Although these were common to ancient Babylon's economy, in John's day that Babylon no longer existed. Yet, like Isaiah, John draws on it as the type of an endtime Babylon, the one setting a precedent for the other (see Figure 37).

Figure 37   **Babylon as a Type for the "Last Days"**

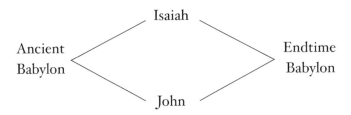

Shipping plays an essential part in the economy of John's Babylon the Great, making her goods accessible to all. A worldwide maritime empire supplies Babylon's lusts until the day she dies. Upon her sudden destruction, every sea captain, all ships' crews, sailors, and those who trade by sea weep and wail at her fiery spectacle. Throwing dust on their heads, they cry out, "Woe, woe to that great city. Because of her, all who had ships at sea became rich, she was so wealthy." Babylon's merchants—the great men of the earth—mourn her fall (Revelation 18:2, 11, 17–19, 23). As hard as it may be to imagine, an entire world economy and all that depends on it entirely and irreversibly passes away overnight.

According to John, God destroys Babylon because she persecutes and oppresses God's people. Because they won't follow her ways, Babylon bullies them. Just as the beast on which she sits makes war against God's holy ones, so she adopts the beast's anti-God attitude. Not only does she deceive the nations with her sorceries, she is guilty of the blood of prophets and saints and all who are slain. Drunk with the blood of martyrs, the great whore suffers God's justice. Even as the beast is cast into a lake of fire and brimstone, so she too falls, burns up, and lives no more. Upon she who corrupted the earth with her adulteries, God avenges the wrongs done to his servants (Revelation 13:7; 14:8; 18:23–19:2, 20).

When Babylon exalts herself over all, ruling the world like an empress, she never imagines that famine, mourning, death, and destruction are her lot. Unless God's people living in Babylon flee in time, they too suffer her fate. To escape her "plagues"—God's curses on Babylon—they must "come out of her" (Revelation 18:4–8). John portrays God's covenant people as a "woman" heavy with child. As soon as she gives birth to a deliverer, she flees into the wilderness to escape the power of the dragon (Revelation 12). The ancient type of that event are the plagues God sent on the Egyptians at the time his people fled Egypt, when Moses, their deliverer, led them through the wilderness to the Promised Land.

The Harlot Babylon Persecutes the Virgin Zion

Numerous parallels between John's Babylon the Great and Isaiah's Greater Babylon suggest that both prophetic writers are speaking about the same endtime scenario. Those parallels are most obvious in the light of Isaiah's Seven-Part Structure, which establishes an endtime setting for Isaiah's prophecy. That structure too identifies Babylon as a "city," a metaphor Isaiah uses to describe a worldwide anti-Zion establishment that is identical with Babylon. Isaiah depicts that city as exalted, arrogant, rowdy, boisterous, oppressive, alien, and chaotic. Its heathen palaces and elite residents, its hordes of hedonists and evildoers, its rude and unruly mobs perish in a fiery holocaust, ending up in the dust.

Isaiah, too, describes the wicked city as a "whore" or harlot, referring to those who rebel against their Maker. Isaiah's Babylon rules as Mistress of Kingdoms, lording it over the people of God. Like John's Babylon, she doesn't fear widowhood or bereavement of children, though both overtake her in "one day"—God's Day of Judgment. Her merchants or "procurers," who drummed up business for her, now abandon her to her humiliating fate. Her statisticians and prognosticators, who measured trends and made hopeful predictions, are as stubble burned in the fire. She who exalted herself over God's covenant people, who was pampered and lived delicately, descends, discredited, into the dust.

The counterpart of Isaiah's wicked city is the City of Righteousness, a holy city (see Figure 38). It is the city of Israel's God, a place of solemn assemblies, an abode of peace. That city—Zion/Jerusalem—survives the archtyrant's desolation of the earth and rises, regenerated, from the dust. Her residents are "holy ones"—saints—whom God delivers in the selfsame hour that he destroys Babylon. God's deliverance of the righteous, in effect, consists of his destruction of the wicked, they being two aspects of the same endtime drama. The righteous city prevails over her wicked counterpart because God is her defense. She gathers God's people to safety at the time the archtyrant desolates the city of chaos.

Figure 38   **Two Juxtaposed Endtime "Cities"**

Babylon—City of Wickedness	Zion—City of Righteousness

As in John's vision, God provides for his people to exit Greater Babylon when its destruction is about to take place. God's servant calls on them to "come out of her," to flee from destruction as at the exodus out of Egypt. They embark on a new wandering in the wilderness to the Promised Land—the land of Zion or Jerusalem. Those events parallel John's depiction of the woman who flees into the wilderness to escape the power of the dragon. God protects her there until Babylon falls and the dragon is bound. John doesn't describe much of what happens to the woman after her wilderness ordeal except that she marries Jehovah, her husband. We get the rest of the story of her deliverance from Isaiah.

Isaiah similarly describes those who escape destruction as a woman. She is the Virgin Daughter of Zion, whom Israel's God preserves from a Sodom-and-Gomorrah type of holocaust. When she repents and returns to him, Jehovah marries her by an everlasting covenant. After that, when the archtyrant lays siege to her, Jehovah protects her and puts down her enemies. Her covenant relationship with Israel's God obliges him to defend her so long as she proves faithful. The people whom Jehovah delivers in that day receive permanent lands of inheritance. Isaiah figuratively depicts that event as the Woman Zion enlarging the site of her tent to make room for her scattered children who return to her.

Prominent among those who fight against Zion—against God's covenant people—are the king of Assyria/Babylon and his alliance of nations. They seek to conquer the world and annihilate God's people by fire and by the sword. Instead, they end up destroying Babylon, the world and its wicked inhabitants. The archtyrant and his war machine are Isaiah's equivalent of John's beast with ten horns. They consist of ten rulers who rise to power at the end of the world who burn Babylon with fire. John's horns, in turn, resemble the ten horns or rulers of the beast Daniel predicts will devour the whole earth. Daniel's "little horn," which makes war against the saints of God, compares with Isaiah's archtyrant.

They seek to conquer the world and annihilate God's people.

Isaiah's Seven-Part Structure makes trade and merchandising an essential feature of Babylon, the port city of Tyre being an integral part of his Greater Babylon. Tyre's shipping industry sustains the global conglomerate that Isaiah identifies as Babylon. Tyre, which the Babylonians "established for shipping," represents the entire sea-faring empire, not just one port. Isaiah depicts Tyre as a "whore" or harlot who hires herself out to all kingdoms on the face of the earth (Isaiah 23:13, 17). Here again, we see Isaiah's influence on John in the light of Isaiah's literary structure. Considering the parallels, the same entities that make up Isaiah's Greater Babylon seem to comprise John's Babylon the Great.

When God stretches out his hand over the sea in judgment, the nations of the world suffer the devastating effects of Tyre's fall. Their merchant ships sound their sirens in alarm when Tyre is laid waste. Tyre's abundant source of revenue is abruptly cut off when her ports of haven are destroyed. Her merchants and traders—the world's princes and celebrities—are humbled and disparaged. Isaiah credits the "Assyrians"—the king of Assyria/Babylon's military machine—with Tyre's downfall (Isaiah 23:1, 3, 8–9, 11, 13–14). Tyre doesn't perish alone, however, but expires together with all who make up Greater Babylon. In the sudden destruction that engulfs Babylon all wicked entities are casualties.

John's Babylon the Great and Isaiah's Greater Babylon thus mirror each other, filling in each other's details when viewed together. The two writers paint endtime scenarios depicting the same series of events (see Figure 39). The Harlot Babylon—a wicked world and its idolatrous society—comes to a fiery end in God's Day of Judgment. The Virgin Daughter of Zion—God's righteous people—miraculously escapes destruction in an exodus out of Babylon resembling Israel's exodus out of Egypt. Ancillary events, such as the archtyrant's world conquest and his final fall, though described using different imagery, parallel each other. John's prophecy, in effect, forms a second witness to Isaiah's.

Figure 39   **The Synonymity of Two Apocalypses**

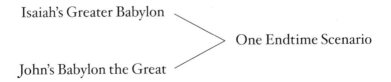

A False Socio-Economic System Sustains Babylon

Personal gain and power—the quest for self-exaltation—are the main driving forces behind Babylon. If these are our driving force also, then we too belong to Babylon. Babylon focuses on the things of this world, not those of God or a better world. Babylon's socio-economic system is based on the manufacture, promotion, and sale of idols—false gods people worship. The prophets define these as the "works of men's hands," inventions of man's own making. Anciently, false gods consisted largely of statues, icons, and fetishes. But Isaiah defines idols in other ways as well: silver and gold, horses and chariots, and prominent persons in society. People may idolize them without being aware of it.

Let us look, for example, at present-day parallels of ancient kinds of idolatry. Isaiah's references to designing, sketching, carving, chiseling, hammering, smelting, casting, plating, welding, and riveting remind us of today's industrial factories. In our society, no less than in ancient Babylon, consumer goods—the works of men's hands—form a vast human enterprise. According to Isaiah, Babylon's idols require "skill and science" or the latest technology to conceive and produce. Even so, they get obsolete and must be replaced by new and more modern ones. They follow popular trends and are expensive to buy. They divide people into rich and poor, depending on who can pay the highest price.

Isaiah satirically parodies the role of idols in Babylon's society. People attribute their success in life to them rather than to God. After all, they provide a decent living for those who manufacture, promote, and sell them. In fact, the entire human establishment revolves around them. The very machinery of Babylon thrives on the profuse production of idols, the fruits of man's resourcefulness and marvelous ingenuity. People covet them and are willing to pay in gold and silver. They lend stature and class distinction to the rich. Small wonder Babylon's entrepreneurs are the icons of society. To them, people kowtow and heap adulation. As the elite of the earth, they live like gods—false gods.

> Those who belong to Babylon don't perceive it for what it is.

Isaiah depicts this preoccupation with idols as false "worship," set in opposition to true worship. The Hebrew verb "worship" (*'ābad*) also means "work" (*'ābad*). Applying this dual meaning, whatever people work at, spend their energies and resources on, that is what they worship. Those who belong to Babylon, however, don't perceive it for what it is. They can't for a moment imagine that they are worshiping idols or that there is a problem with what they do. They carry their idols on their persons, they place them in their homes, they idolize and adore them, yet they don't discern that it is idolatry. Materialism, like any other culture, seeks to perpetuate itself and provides its own rationale.

A spiritual blindness—John calls it drunkenness—afflicts all who indulge in idolatry. Becoming physically distracted and beguiled by a counterfeit brings with it evil consequences. Isaiah thus condemns Babylon's materialism in contemptuous terms: "All who manufacture idols are deranged; the things they cherish profit nothing. Those who promote them are themselves sightless and mindless, to their own dismay. Who would fashion a god or cast an idol that cannot benefit them? Their whole society is confused; their fabricators are mere mortals . . . . They have become unaware and insensible; their eyes are glazed so they cannot see, their minds are incapable of discernment" (Isaiah 44:9–11, 18).

The contest between the false gods and true God extends beyond material lusts verses spiritual fulfillment. No god that men make is able to deliver them in the day of calamity. There comes a moment of truth—the end of the world—when everyone will recognize who is God and who isn't. Isaiah predicts that those who rely on idols will realize their error too late: "As one, the makers of inventions retreated in disgrace, utterly dismayed and embarrassed" (Isaiah 45:16). Their false gods couldn't save them (see Figure 40). Instead, they caused them to fall prey to the archtyrant's propaganda, blinding them to his evil designs. Preoccupied with their idols, they lost sight of Israel's God, their only Savior.

Figure 40   **False Gods Versus the True God**

False Gods	True God
—Unable to Save	—Able to Save

Isaiah observes that God's people's "land is full of idols—they adore the works of their hands, things their own fingers have made." But in the day of his coming to reign on the earth, Israel's God "will utterly supplant the false gods. Men will go into caves in the rocks and holes in the ground from the awesome presence of Jehovah and from the brightness of his glory, when he arises and strikes terror on earth. In that day men will throw away to the moles and to the bats their idols of silver and gods of gold which they have made for themselves to adore" (Isaiah 2:8, 18–20). In God's Day of Judgment "those who trust in idols and esteem their images as gods will retreat in utter confusion" (Isaiah 42:17).

Infatuation with idols grips people like a disease.

Even when faced with the effects of their idolatry—the curses of the covenant—infatuation with idols grips people like a disease. Of idolaters, Isaiah says, "They are followers of ashes; their deluded minds have distracted them. They cannot liberate themselves [from them] or say, 'Surely this thing in my hand is a fraud!'" (Isaiah 44:20). Such souls see no connection between their misfortunes and a lifestyle defiled by idols. Locked into a system that seems to work, they can't conceive of anything else. Although Babylon's flaws are evident, her faults exposed for all to see, people can't escape her bewitching spell. When her idols are razed to the ground, a majority of humanity perishes with them.

Israel's God addresses the Harlot Babylon: "Secure in your wickedness, you thought, 'No one discerns me.' By your skill and science you were led astray, thinking to yourself, 'I exist, and there is none besides me!' Catastrophe will overtake you, which you will not know how to avert by bribes; disaster will befall you from which you cannot ransom yourself: there will come upon you sudden ruin such as you have not imagined" (Isaiah 47:10–11). Of those who follow economic indicators and project popular trends, Isaiah adds, "See, as stubble they are burned up in the fire, unable themselves to escape the hand of the flame. . . . Each deviates his own way; none is there to save you" (Isaiah 47:14–15).

Modern Idolatry Mirrors Ancient Counterparts

Isaiah covers a wide spectrum of idolatry, not only the "works of men's hands." In fact, the nature of idol worship has changed little from his day to ours. As Moses teaches, one of God's main prohibitions to his people is the making and worshiping of "images," "likenesses," or "pictures," things that deflect them off the path leading to salvation (Exodus 20:4; Deuteronomy 4:16). Obsession with *images* leads to lives lived in unreality. It prevents people from realizing their divine potential and makes them vulnerable to intrigues by enemies. Images are enticing as a form of idolatry because they capture the imagination, so that people "worship the creature rather than the Creator" (Romans 1:25).

Ancient Israelites, contrary to God's law and word, made likenesses of the god Baal and set them up in houses of Baal. They put up shrines in their own homes and in the houses of their gods. Consequently, God subjected them to their enemies, giving aliens power over his people (Judges 2:10–23; 10:6–16). Yet they continued preoccupying themselves with images, growing more and more depraved. They loved and lusted after pictures of the elite of Babylonian society, images in color, of people attired in the finest fashions (Ezekiel 16:17–18; 23:14–16). Paradoxically, the images people could *see* were more real than their God, whom they could not see. But that was the test of their faith.

People "worship the creature rather than the Creator."

In God's Day of Judgment that signals the end of the world, men will be compelled to "have regard to their Maker and their eyes look to the Holy One of Israel, and regard not the altars, the works of their hands, the idols of prosperity and the shining images. In that day their mighty cities will be as the deserted towns of the Hivites and Amorites, which they abandoned before the Israelites during the desolation" (Isaiah 17:8–9). As God's people had conquered the Baal-worshiping Canaanites, so others now conquer them. But God forgives their idolatry when they destroy their idols. "Because [of them] the defended cities lie forlorn, deserted habitations, forsaken like a wilderness" (Isaiah 27:9–10).

It isn't difficult to see parallels of ancient image worship in our modern society. Our images may be more sophisticated than those of our forebears but we love them equally well. Today's movie theaters resemble "houses of Baal," where people worship at his shrine and lust after likenesses. TV sets parallel personal shrines at which we adore pictures of the elite of Babylonian society, images in color, of people attired in its finest fashions (see Figure 41). Our attention easily gets distracted from the true God to such substitutes, as we worship the creature rather than the Creator. The images arouse our baser natures; the more we give them license, the more corrupt we become—like the images themselves.

Figure 41   **Modern Manifestations of Baalism**

The Baal-Anath Epic of Ugaritic literature depicts alternating scenes of violence and sex that were relived in real life by people who took their cue from the Baal myth. Pornographic imagery accompanied their performance. The myth so incited Israelites who exposed themselves to it that even after the wonders God had performed—in releasing them from bondage and leading them to the Promised Land—they committed immoral acts with heathen nations (Numbers 25:1–9). Consequently, God punished those who persisted in this corrupt cult by empowering their enemies against them. These eventually deported his people entirely out of their land. Too late, they realized the error of their ways.

In the Ugaritic myth the hero-god Baal is authorized by a higher authority, El, to compel the villain-gods Yamm/Nahar (Sea/River) and Mot (Death) to comply with Baal's rule or face him in a confrontation. Yamm/Nahar and Mot are forces of chaos who will make trouble for Baal and for the world if Baal doesn't subdue them. They resist Baal and each fights him to the death. Various cohorts help Baal and his rivals in their life-and-death struggle. The versatile craftsman Koshar fashions the weapons Baal uses against his enemies. These weapons can kill, injure, or maim from a distance. As the central figure of this drama, Baal literally kicks up a storm, he being the god of lightning and thunder.

Still, Baal suffers setbacks. He stares death in the face and at one point appears completely overpowered. But with the timely aid of his violent consort Anath he escapes the clutches of death and wins the victory at the last. The myth credits Baal with restoring order in the world, everyone profiting from his extraordinary prowess. Sexual relations between him and Anath, hitherto hampered by adversity, now receive full expression. Explicit scenes of the violent exchanges between the hero and his rivals, and of the victor's sexual acts, form the substance of the narrative. Variations of the story, such as Baal-Peor, Baal-Berith, Baal-Zebub, and other Baals, existed in different regions of Canaan.

We recognize the plot that animates many movies in our media.

Comparing Baalism with anything in the world today, we recognize the basic plot that animates so many movies in our media. Their success seems to lie in the quantities of violence and sex they portray. The hero and his helpers are authorized to kill and do as they please so long as they subdue the enemy and restore order. They do battle using weapons that kill and injure from a distance, that strike like lightning and clap aloud like thunder. In performing his bizarre task, the hero endures setbacks, has close encounters with death, yet help always arrives in the nick of time, often by a woman driven to violence. In these stories, explicit scenes of violence and sex abound as they do in the Baal myth.

The spilling over of violence and sex from fictitious dramas into real life occurs as commonly today as it did among the Canaanites. By legitimizing carnality in their culture the Canaanites marked themselves ripe for destruction. Through the media in our everyday lives, persons enter our homes and minds to perform acts we would abhor in real life. The pornographic images, the licentious manner of the characters, their distorted standard of values, and their disposition to violence—all subvert and pollute our minds (see Figure 42). By indulging them we disdain God's standard of "stopping [our] ears at the mention of murder and shutting [our] eyes at the sight of wickedness" (Isaiah 33:15).

Figure 42   **Twin Traits of Baalism, Today as Anciently**

Disposition to Violence

Sanctioning of Carnality

Mimicking their fictitious heroes, men violate others' rights: "Your palms are defiled with blood, your fingers with iniquity; your lips speak guile, your tongue utters duplicity. None calls for righteousness; no one sues for an honest cause. They rely on empty words, deceitfully spoken; they conceive misdeeds, they beget wickedness. . . . Their works consist of wrongdoing; they manipulate injurious dealings. Their feet rush after evil; they hasten to shed innocent blood. Their thoughts are preoccupied with mischief; havoc and disaster follow in their wake. They are unacquainted with the way of perfection; integrity is not within their bounds. They have made crooked their paths" (Isaiah 59:3–4, 6–8).

The Harlot Babylon not only represents a wicked category of God's people, but she also symbolizes individual adulterous women whose "nakedness will be exposed" and whose "shame uncovered" in God's Day of Judgment (Isaiah 47:3). Israel's God, therefore, addresses these persons as he does his wicked people as a whole: "Behind doors and facades you have put up your emblems, and have exposed yourself to others than I: mounting your bed, you have laid it wide open. . . . But I will expose your fornication and the wantonness of your exploits. When you cry out in distress, let those who flock to you save you! A wind will carry all of them off; a vapor will take them away" (Isaiah 57:8, 12–13).

Modern "Baals" and "Anaths," however, are but a few among many human idols whom Isaiah condemns. Through a play on words he identifies prominent people in society as "idols." Using terms that possess multiple meanings (*ēlâ; 'ēlîm; ḥasôn; bāḥar; ḥāmad*), Isaiah implies that people idolize "celebrities" and "bigwigs." People are "enchanted" and "captivated" by them and demonstrate "covetous desires," "fawning adulation," and "carnal lust" toward them. The human idols, meanwhile, exercise "immunity" from the law on account of their wealth, power, or fame. But in the end they and their enterprises constitute the "spark" that sets off a fiery conflagration of the wicked (Isaiah 1:29–31).

> Isaiah identifies prominent people in society as "idols."

Isaiah predicts that God will "make all glorying in excellence a profanity and the world's celebrities an utter execration" (Isaiah 23:9). He accomplishes that feat through the ultimate human idol himself—the king of Assyria/Babylon. That archtyrant condemns to the fire the false gods of all peoples (Isaiah 10:10–11; 37:18–19). As Daniel foretells, he regards no god other than himself but "magnifies himself above all" (Daniel 11:37). Under his tyranny human gods now worshiped, exalted, extolled, glorified, revered, idolized, and adored will be but "despised broken idols" (Jeremiah 22:28). Movie stars, rock stars, sports stars, superstars, tycoons, barons, and bigwigs will be a thing of the past.

Just as idolatry corrupted God's people in the past, so it does today. Isaiah predicts that God "has in store a day of commotion and trampling and riot in the Arena of Spectacles" reminiscent of modern sport events (Isaiah 22:5). Spectator sports in large part influenced the downfall of the Roman Empire as the elite and the masses alike were caught up in the frenzy of the games. Stadiums holding hundred of thousands of spectators, with gladiators disciplined and groomed for contests of skill combined with brute strength, characterized sports Roman style. Contestants became household names, adored by women as gods. People knew them by their personal statistics and professional record.

Great bands of musicians, organized in festal processions, blared on trumpets before and during the games. People made predictions on their outcome, betting money on the results. Huge unruly crowds waved handkerchiefs, shouted advice, disapproval, or insults, rising up from their seats in moments of suspense. As contests neared their conclusion, the fervor of the crowds reached fever pitch, accompanied by calls for blood. People debated the results long after the events. In like manner, the fanfare and pageantry we impose on games today, the vast resources of money and man-hours we devote to professional sports, betray an entrenched cult, a full-blown diversion from life's real contest.

Professional sports betray a diversion from life's real contest.

Isaiah describes "harps and lyres, drums, flutes, and wine" at God's people's banquets and entertainments: "They regard not what Jehovah does, nor perceive his hands at work. Therefore are my people taken captive for want of knowledge; their best men die of famine, their masses perish with thirst. Sheol [Hell] becomes ravenous, opening her mouth insatiably; into it descend their elite with the masses, their boisterous ones and revelers. Mankind is brought low when men debase themselves, causing the eyes of the high-minded to be downcast" (Isaiah 5:12–15). In God's Day of Judgment "the rhythm of drums ceases, the revelers' din stops, and the pulsating of lyres comes to an end" (Isaiah 24:8).

One way people anciently debased themselves was through music that "ravished the soul." The Books of Adam and Eve relate how, before the Flood, the descendants of Cain, who lived on the plain, enticed the people of God to come down from the mountain where they dwelt apart. In the days of Jared (whose name means "Going Down"), most descended the mountain, lowering themselves to the level of the Cainites. Carnal lusts overcame them, for which the Cainites' music had conditioned them. When, in remorse, some tried to return, they weren't able. Having "descended from glory," they had estranged themselves from being the people of God (2 Adam and Eve 20–21) (see Figure 43).

The account explains how a man named Genun, whom Satan inspired, made trumpets, horns, stringed instruments, cymbals, psalteries, lyres, harps, and flutes. When Genun and his musicians played the instruments, "Satan came into them, so that out [of them] were heard beautiful and sweet sounds that ravished the heart." The music's intensity and momentum, when played at all hours by impassioned bands of artists, inflamed people's hearts and won them over. Performing daily at the foot of the mountain, the people of Cain "burned as with fire" as Satan "increased lust among them." After a year of exposure to the music, many of God's people went regularly to look down at the musicians.

Satan then taught Genun to design colorful costumes. To God's people who came to be entertained, the Cainites "shone in beauty and gorgeous apparel, gathered at the foot of the mountain in splendor, with horns and dazzling dresses." Over time, in spite of Jared's warning that if they descended God wouldn't let them return, few remained. For "when they looked at the daughters of Cain, at their beautiful figures, at their hands and feet dyed in color, tattooed in ornaments on their faces, the fire of sin kindled in them." For "Satan made them look most beautiful," so that people lusted after each other like ravenous beasts, committing abominations and falling into defilement (2 Adam and Eve 20–21).

Figure 43   **The Evil Effects of Idolatry**

Carnality and Lust

Alienation from God

Spiritual Blindness & Deafness

Loss of Covenant Blessings

Unreality and Self-Deception

Subjection to Forces of Chaos

Dispossession & Disinheritance

When we view the physical descent of God's people from the mountain as symbolizing spiritual descent, the account describes a modern subculture. Witness a concert by any well-known rock group. The spectacle they create—its fantasy, frenzy, and hysteria—appeals to the basest of human emotions. The physical appearance of the musicians—their gaudy and glittering attire, their lewd and suggestive gestures—parallel in every way the Cainites whom the Books of Adam and Eve portray. As Isaiah predicts, "The look on their faces betrays them: they flaunt their sin like Sodom; they cannot hide it" (Isaiah 3:9). These and other forms of idolatry, too many to mention, reveal how far we have fallen.

The Rebellious among God's People Join Babylon

Those who evidence "disloyalty" and "rebellion" toward God among his people form a sizeable contingent in Isaiah's

Babylon category. The historical type of this blending into Babylon is Judah's exile to Babylon around 600 B.C. At that time many Jews assimilated into Babylon's materialistic society. Although some returned to Jerusalem to resettle the land, most chose to stay. That event—of many of God's people merging into Babylon while some return to the Promised Land—repeats itself at the end of the world. Gazing far into the future, beyond ancient Babylon to the "last days," Isaiah sees a similar assimilation and return, thus dividing God's people into "Babylon" and "Zion."

When Jehovah appoints Isaiah as a "hardener of the heart," Isaiah too serves as a type of the future. After God's people become alienated and transgress against him, Jehovah sends Isaiah to warn of adverse consequences and to call on them to repent. In response many harden their hearts and rebel even more. By thus rejecting God's word they unwittingly seal their own doom: Israel's God hands them over to the tyrannical king of Assyria. Those who renew their allegiance to Jehovah, on the other hand, escape the same destruction that befalls those who rebel. Relying on Israel's God—on the protection clause of his covenant—they are miraculously delivered and their enemies are put down.

In a second, *composite* fulfillment of these two different scenarios God appoints his endtime servant to preach repentance to his people Jacob/Israel who live in Greater Babylon. As noted, Jacob/Israel is that pivotal category from which some ascend to Zion/Jerusalem and others descend to Babylon. In response to the servant's mission many renew their allegiance to Israel's God and "come out" of Greater Babylon. Others harden their hearts and remain behind (see Figure 44). Those who receive the servant's message ascend the ladder while those who reject it descend. By forsaking their God, and ultimately fighting against Zion, those who descend complete their merger into Greater Babylon.

Figure 44   **The Servant's Mission—A Composite of Types**

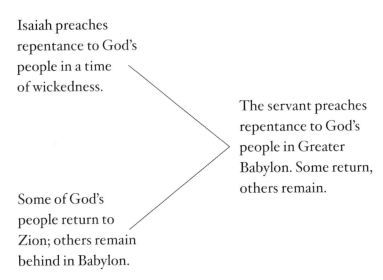

Isaiah preaches repentance to God's people in a time of wickedness.

The servant preaches repentance to God's people in Greater Babylon. Some return, others remain.

Some of God's people return to Zion; others remain behind in Babylon.

Isaiah describes God's people who descend as a "whore" or harlot. That imagery identifies them with Greater Babylon, also called a "whore" or harlot. In effect, God's rebellious people do all that Babylon does and thus suffer the same fate. They regard evil as good and good as evil. They devise schemes to exploit and defraud the needy. They rob and commit murder to get power and gain. They acquit the guilty for a bribe and deny justice to the innocent. They hurl insults and false accusations. They rely on one another instead of on God. They indulge in liquor and amusements and linger at night parties. They commit perverse and immoral acts. Isaiah therefore calls them "Sodom" and "Gomorrah."

God's wicked people include corrupt political leaders who dupe and mislead the masses. They draft and enforce oppressive legislation, depriving the poor of God's people of their rights. They include religious leaders who misuse their ecclesiastical authority, who ostracize believers for being zealous for God. They practice hypocrisy and preach misleading things about God, leaving the hungry soul empty, the thirsty soul deprived.

They include cultists who engage in sexual orgies and the ritual sacrifice of children. They delight in despicable acts, in committing abominations, deliberately desecrating what is sacred. By putting God out of their lives, they extinguish the divine spark within them.

When the world enters a countdown no comfort zone remains.

Isaiah's Seven-Part Structure, therefore, contrasts two opposite groups of people as two Cities, two Women, and as Babylon and Zion. And it contrasts two covenants affiliated with them that express each entity's ideology. One is a "Covenant with Death," an inherently self-destructive mechanism. The other is a Covenant of Life, God's promise of eternal life. One consists of reliance on man's counsels and schemes, on human agreements—on the "arm of flesh." The other consists of adherence to God's law and word as contained in scriptures and as his servant reveals it. At some point everyone makes a choice for or against God. When the world enters a countdown no comfort zone remains.

Those who willfully choose evil over good precipitate God's endtime judgment. By rejecting God's word, relying instead on their own ideas, they bring about their own damnation. The law people keep or fail to keep determines their imminent fate. Instead of choosing life—deliverance from destruction and a millennial peace—many choose death at the hands of the archtyrant. God's servant acts as the catalyst of this endtime division of people throughout the world. They either respond to the servant's message by complying with God's law—thus qualifying for deliverance—or by rebelling against God and all that he represents. Like those who responded to Isaiah, humanity divides in two.

Making wrong choices causes people to regress spiritually, to move down the ladder. It causes a lack of cognitive awareness so that they can't see clearly but lose the light they once had. Culturally based choices bind people to cultural constraints designed to preserve the system, most often Babylon's status quo. They serve the establishment; the establishment doesn't serve them. Over time they grow ignorant of anything but Babylon. By choosing poorly—by aborting life's tests—they forfeit being reborn on higher levels. Isaiah characterizes Babylon this way: "I exist, and other than me there is nothing!" (Isaiah 47:10). In the minds of its self-serving citizens, there is only Babylon, nothing more.

Like Lot's wife, who died with the wicked in the holocaust of Sodom and Gomorrah, people in the Babylon category cannot or will not make a paradigm shift. Heedless to new, emerging realities, they can't imagine that the end of their world draws near—the end of Babylon. Losing touch with the source of their salvation, they position themselves out of reach of deliverance. By rejecting the true God, who offers all the ability to choose for themselves, they fall into the hands of a false god, the king of Assyria/Babylon. Like an abuser who won't nurture or protect his children, the archtyrant cruelly slays them. Like the depraved leader of a satanic cult, he perversely sacrifices his own.

———————————————

Postscript: The prophet Malachi is describing lower categories of God's people when he quotes them as saying "It is futile to serve God. What do we gain by fulfilling his requirements and acting somberly before Jehovah of Hosts? Nowadays we sustain the arrogant. Evildoers are entrenched, and even those who provoke God escape free!" But Malachi adds "Then those who feared Jehovah spoke often with one another, and Jehovah listened and heard. And a Book of Remembrance was written in his presence concerning those who fear Jehovah, who meditate on his name. 'These will be mine,' says Jehovah of Hosts, 'in the day that I make up my treasure. And I will spare them as a man spares his son who serves him. Then you will see the difference between the righteous and the wicked, between those who serve God and those who don't serve him'" (Malachi 3:13–18).

Malachi adds that those who fear God, who speak often "with one another" (because they can't speak freely of spiritual matters for fear of recrimination), will tread the wicked as ashes under their feet in God's Day of Judgment. God will set the evildoers and arrogant ablaze in the "great and dreadful Day of Jehovah," a day that "burns like a furnace." To those who serve God, on the other hand, the "sun of righteousness" rises "with healing in its wings," and they "grow up as calves of the stall" (Malachi 4:1–3, 5). The contradictory human conditions that herald God's Day of Judgment constitute a test of people's loyalties to their God. The wicked "sin now and pay later" while the repentant pay now and later rejoice. Insiders cash in, oppressing the poor, but end up robbed of their riches, while those who prove loyal to him, God prospers (Malachi 3:5–12).

4

Jacob/Israel,
Believers in a Creator–God

*Jacob/Israel represents a beginning point on the spiritual ladder
to heaven. Ancient Israel's exile from the Promised Land sets the
stage for endtime Israel's return. Those who dispersed into the
nations of the world renew their allegiance to God and ascend
the ladder. They return in two pilgrimages to the Promised Land.
Their curses turn into blessings.*

Jacob/Israel represents the most basic level on the spiritual
ladder to heaven. It consists of believers in the God who created
the heavens and the earth but it is made up of more than only
Jews, Christians, or Moslems. It encompasses all those whom
God has created to be his people, whom he asks to be loyal to
him and to learn who he is. It includes God's people who, over
many centuries, assimilated into the nations of the world, who
lost their identity as Israelites yet maintained a belief in God.
It consists of those who acknowledge God as their Maker but

who don't subscribe to much beyond that. In an endtime setting Jacob/Israel comprises people of all nations whom God seeks to reclaim.

As mentioned, Jacob/Israel is a key pivotal category of God's people. From there they either go up or down the ladder. At the end of the world many ascend to Zion/Jerusalem while many more descend to Babylon. Through his servant, and through other servants who labor with him, Israel's God challenges Jacob/Israel to cease clinging to a false idea of him, to do more than merely believe that he exists. They must choose between the true God—their Savior—and the false gods who cannot save. God asks them to renew their allegiance to him and keep his law and word. As the end of the world approaches Jacob/Israel cannot remain where it is. Everyone on that level must either ascend or descend.

To rehearse what we learn from Isaiah's Seven-Part Structure, people go one of two ways, experiencing either "ruin" or "rebirth," "punishment" or "deliverance," "humiliation" or "exaltation," "suffering" or "salvation," "disinheritance" or "inheritance" as their final state. They either face spiritual and physical subjection to enemies or see spiritual and physical redemption and a millennial peace. Like the two lowest categories, Jacob/Israel disappears at the end of the world. The earth itself ascends from the Jacob/Israel level to that of Zion/Jerusalem (see Figure 45). A new era dawns for all who ascend with it, for all who maintain "loyalty" to God and "compliance" with the terms of his covenant.

Just as signs and miracles accompanied Moses' ministry to God's people at their exodus out of Egypt, so signs and miracles accompany the servant's ministry to the nations of the world. If, like Pharaoh, we reject these and fight against the God of Israel, then we align ourselves with Babylon and come under condemnation. The full measure of plagues or curses that befalls the wicked in God's Day of Judgment then falls on us. All who violate the rights of God's people inevitably suffer "ruin." At the end of the world, God destroys Babylon and delivers Zion/Jerusalem. Jacob/Israel ceases to exist; it disappears into categories above or below. Only Zion/Jerusalem and categories higher survive.

Figure 45   **The Earth's Descent and Ascent**

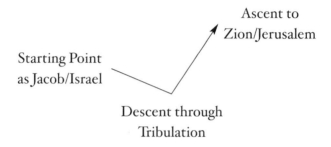

From the chaos that overwhelms the world at Babylon's destruction arises a nobler civilization that spreads throughout the earth. The earth renews its vitality after Babylon descends "into the dust" (Isaiah 47:1). "Dust," "chaff," "debris," "fire," "smoke," "ashes," and other chaos motifs describe the ultimate "ruin" of the wicked, denoting the physical disintegration of peoples and institutions into their elemental state—into non-entities. Zion/Jerusalem's rising "from the dust," on the other hand, signifies the "rebirth" or re-creation of God's covenant people and their divine institutions (Isaiah 52:2). It gives us a picture of God's people emerging, transformed, on a higher spiritual and physical plane.

A final time of testing precedes this end-of-the-world or end-of-Babylon scenario. God gives all peoples a last opportunity to ascend by renewing the covenant. To survive destruction Jacob/Israel must "repent" and "return." If we make that transition we may look forward to a more wonderful future than we can imagine. As most start off life's journey on the Jacob/Israel level, it is a natural step forward in our growth to ascend to Zion/Jerusalem. People in the Babylon category, too, may still do so, although probably few will. To ascend two levels within so short a time would be difficult but not impossible. A biblical precedent for such a sudden about-face were the people of Nineveh.

Ambivalent Believers Awaken to Their Identity

Isaiah predicts an endtime scenario beginning with God's people finding themselves exiled from the Promised Land. That exile occurred in two stages: (1) the Ten Tribes of the northern Kingdom of Israel were banished into Mesopotamia in the late eighth century B.C.; and (2) the Jews of the southern Kingdom of Judah were deported to Babylon more than a century later. An apocryphal account states that the Ten Tribes later migrated north of Mesopotamia. After counseling together, they traveled a year and a half's journey beyond the River Euphrates (4 Ezra 13:40–45). That would have taken them into eastern and western Europe, dispersing Israelite lineages throughout those lands (see Figure 46).

As God's people multiplied and spread, moreover, they mingled with Gentiles or non-Israelites. The Jewish Diaspora among many nations is an example. A tenth of every generation of Jews alone has assimilated into the Gentiles and is no longer known as Jewish. While many Israelites, like the Jews, may have retained some sort of ethnic identity, most lost their Israelite connection. That isn't surprising considering the vagaries of history and the migrations of peoples throughout the earth. It is little wonder, then, that Israel's Ten Tribes have become lost from history. Isaiah and other prophets, however, tell us that they are destined to reemerge together with many Israelites in the "last days."

Figure 46   **Migration of the Lost Ten Tribes**

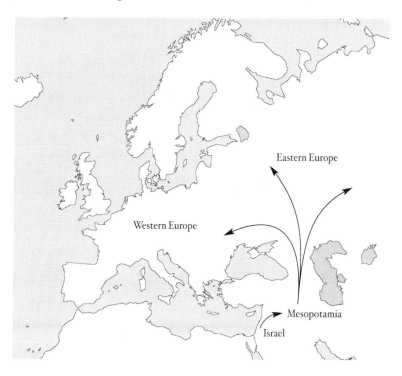

Today, after nearly three millennia of exile, God's people are most likely so far dispersed that every nation, kindred, tongue, and people is infused with the lineages of Israel as the prophets foretold. That assimilation sets the stage for a key part of Isaiah's endtime scenario to commence: Jacob/Israel—a worldwide category of God's people—renews its allegiance to Israel's God and prepares to return home at the end of the world. Jehovah will "assemble the exiled of Israel and gather the scattered of Judah from the four directions of the earth" (Isaiah 11:12). A reawakening of peoples to their Hebrew roots in that day causes some to name themselves "Jacob" and others "Israel" (Isaiah 44:5).

Born in exile—dispersed among the nations of the world—and finding themselves alienated from the God of Israel, their

Maker, the Jacob/Israel category has more to overcome than if the blessings of God's covenant had remained in force. To repent of transgression and return to the privileges of their righteous ancestors, the endtime generation of God's people must put forth more effort to restore those blessings than if they had been born into a state of blessedness. In other words, they must struggle through a *descent phase* before being able to ascend to a higher spiritual and physical plane (see Figure 47). Their disadvantaged state may thus be used to advantage as a means toward ascent.

Figure 47   **Exile and Return as Descent and Ascent**

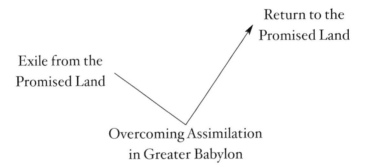

Moses foretold such a scenario long before God's people went into exile. After pronouncing the blessings and the curses of the covenant, Moses counseled them to keep the law of the covenant, to choose life instead of death. Nevertheless, having foreseen Israel's falling away, he predicted they would go into exile and be scattered among all nations. There, they would adopt strange customs and beliefs. But Moses also predicted that at the end of the world—"in the last days"—they would "repent" and "return." When they again kept the terms of the covenant God would gather them from wherever he had scattered them, and they would repossess the lands of their inheritance (Deuteronomy 28–30).

From a historical standpoint it didn't matter that most of God's people had lost their connection with the Promised Land and ended up dispossessed. By resuming their covenant identity at the last, they could yet participate in God's redemption of humanity. God anticipated Israel's exile and dispersion in the past and used it to reclaim all nations and peoples in the future. In spite of ancient Israel's rebellion and apostasy all things could still turn out for the best. God could turn evil into an even greater good than had existed before. What began with a cursed consequence of ancient Israel's breaking of the covenant could end with a blessed consequence of modern "Israel's" renewing the covenant.

> God could turn evil into an even greater good than before.

The very names "Jacob" and "Israel" throw light on this process. Isaiah depicts them as two distinct groups within a single category of people. We recall that Jacob, father of the nation of Israel, received the new name "Israel" upon proving loyal to his God, when God confirmed his covenant with him. At that time Jacob made the transition to a higher spiritual level. The same principle applies to every other level of the spiritual ladder, of which Jacob serves as a type. In Isaiah's paradigm "Israel" represents those who have renewed the covenant but who haven't yet ascended. "Jacob" represents those who believe in God but who haven't yet renewed the covenant. Jacob/Israel thus has two sub-groups.

Both groups, however, may ascend to the next level by keeping God's law and word. That includes "repenting" of transgression and "returning" in a new exodus out of Babylon. Although God's warning to all nations before his Day of Judgment goes unheeded by much of humanity, a small percentage of people throughout the earth responds to the wake-up call. Isaiah compares those who survive destruction to a tithing of the people. As the Israelites anciently gave a tenth of their gains to God, so a tenth of his people will in that day attain the Zion/Jerusalem level. God will confirm his covenant with them, delivering them from death and bestowing on them the blessings of his covenant.

God's Servant Fulfills a Mission to the Nations

God sends his servant and others who assist him to bring people on the Jacob/Israel level initially to Zion/Jerusalem. God appoints persons in higher categories to minister to those lower to lift them up. God's sons/servants, and also Zion/Jerusalem, ascend the ladder at the end of the world by ministering to Jacob/Israel. At that time people everywhere receive the chance to ascend in a way never before made possible and never to occur again. Strong forces for and against God's people—for and against God—will test people everywhere to the utmost. Those who minister to lower levels will assist as many as they can to experience "rebirth" after they have suffered "ruin" and oppression in Babylon.

As we might expect, the most valiant individuals in Isaiah's endtime scenario ascend highest on the ladder to heaven. Their commitment to serving God by serving their fellow human beings goes beyond just being good neighbors. As the greatest example of service toward his children, Israel's God is their role model. Isaiah describes him as the "Holy One" (Saint) and "Valiant One" (Hero) of Israel, emphasizing the divine attributes that get his people up the ladder. It is no accident, therefore, that those whom God delivers at the end of the world are also called "holy ones" (saints) and "valiant ones" (heroes). These and similar godlike traits qualify them as God's elect (Isaiah 10:20; 13:3; 60:16).

Israel's God is the greatest example of service.

Long ago Moses labored with the Israelites in the Sinai wilderness to accomplish the same thing but they weren't able to live up to it. Israel's God offered them the higher law—the terms of his covenant on the son/servant level. He called them to be a "royal priesthood," to minister his salvation to the rest of humanity. For them, it constituted an opportunity for spiritual service, not a bid for political elitism. But instead of accepting God's call, they hardened their hearts and reneged on their mission of ministering to the world. Isaiah laments that God's people "have not wrought salvation in the earth" to the extent they should have, neither anciently nor even at the end of the world (Isaiah 26:18).

In Moses' day seventy elders of Israel's congregation "went up" or "ascended" to that ministering level. They saw God on Mount Sinai and ate and drank in his presence (Exodus 24:9–11). Their physical ascent on the mountain symbolized their spiritual ascent that preceded it (see Figure 48). These seventy elders functioned as servants of God together with Moses. The spirit of prophecy rested on them as it did on Moses, lending them the power and wisdom to minister to God's people (Numbers 11:16–17, 24–25). Isaiah predicts a new version of that type at the end of the world: assisted by other servants or "elders," God's servant finally brings to pass the salvation of humanity that Moses foresaw.

Figure 48   **Ascent into God's Presence Is Ultimately Physical**

Spiritual Ascent   ⟶   Physical Ascent

According to Isaiah, God raises up his servant when the world is spiraling in a spiritual downturn—when God's people are buying wholesale into the ideology of Babylon. Isaiah's ministry was a type of that scenario. So was the time before the Flood, when wickedness and violence prevailed throughout the earth. At that time God destroyed the earth's inhabitants by water, saving only Noah and his family. At the end of the world he destroys the earth's inhabitants by fire, saving only those who heed his warning to prepare. Like Noah, we obtain deliverance when we observe God's law and word. By yielding to a wisdom higher than our own we show our loyalty, especially through the hard times.

Israel's ancient pilgrimage to Jerusalem was a type of Jacob/Israel's ascent. At certain feasts of the year, such as Passover and Tabernacles, God's people "went up" or "ascended" to Jerusalem to receive divine instruction and offer sacrifice at the temple. Isaiah depicts Israel's return from exile to the Promised Land as just such a pilgrimage. The physical journey to Zion or Jerusalem at the new exodus out of Babylon symbolizes the spiritual journey that precedes it. The Hebrew word for "pilgrimage" (*ălîyâ*) also means "ascent" (*ălîyâ*), expressing our inborn desire to attain a higher, transcendent state. Those who return to Zion or Jerusalem in the endtime pilgrimage are those who *ascend* spiritually.

In his day Isaiah served a symbolic role as a "sign and portent" of calamities to come upon Egypt and Cush (Isaiah 20:3–4). That becomes the type of a comparable role by God's servant in the "last days." For three years Isaiah testified that the king of Assyria would take captive the people of Egypt and Cush, typifying a similar three-year warning to all nations at the end of the world. Isaiah lumps Egypt and Cush together with other nations comprising Greater Babylon, all of whom participate in a tragic finale. From the time the servant begins his mission Babylon has a three-year "lease" of time in which to repent before God brings upon it three years of judgment (Isaiah 16:14; 37:30) (see Figure 49).

In the books of Daniel and John that time period is three and a half years. The difference may not be significant—Isaiah's three years of God's judgment may simply be a part of Daniel's and John's three-and-a-half years. Three years of warning followed by three of judgment may also be part of a seven-year distress cycle such as occurred anciently in Israel and Egypt. The important thing to know is that everything that happens at the end of the world possesses a type or types in the past, so that familiarity with Israel's history gives us the advantage of knowing how future events fall out. We may indeed survive the times ahead, but it will still require an uncommon degree of resourcefulness.

Figure 49   **Isaiah's Endtime Scenario**

Three Years of Warning	→	Three Years of Judgment	→	Millennium of Peace

Spiritual Conversion Precedes Physical Return

First of all, God's servant fulfills a spiritual mission to the nations of the world. God sends him "to preach to those who have grown weary a word to wake them up," suggesting they have fallen away from God and from an awareness of being his people (Isaiah 50:4). Isaiah says they have grown "blind," "deaf," and willfully ignorant. They are "uncomprehending" of the things of God and don't connect their misfortunes to the way they live (Isaiah 42:18–25). They "have eyes but see not, ears but hear not." They believe God has forgotten them even as they forget him. But Isaiah asserts that it is their sins and iniquities that "separate them from God" so that he doesn't hear them (Isaiah 59:2).

He asks "Who is it that hands Jacob over to plunder and Israel to despoilers if not Jehovah, against whom [they] have sinned? For they have no desire to walk in his ways or obey his law" (Isaiah 42:24). In spite of all God does for his people they still question his love for them: "Why do you say, O Jacob, and speak thus, O Israel: 'Our path is obscured from Jehovah; our cause is overlooked by our God'?" (Isaiah 40:27). Although they believe God doesn't care for them, he reassures them: "But, you, O Israel, my servant, Jacob, whom I have chosen, offspring of Abraham my beloved friend . . . to you I say, 'You are my servant; I have accepted you and not rejected you'" (Isaiah 41:8–9).

Almost all of God's people have fallen into a deep sleep.

After centuries of assimilation into the nations of the world, in other words, almost all of God's people have fallen into a deep sleep. They have grown weary and forgetful about keeping God's covenant while under Babylon's magic spell. At the end of the world the servant breaks the spell, waking the Virgin Daughter of Zion from the sleep of death. He leads God's people to safety in the place Zion or Jerusalem at the very time the Harlot Babylon is destroyed. Like the heroine of fairytales, God's people must follow a wisdom higher than their own if they would "live happily ever after." Those who reject divine guidance end up as villains or other reprobate characters in the annals of human history.

Fairytales, in fact, closely parallel Isaiah's endtime drama. At that time every ancient archetype makes an appearance on the world stage. Fairytales portray the same categories of people on the spiritual ladder that Isaiah does (see Figure 50). The Virgin Daughter of Zion—God's people who ascend—plays the part of the heroine. The servant acts the part of the hero or prince. The Harlot Babylon, the witch. The king of Assyria/ Babylon, the ogre or giant. God's emissaries on the level of seraphim, fairies. Babylon's reprobates, ugly stepsisters. Jacob/ Israel, generic characters. The heroes and villains of the Book of Isaiah may have their counterparts in fable but their endtime roles are real.

As mentioned, God's servant fulfills many roles at the end of the world. God appoints him as "a witness to the nations, a prince and lawgiver of the peoples" (Isaiah 55:4). In these roles he resembles Moses, except that the servant's mission is to all the world, not just Egypt or Israel. The servant releases God's people from spiritual blindness before releasing them from physical captivity. Like Moses, he instructs them in the law of the covenant and word of God before leading their return to the Promised Land. God requires that they obey the terms of his covenant before he can bless them as promised. Although God's salvation is free, it isn't easy to develop faith enough to comply with his will.

Figure 50   **Parallels with Fairytale Archetypes**

The Virgin Daughter of Zion—the Heroine

God's Endtime Servant—the Hero or Prince

The Harlot Babylon—the Evil Stepmother or Witch

The King of Assyria/Babylon—the Ogre or Giant

Angelic Emissaries—Fairies or Secret Helpers

Babylon's Reprobates—Ugly Stepsisters

Jacob/Israel—Generic Characters

As with the heroine of fairytales, it takes courage to walk alone with God through the "suffering" and "humiliation" of a *descent phase* before getting a glimpse of "salvation" and "exaltation." While the Woman Zion—the heroine in Isaiah's endtime scenario—represents God's covenant people as a whole, she also represents individuals. Zion/Jerusalem's journey as a nation is the sum total of many persons following the same path to God. While we encounter villains such as the king of Assyria/Babylon, and heroes such as the servant in the closing drama of

God's people, we also encounter our personal ogres who make our lives miserable, if we let them, as well as our personal princes and mentors.

Whatever invites us to love God, to covenant with him to keep his law and word, is of God. And whatever entices us away from God, to break faith with him, is evil. As in fairytales, however, reality isn't always what it seems. In the eyes of the world the wicked stepmother—the Harlot Babylon—appears respectable, while God's servant and his associates meet with contempt. On the other hand, if the heroine divulged the fact that she was visited by fairies she would be laughed to scorn. Similarly, when Joseph's brothers learned of his prophetic dream they hated him all the more. In living God's law, then, we walk a fine line between keeping our own counsel and standing up for what we believe.

> As in fairytales, reality isn't always what it seems.

God appoints his servant to minister to his people only after the servant has passed through his own "suffering" and "humiliation" that constitute *his* test of loyalty to God. No one is born a prince or savior all at once, but he attains that state step by step as he keeps the terms of God's covenant. Like the beast in *Beauty and the Beast*, the servant and all who ascend must conquer their own demons before becoming capable of ministering to others. "Salvation" and "exaltation" on the highest levels of the ladder follow "compliance" with God's will instead of the perverse self-will of one's lower nature. The servant's passing tests of "loyalty" qualifies him to teach God's law and word to God's people.

The servant's ministry results in "the deaf hear[ing] the words of the book"—the Book of Isaiah and other sealed books—and "the eyes of the blind see[ing] out of gross darkness" (Isaiah 29:18). The servant's task is to "open the eyes of the blind, to free captives from confinement and from prison those who sit in darkness"—to deliver those who still find themselves in a cursed condition (Isaiah 42:7). At that time "they who erred in spirit will gain understanding and they who murmured accept instruction" (Isaiah 29:24). They will return to Zion from far-flung lands of exile. They will walk through wildernesses, mountains, seas, rivers, and even through fire (Isaiah 11:10–16; 43:1–8; 49:8–12).

The servant's spiritual ministry precedes any physical fulfillment of endtime prophecy. God sets up tests of faith for his people, which, if they pass, qualify them for his promised "deliverance." Just as anciently the spiritual apostasy and "rebellion" of God's people preceded their physical exile, so at the end of the world the spiritual conversion and "compliance" of God's people precedes their physical return (see Figure 51). God's servant and his associates bring about this reversal of circumstances, saving humanity from utter desolation. Without God's intervention and his people's positive response to it, the whole world in its wicked state would remain under a curse—the curse of a broken covenant.

Figure 51   **Israel's Former and Latter History**

Spiritual Apostasy ⟶ Physical Exile

Spiritual Conversion ⟶ Physical Return

God's Curses Are a Prelude to God's Blessings

All blessings from God, including the endtime salvation of his people, come from keeping the terms of his covenant. As mentioned, the blessings and curses of the covenant never fail; they are as relevant today as when Moses first pronounced them in the Sinai wilderness. Blessings, or good fortune, follow keeping God's law, while curses or misfortune follow its breaking.

Divine protection from a mortal threat, together with permanent lands of inheritance and an enduring posterity, constitute three fundamental blessings of the covenant. Isaiah, therefore, describes God's covenant as a divine assurance of blessedness, both in this world and in the world to come (Isaiah 54:2–3, 5–10, 13–17; 55:1–3).

When Israel broke the covenant God exiled his people from the Promised Land. Still, they had obtained the land in the first place by *keeping* the law of the covenant. Although God had promised the land to Abraham, Isaac, and Jacob—Israel's progenitors—their descendants inherited it only when they *themselves* kept the terms of the covenant. Other curses, too, followed breaking the covenant: famine, disease, invasion, desolation, bondage, persecution. These evil effects have continued from ancient times except where people have again kept God's law and word. By remaining ignorant of his covenant, therefore, people perpetuate the curse and remain "blind" and "deaf" to life's divine purpose.

> God's covenant is a divine assurance of blessedness.

Ascending to Zion/Jerusalem may thus first of all mean coming to terms with centuries-old covenant curses. It may involve settling a long-standing debt of "punishment," getting rid of a burden of guilt accumulated by the generational breaking of God's law. That is where Isaiah's principle of "ruin" before "rebirth," "disinheritance" before "inheritance," "punishment" before "deliverance," "suffering" before "salvation," and "humiliation" before "exaltation" comes into force. We have to pay a price that banishes the curse. How do we do that? By renewing the covenant and keeping its terms—by living God's law, even the lesser law. God acknowledges us as Zion/Jerusalem when we merit the name.

When people of Jacob/Israel make that transition—giving up their false gods for the true God—they experience a metamorphosis, a change of identity. From then on they become a *covenant people*. Isaiah compares that transition to the Woman Zion—God's wife—having "served her term" as in a pregnancy (Isaiah 40:2). God's people are delivered or reborn on a higher level. They are no longer called Jacob or Israel, which signifies a provisional category of God's people. Jacob/Israel isn't blessed by God, experiencing "deliverance," "salvation," "inheritance," and so forth. Zion/Jerusalem is. The Jacob/Israel level is merely a proving ground for ascent to the first level of blessedness (see Figure 52).

Figure 52   **Isaiah's Three Levels of Blessedness**

Seraphim—Third Level of Blessedness

Sons/Servants—Second Level of Blessedness

Zion/Jerusalem—First Level of Blessedness

Jacob/Israel—A Provisional Category of God's People

Isaiah thus depicts God's spouse as having "expiated her iniquity," as having "paid double for all her sins" (Isaiah 40:2). That shows, first of all, the transition from Jacob/Israel to Zion/Jerusalem. At that point—in the "last days"—God's people pay off a long-term liability for "punishment," obtaining a reversal of the curses of the covenant. They experience a release or "deliverance" from all kinds of misfortunes. By suffering an inherited cursed condition while faithfully keeping the law of the covenant, God's people pass their test of loyalty. God reverses the curse, changing it into a blessing. By following this pattern God's people (and individuals) can make use of a bad situation and turn it to good.

A type of such a reversal of circumstances is Abraham, who was born in Babylonia into a cursed condition. His father Terah made and sold idols, and his people were idolaters. A famine or curse covered the land. Abraham, however, was determined to serve the true God and thus incurred his people's displeasure. When they tried to kill him, he moved away and met Melchizedek, his ancestor, the priest-king of Salem. Abraham acknowledged Melchizedek's priesthood—his authority to act in God's name— and obtained his own ministry. In that instance Melchizedek became a type of God's endtime servant, who performs a similar role to Abraham's descendants who exit Greater Babylon (see Figure 53).

Figure 53

An Ancient Type of the Servant's Endtime Ministry

Melchizedek   ⟶   Abraham

God's Servant   ⟶   Abraham's Descendants

Abraham's journey from Babylonia to the Promised Land was as much an escape from peril as it was a blessing stemming from his loyalty to God. Abraham broke with a carnal, materialistic culture, loving God more than idols. By so doing he became a type and model of his descendants. God urges his people to "look to Abraham your father"—by repenting of evildoing and returning to the Promised Land (Isaiah 41:8–9; 51:2). Their exodus to Zion from the ends of the earth consists of a similar escape from peril and a reward of righteousness. Like Abraham, those who ascend to Zion/Jerusalem receive lands of inheritance to be handed down to their descendants from generation to generation.

God saved not only Abraham from a cursed condition, moreover, but others together with him who followed him to the Promised Land. In that sense Abraham served as a savior or deliverer to some who might have otherwise have died from the famine had they stayed in Babylon. Accordingly, God's sons/servants, and also seraphs, perform saving roles to God's people in Greater Babylon at the end of the world. By ministering to others, endeavoring to lift them higher, they prepare them for the journey to Zion or Jerusalem. In that day all levels of the spiritual ladder, not just the highest, perform in order for God's plan to work. God saves both those who minister and those whom they serve.

God reverses the curse, changing it into a blessing.

A type of this scenario was the escape of Abraham's nephew Lot and his daughters from Sodom when God destroyed the cities of the Plain. God delivered Lot for Abraham's sake (Genesis 19:29). But he delivered Lot's daughters for Lot's sake. The rest of the land's residents, whether family or not, perished in the fire. In the endtime version of those events many escape the burning of Greater Babylon for the sake of individuals on higher levels. God's sons/servants, and beyond them, seraphs, directly influence this endtime "salvation." Although Zion/Jerusalem qualifies for "deliverance" by keeping the terms of God's covenant, God nevertheless intervenes to save his people for his servants' sake.

Ascent to Zion/Jerusalem Can Be Sooner or Later

The commencement of the "last days" finds people on different spiritual levels and in different stages of ascent. Not all who reach Zion/Jerusalem or levels higher at the end of the world do so at the same time or in precisely the same manner. In that time of flux big changes are set in motion, causing many people to react differently. Some take more time than others to advance from one phase to the next. Persons in upper categories, too, are then ascending, the same as those to whom they minister. Because God gives everyone the freedom to choose, some progress rapidly while others linger behind. To accommodate these differences God makes provision for all to ascend at their own pace.

Thus, two "pilgrimages" to the Promised Land—made up of two separate groups who come out of Jacob/Israel—occur proximate to the end of the world. Each *physical* pilgrimage follows a group's *spiritual* ascent. The first group attains the Zion/Jerusalem level and levels higher in direct response to the servant's performing his mission to Jacob/Israel, God's people dispersed throughout the earth. Assisted by additional servants, God's servant convinces many to establish a covenant relationship with Israel's God. That first group participates in an exodus out of all nations on the eve of a Sodom-and-Gomorrah type of destruction. Those on the level of seraphs gather them home to Zion or Jerusalem.

The second group makes a similar "pilgrimage" to the Promised Land but not until after the millennium of peace has begun. Its spiritual ascent to Zion/Jerusalem occurs *during* God's Day of Judgment—between the time the first group leaves in the exodus and the end of the world. This second group doesn't respond to the servant's summons—doesn't heed God's warning and wake up in time to avoid calamity. Instead, it attains the Zion/Jerusalem level through the school of hard knocks. Consequently, it has to wait for a second chance to make its return. As it suffers through God's Day of Judgment, its spiritual ascent nonetheless qualifies it for the physical ascent that follows (see Figure 54).

Figure 54   **Two Endtime Pilgrimages to Zion/Jerusalem**

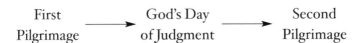

First Pilgrimage ⟶ God's Day of Judgment ⟶ Second Pilgrimage

The second group's passing through "outer darkness"—the chaos of God's Day of Judgment—actually helps it ascend to the next level. It undergoes "ruin" before "rebirth," "punishment" before "deliverance," "suffering" before "salvation," etc., by wading through the worst times in human history. The "last days" may be short but they are intense, acting as a refiner's fire for those who don't at first heed God's warning. Yet, because they don't descend to Babylon, God still protects them, but indirectly. Better to ascend to Zion/Jerusalem late than never! Those whom God protects directly—by overshadowing them with his cloud of glory—go through their refiner's fire *before* his Day of Judgment.

A type of two or more pilgrimages to Zion or Jerusalem occurs anciently when the Jews return from Babylon in two or more migrations. Some lead the way, building the second temple, while others come some years later. In Isaiah's endtime scenario the first to return to the Promised Land also build the temple. They assist the servant to build the new, millennial temple, just as the Jews helped Zerubbabel to build the second one. Then, after Babylon is destroyed and the millennial age has begun, the first wave does for others as the servant and his associates did for them: they go out and lead home the second wave from throughout the earth in a second pilgrimage to Zion (Isaiah 60:1–7; 66:18–20).

Repentance/Return Leads to Healing/Salvation

In a real sense we ascend the ladder to heaven as we experience spiritual renewal or *healing*. That happens when we respond appropriately to God. God leaves it to us to answer his invitation to come to him with all our hearts. But as our awareness of his reality increases—when we live the law of his covenant—we experience the peaceful, healing influence of his Spirit. God "pours out his Spirit" on us insofar as we are willing to receive it. That results in a spirituality that proceeds from one phase of loyalty to the next. The valleys and plateaus we pass through on our journey correspond with increasing levels of healing or regeneration—with successive births or rebirths on ever higher levels of ascent.

After we ascend we are no longer as we were. We are still ourselves, but we are remade closer to God's image and likeness. The same applies in an opposite sense. Those who descend, too, change. We never stand still because time itself moves forward. After we ascend or descend we don't think and act exactly as before. In that sense being "born again" means functioning on a higher plane, living a higher reality. As we ascend God broadens our understanding even as he imbues us with his power. Conversely, "dying" to one's level means living a lower reality (see Figure 55). Our understanding diminishes to the degree we descend. We lose our vitality and become spiritually, and perhaps physically, ill.

Figure 55   **Humanity's Choice of Life or Death**

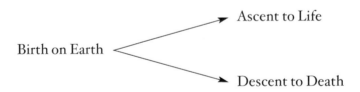

Isaiah equates "salvation" with healing. For example, God smites Egypt by the hand of oppressors in order to *heal* it. As a result, the Egyptians repent, appeal to God, and covenant with him by sacrifice. At that point God responds to their pleas and "heals" them, sending a savior who delivers them (Isaiah 19:19–22). Elsewhere Isaiah describes healing as the result of "seeing with the eyes, hearing with the ears, understanding with the heart, and repenting" (Isaiah 6:10). To "repent," by definition, means to "return" to God, who stands at the top of the ladder.

Such repentance occurs step by step. Until we reach the top, the "gate of heaven," there remains something to repent of (Genesis 28:12–17).

In his role of suffering Savior, Israel's God brings to pass our healing. Isaiah notes that "the price of our peace he incurred, and with his wounds we are healed" (Isaiah 53:5). Jehovah takes our guilt upon himself so that we might not suffer the effects of justice if we repent. God says "You have burdened me with your sins, wearied me with your iniquities. But it is I myself, and *for my own sake*, who blot out your offenses, remembering your sins no more" (Isaiah 43:24–25; emphasis added). As is shown in Chapter 8, Jehovah answers for our transgressing the law of his covenant provided we repent. The key to our healing and "salvation," therefore, is that God forgives us as we again keep his law.

On our journey up the spiritual ladder, the higher we ascend the closer we get to God and more like him we become. Conversely, the lower we descend the farther away we get from God and less like him we become. God says "As the heavens are higher than the earth, so are my ways higher than your ways and my thoughts higher than your thoughts" (Isaiah 55:9). But he counsels the wicked to whom he is speaking to forsake their ways and thoughts and to conform to his. He invites all to "Come unto me . . . that your souls may live!" (Isaiah 55:3, 7). As we prove loyal to him through life's trials we "see" and "hear" much more than before. Our understanding increases to the degree we love God.

Each rebirth resembles an awakening to a greater awareness.

Becoming like God, then, doesn't consist so much of adopting new ideas but of discarding old ones that impair our view, that render us prisoners of prejudice. Each time we pass through the refiner's fire and complete a new cycle of *descent before ascent* we peel off another layer, like a serpent shedding its skin or like a fruit whose outside hides its inner sweetness. Healing thus consists largely of *unlayering*, unbinding the "bands of iniquity," giving the inner child of God a new lease on life. Each rebirth on a higher level resembles an awakening from sleep to a new awareness. As we ascend we become a new manifestation of the divine already abiding within us—a true son or daughter of God.

People in the Perdition category, on the other hand, such as the king of Assyria/Babylon, reach a point of no return in their slide down the ladder until they are incapable of repenting. The "bands" of their iniquity—their coarse outer layers—harden until they can't be broken. When people cut themselves off from God their disease progresses until it is incurable. They descend into the "Pit of Dissolution" (Isaiah), also called the "Bottomless Pit" (John), which we may liken to a black hole (see Figure 56). God cuts them off "root and branch": they can claim no ancestry, and they leave no posterity. Their curse—like Sodom's—is irrevocable. For them, it would have been better not to have been born.

Figure 56   **A Point of No Return on the Ladder to Heaven**

Entry at God's Gate

Acceleration to Heaven

Beginning of Ascent

Point of Inertia

Beginning of Descent

Acceleration to Hell

Point of No Return

Dissolution in the "Pit"

People in the next-lowest category—Babylon—can still repent and return but must suffer the consequences of their actions. The results of transgression remain until their iniquity is "expiated." Just as the child born to a drug abuser suffers the effects of its parent's sins, so curses accumulate until someone goes through "withdrawal." But the curses themselves may lead to repentance. When offenders take what is coming to them, drinking the cup of God's wrath, they may grow aware of the magnitude of their crime. By suffering God's "punishment" they learn about justice. In the end, they may yet become believers—the hard way. The first step in their healing is to acknowledge that God exists.

As they ascend, people in the Jacob/Israel category take healing a step further than those of Babylon. By aligning themselves with Israel's God in a covenant relationship, they tap into God's "deliverance" and "salvation." He empowers them by his Spirit to overcome obstacles. He turns their weaknesses into strengths, their darkness into light, their chaos into creation. That relationship works both ways: as we experience God's love it warms our hearts and we respond by deepening our loyalty. This may take us to levels we never knew existed. The mysteries of God are accessible to those who deeply desire to know. To be healed or made "whole" we must love and grow like him who gave us birth.

Postscript: Evidently, a problem we all face comes from within not from without. We set limits on our intelligence, being "willfully ignorant" of anything more than what we believe we already know. We retreat into our comfort zone in the very moment life beckons us onward and upward. But it is clear from Isaiah that we *will* be discomfited one way or another sooner or later. So choosing now to progress seems a better way to go than letting ourselves regress by not keeping up with God's design.

I used to wonder who the "Sons of Belial" were of whom the prophets speak so repugnantly. I understood they were "damned souls," persons under some kind of curse. King David calls them "thorns" that will be "utterly burned with fire" in God's Day of Judgment. I later understood that "Belial" is a Hebrew compound of *bĕlî*, meaning "not" or "without," and *ya'al*, meaning "ascend." "Sons of Belial," therefore, refers to those who don't ascend—Isaiah's Babylon category—people cursed indeed!

But let's assume I'm "a born-again believer." Now have I spiritually arrived? Answer: If I'm content to remain Jacob/Israel and ascend no further, yes. But Isaiah teaches there's a world of difference between that and being born again as Zion/Jerusalem, and between that and being born again as sons/servants. Aren't we constantly either awake or asleep, enlightened or darkened, born again or dying? Dare I say "I will go thus far and no more" when God says the sky—or, rather, heaven—is the limit?

5

ZION/JERUSALEM, GOD'S COVENANT PEOPLE

Zion/Jerusalem keeps the terms of God's covenant. Covenant curses turn into covenant blessings for those who prove loyal to Israel's God. Zion/Jerusalem passes three tests of loyalty and escapes the fiery desolation of Babylon. God's righteous people ascend the ladder and inherit Paradise. Cosmic parallels depict the spiritual journey of God's people to heaven.

People who attain the Zion/Jerusalem level arrive at an important milestone in their lives. Like most persons born on the earth, they started as Jacob/Israel and advanced beyond that basic level to a new high. It now comforts them to know for sure that an upward path exists, that there is a higher reality than the one they knew. Otherwise they might still harbor doubts, concluding that their corrupt condition in life is all there is. After a few failed attempts to ascend they could have become convinced there is no such thing as spiritual ascent, with the nonbeliever protesting "Bah, humbug!" Now, ascent is a reality, not an altered state but an alternative status with God from what the world has to offer.

It is one thing to believe in God and quite another to make a covenant with him. When God covenanted with Israel anciently—that if his people would keep his law and word he would be their God and they would be his people—he gave them the chance to be blessed above all other nations on earth. If they transgressed the terms of his covenant they could still be forgiven their sins by "repenting" of wrongdoing and "returning" to God. Rituals in the Law of Moses ensured the purification of transgressors who renewed their loyalty to God. Although Isaiah shows that Jehovah's atonement for transgression implies that such rituals were purely symbolic, still, God's covenant would remain in force.

Covenanting with God—establishing allegiance to the same God of Israel who covenanted with his people in the past—sets believers apart from all others. Through that formal covenant relationship one finds forgiveness of sins, covenant blessings such as earthly prosperity and divine protection, and the beginning of a spiritual journey that leads into God's presence. Covenant curses, whether self-inflicted or inherited from preceding generations, can now be reversed. Even humanity's mortal state—the curse inherited from Adam and Eve that gives us our disposition to evil as well as good—loses some of its sting. Blessings flow when a people become God's people and he becomes their God.

Although they may be born into a cursed condition through no fault of their own, people in the Zion/Jerusalem category rise above the curse and turn it into a blessing. They use their disadvantaged state to advantage by dealing appropriately with adversity. Struggling against evils, they grow stronger, surmounting obstacles instead of being defeated by them. God strengthens them to overcome when they call on him for help.

Because they covenant with him and prove loyal through trials, he is *bound* by the terms of the covenant to deliver them. Their experience with God convinces them he is there for them. As he saves them again and again, they move from faith in him to certain knowledge of his love.

As they prove loyal through trials, God is *bound* to deliver them.

Getting that far, however, may be far enough for some people, at least for a time, although time itself moves forward. As God's blessings take effect many rest on their laurels, content to enjoy their blessed state. Passing tests of loyalty to attain the Zion/Jerusalem level seems more difficult for some than others, perhaps because a few of God's children start earth's journey further ahead in their ascent. As just a young man, for example, Isaiah sees Jehovah in the temple, placing him almost immediately on the son/servant level. What takes many a lifetime, some appear to be born to as an inherited privilege. God puts such persons in strategic places to help others attain their spiritual goals.

For many of us, getting to the Zion/Jerusalem level is the exciting first step in an ever-accelerating spiritual climb. Having once tasted the fruits of our faith, we are eager to ascend again. Seeing a new door open as the old one closes makes us want to explore the next challenge. Each attempt to ascend leads into fresh yet somehow familiar territory, introducing a new set of rules as ancient as eternity that regenerates us even more than before. It is deeply satisfying to metamorphose as from a caterpillar to a butterfly. Just as at the end of the world God re-creates the earth, making it a new Paradise, so he re-creates all who ascend, transforming them into "new creatures," closer to his image and likeness.

Once we ascend a level on the ladder we may remain there or ascend yet further unless we descend by rebelling against

God. Because we ascend to any spiritual level only as fast as we overcome covenant curses, we advance only as far as God empowers us against evil. God does his part because of our covenant relationship with him, provided the covenant is on *his* terms. He responds to his people's needs to overcome every obstacle when they observe *his* law and word, not those of men. In that manner we ascend from one victory to the next. Humanity's fascination with climbing mountains reflects our natural inclination to ascend to the highest pinnacle and our inborn belief that we can do it.

Cosmic Parallels Reflect Our Spiritual Journey

As the prophets use cosmic phenomena to portray spiritual states, we find that cosmic bodies parallel people's ascent on the ladder. Different categories of people compare with different categories of heavenly bodies. Some reflect God's light, or the light of others, while some, like God's servant, are themselves a "light," Israel's God being the brightest "Light" of all. Persons on the highest levels compare with stars in the heavens: God calls each by name just as he calls his sons/ servants by name, and they follow his every command. Each time a person ascends a level he receives a new name, reflecting a new spiritual phase. The names Jacob/Israel and Zion/Jerusalem express that progression.

The transition from "ruin" to "rebirth," "suffering" to "salvation," "humiliation" to "exaltation," etc. each time we ascend the ladder demonstrates a cyclical pattern in the celestial journey of God's children. It shows that human life, like the cosmos, is cyclical in nature. A heavenly pattern governs human affairs, with which people can align themselves or from which they can deviate, as they choose. That cyclical pattern makes it necessary to pass through "ruin," "suffering," "humiliation," etc. all over again even after experiencing "rebirth," "salvation," and "exaltation," the reason being that the higher we ascend the lower we temporarily descend while passing tests of loyalty (see Figure 57).

Figure 57   **The Higher the Ascent, the Lower the Descent**

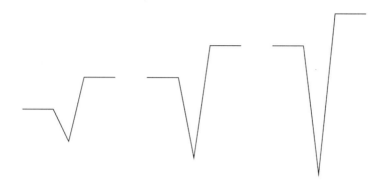

Before God calls someone to the seraph level, for example, that person must prove, by passing through trials, that he or she will use God's power in God's service. The Perdition category shows how people abuse power to promote themselves and their own agendas. Yet, without such people choosing evil rather than good there would be fewer challenges for those who ascend. God, therefore, won't imbue with power a person on the highest levels until, like Isaiah, he proves unselfish in keeping the terms of God's covenant. Although we never lose the freedom to choose, God "confirms" us in righteousness, or in righteous doing, when, like his angels, it becomes natural for us to choose right.

Our journey through life, then, is not just cyclical—passing through experiences that repeat themselves—it is also climactic, passing through experiences that intensify. By their very nature they demonstrate our divine potential as children of God. The history of God's people in general, of individuals born on the earth, and of the earth itself, continues in ever-expanding and more elevated circles unless one chooses to descend. The ancient Maya understood the inseparable relationship of humanity to the cosmos. They saw human history as cyclical, not linear. What happened in the past would happen again but on a larger scale. The past thus serves not just as a type but as a microcosm of the future.

Seasonal changes—the earth's "death" in winter and regeneration in summer—testify of life's cyclical pattern. Isaiah often uses such imagery from nature. Those whom the servant empowers, for example, he calls the "oaks of *righteousness*" (Isaiah 61:3; emphasis added). An oak tree, however, loses its leaves in the fall and sprouts new ones in the spring as it grows in stature. It experiences *descent before ascent*. Its "humiliation"—as it loses the leafy glory it had gained—precedes its "exaltation" as it grows even mightier than before (see Figure 58). A cyclical pattern in our physical lives, too, forms a type of our spiritual lives as when we become ill but recover more immune to a disease than before.

Figure 58   **Physical Growth as a Type of Spiritual Growth**

God's re-creation of the earth—after it reverts to chaos in the Day of Judgment—reflects the cyclical pattern. The earth has gone through previous such changes, as from the dinosaur age to that of man, and from before the Flood to after it. Catastrophes accompany each change. Using the literary pattern of alternating themes of chaos and creation, Isaiah shows God's creation narrowing from things of a broad nature, such as the earth, to individuals whom God creates, then re-creates (Isaiah 40:12–17, 21–31). Isaiah's prediction of new heavens and a new earth in conjunction with the endtime "rebirth" of God's people, too, speaks of ongoing human and cosmic transformations (Isaiah 65:17–18).

Zion/Jerusalem's rising "from the dust" to sit on her throne demonstrates such a cyclical transformation (Isaiah 52:1–2). It implies first of all that God's people who ascend must pass through a chaotic state—through "ruin," "suffering," "humiliation," etc.—in order to rise, regenerated like the phoenix, from the ashes. To sit on a throne, moreover, implies power and authority from God. But Isaiah teaches that this power increases as one ascends the ladder. In contrast to Zion/Jerusalem, for example, Jacob/Israel and people in descending categories are "blind" and "deaf." So long as they don't "repent" and "return" by keeping the terms of God's covenant they are unfit to govern others.

Zion/Jerusalem's rising "from the dust," in fact, forms a part of a much larger pattern that encompasses higher spiritual categories. Not only Zion/Jerusalem but also God's sons/servants, seraphs, and, as is shown in Chapter 8, even Jehovah, rise "from the dust" to sit on their thrones on ever ascending levels of the ladder. This pattern teaches that life consists of an entire series of births and rebirths into higher states of being that involve a kind of death of the former self. Lastly, because both human and cosmic bodies are composed of "dust," that term links our lives inseparably to the cosmos. The fact that our spirits are clothed in this element means that ascent is ultimately physical as well as spiritual.

Isaiah's linking astronomical and theological concepts suggests we have much to learn by observing our celestial environment. Just as a person's transformation doesn't end when he ascends a level, neither does the earth's or that of other heavenly bodies. In cosmic phenomena one might expect that the massive explosion of a giant star would mean the end of its huge mass as it disintegrates into billions of shooting globules. For that reason a supernova was thought to be the death of a star, which in one sense it is. In another sense something else occurs. Not only does the star remain—in a metamorphosed state—but entire new star systems are born, beginning countless new cycles of existence.

> Like cosmic bodies, we experience progression or regression.

So also, when divinely guided, everyone's journey unfolds through a series of spiritual and physical evolutions. When we see some people happy and others in turmoil we can't judge either one. Some may be enjoying the blessings of having ascended, experiencing a period of peace and joy. Others may be involuntarily descending through trials before rising higher. Treating unkindly someone who is down could cause him to abort his "rebirth." Like cosmic bodies, we are in various stages of progression or regression, and it is unrealistic to expect all to be the same. Different conditions in our physical bodies, upbringing, circumstances, and so forth make it impossible to truly judge anyone.

Persons in an ascending mode are less likely to be critical of others when they see misfortunes occurring to them than will those who are in a descending mode. Job's companions were convinced Job was guilty of transgression when they saw the evils that befell him, which consisted of common covenant curses. But Job was blameless of the things they accused him of. In fact, Job was a type of the future Messiah and of all who suffer innocently as part of their *descent before ascent*— passing through "ruin" before "rebirth," "suffering" before "salvation," "humiliation" before "exaltation," etc. Accordingly,

God "blessed the latter end of Job more than his beginning" (Job 42:12) (see Figure 59).

Figure 59 **Job as a Type of Descent before Ascent**

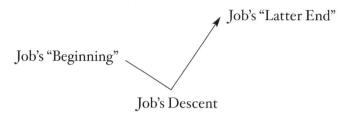

Why Job should suffer covenant curses in the first place is answered in Chapter 6, which discusses the savior roles persons on higher levels perform on behalf of others. While the curses were not Job's own, they may have accrued from former generations, from the lavish lifestyle of his children, or from his community. Because he was blameless, Job overcame the curses instead of being overcome by them—like one who rides an enormous wave compared to one whom it engulfs; or like Shadrach, Meshach, and Abednego, who walked through the same fire that slew those who threw them in. The guilty suffer covenant curses as "punishment" but to the innocent they are a means toward "deliverance."

When we learn to internalize things that happen in our lives, and how God deals with people according to their individual choices and circumstances, we experience a succession of spiritual awakenings. We become more tolerant, seeing in others a reflection of ourselves. Although they may be on different spiritual levels than we are, we can appreciate their struggles the same way we do our own. Just as it takes all kinds of heavenly bodies to make up the cosmos—each of which is essential to the whole—so it takes all kinds of people to make God's plan work for our "salvation" and "exaltation." If like Job we rise above our trials as we minister to others, we, like him, will "see God" (Job 19:26).

By ministering to one another we acquire God's character traits.

Beginning as infants, human beings progress from being totally dependent on others to acting with increasing independence within expanding sphere of influence. As we mature physically we follow God's pattern by participating in God's creation. We "beget" or "give birth" to others as they begin new physical and spiritual cycles, thus aiding their chances for ascent. Isaiah teaches that the process of ministering and being ministered to on ever-ascending levels leads to our celestial "exaltation." By that means—by ministering to one another—we acquire God's character traits. We learn more and more to follow the pattern of God himself as he calls us to serve others of his children in his name.

Alternatively, being "damned in hell" means lapsing to the point of having one's progress stopped or "dammed"—of being unable, or making it difficult, to ascend. We create a hell for ourselves by our own foolish actions. We refuse to follow God's pattern of ascent and instead deny our love and service to others and turn in on ourselves—like fruit that rots from the inside out. Neither heaven nor hell waits until the next life. We create it for ourselves on the earth and it extends right on into the next phase of our existence. No ones ruins our lives for us but we destroy our own lives, whereas every undeserved "ruin" in the course of complying with God's will leads to "rebirth" when we pass the test.

God's People Receive the Servant's Message

God's servant, who initiates the endtime ascent of God's people, appears on the scene when Babylon threatens to drown humanity in a flood of idolatry. God intervenes to deliver his people from spiritual degradation and from bondage to Babylon's ruling elite before they are overwhelmed. In that way God honors his promise to Abraham, Isaac, and Jacob, his people's progenitors, that he would preserve their posterity on the earth. Just as in Egypt he "remembered" his covenant with Abraham, Isaac, and Jacob and raised up Moses to deliver them, so he raises up his servant to deliver them out of bondage at the time the archtyrant consolidates his power, intending to commit global genocide.

Isaiah's literary devices depict the servant as God's answer to the archtyrant's evil plans. Just as God sent Moses to deliver his people from the oppression of Pharaoh, so the servant appears after the king of Assyria/Babylon comes to power. The Bible contains many types of the servant's contest against the archtyrant and his armies, including Joshua's vanquishing the Canaanites, Gideon's routing the Midianites, and David's slaying the Philistines (see Figure 60). When God empowers him, the servant proves more than a match for the archtyrant's might. While the archtyrant pretends to be the savior of the world, even God incarnate, in reality he is the world's destroyer and but another false god.

Figure 60   **Types of the Servant's Contest against the Forces of Chaos**

Abraham—Spoiling the Northern Kings

Moses—Subduing the Amalekites

Joshua—Vanquishing the Canaanites   God's Endtime Servant

Gideon—Routing the Midianites

David—Slaying the Philistines

Cyrus—Conquering the Babylonians

God sends his servant and those who assist him to be saviors of his people, just as Moses and Israel's judges served as saviors to his people anciently. Moses delivered them from hostile forces when they fled Egypt and wandered in the wilderness to the Promised Land. Israel's judges delivered them from enemies after they had inherited the land. Additional such types include Abraham's saving his allies from the alliance of northern kings and his interceding with God on behalf of the righteous in Sodom. Isaiah teaches that God intervenes at the end of the world according to such precedents from the past. When something deviates from these types we can know with certainty that it is not of God.

Just as Moses, Joshua, and King Josiah renewed God's covenant with his people, so does God's servant at the end of the world. God's law and word are the terms of the covenant from which all blessings flow, whether to ourselves or to our descendants. Just as Moses and Israel's prophets taught the terms of the covenant, so do the servant and his associates. Their selfless service accomplishes for God's people what they cannot do for themselves. As such types show, only persons higher spiritually can lift those lower, instructing them in part by the force of their example. God manifests his love for his people through the ministry of "angels"—persons on or approaching the level of seraphs.

Only persons higher spiritually can lift those lower.

Those who receive the servant give heed to his warning of coming calamities, trusting in God rather than in man and his idols when destruction threatens. They cling to God's covenant in the face of hardships. They include the ethnic lineages of God's people but also many whose Israelite ancestors long ago assimilated into the nations of the world. People looking to God for deliverance will respond spontaneously to the servant's ministry, recognizing him intuitively as sent from God. God appoints his servant as a "light to the nations, a covenant of the people" (Isaiah 42:6; 49:6, 8). His mission is to turn their darkness into light, to bring them out of Babylon, first spiritually and then physically.

Predicting the coming of his servant, God says "To Zion, he will be her harbinger; I will appoint him as a herald of tidings to Jerusalem" (Isaiah 41:27). As God's people ascend to Zion/Jerusalem, they, in turn, teach those still on the Jacob/Israel level, assisting them to ascend also: "Scale the mountain heights, O Zion, herald of good tidings. Raise your voice mightily, O Jerusalem, messenger of good news. Make yourself heard, be not afraid" (Isaiah 40:9). When the archtyrant lays siege to God's covenant people, they trust in God to deliver them: "The Virgin Daughter of Zion holds you in contempt; she laughs you to scorn. The Daughter of Jerusalem shakes her head at you" (Isaiah 37:22).

Isaiah teaches that in the "last days," when God's people repent of transgression and return from exile, "many peoples will go, saying, 'Come, let us go up to the mountain of Jehovah, to the house of the God of Jacob, that he may instruct us in his ways, that we may follow in his paths.' For out of Zion will go forth the law, and from Jerusalem the word of Jehovah" (Isaiah 2:3). The work of God's endtime servant and his associates leads many of God's people to ascend the ladder and to survive the archtyrant's cleansing of the earth: "Then will they who are left in Zion and they who remain in Jerusalem be called holy—all who were inscribed to be among the living at Jerusalem" (Isaiah 4:3).

Analogies Occur between the One and the Many

Linked ideas throughout the Book of Isaiah demonstrate how God's people respond to the servant's message. Those who acknowledge the servant do as he does. As the servant keeps the terms of God's covenant, so do they. When they live God's law for its own sake, not for the sake of reward, God blesses them as he blesses his servant. Because he keeps God's law and word as far as humanly possible, the servant personifies *righteousness* and serves as an exemplar of righteousness. Those who do what the servant does, therefore, are called the "followers of righteousness," those whom "righteousness"—God's servant— leads in the new exodus out of Greater Babylon (Isaiah 41:2; 51:1, 7; 58:8).

As the servant declares good tidings to the nations of the earth and isles of the sea, so do they. As he releases God's people from bondage and oppression, so do they. As he patiently endures shame and insult for God's sake, so do they. As he calls on the name of Jehovah and fulfills all his will, so do they. As he trusts in his God in the face of perils and opposition, so do they. As he is not disgraced but vindicated by God in the end, so are they. As he refutes the wicked who wrongfully accuse him, so do they. As he restores ancient ruins and rebuilds God's temple, so do they. As he gains grace and honor in the eyes of God, so do they. As he joyfully celebrates God's salvation, so do they.

As God answers and guides him, so he does them.

As God calls his servant from afar to the Promised Land, so he calls them. As God chooses him to be his servant, so he chooses them. As God anoints him and fills him with his Spirit, so he does them. As God appoints him as a witness to the nations to testify of him, so he does them. As God opens his ear and instructs him, so he does them. As God answers and guides him in all he does, so he does them. As God heals and consoles him in the hour of his distress, so he does them. As God helps him face hardships and validates his ministry, so he does them. As God grants him an everlasting inheritance as a reward for shame, so he does them. As God gloriously endows him, so he does them.

The wicked of God's people, on the other hand, do the opposite of what the servant does (see Figure 61). He rejects evil and chooses good but they choose evil and reject good. He inquires of the living God for guidance but they conjure up the dead. His ear is open but theirs are closed. He possesses wisdom and understanding but they are wise in their own eyes. He judges justly but they acquit the guilty for bribes. He calls on God and relies on him but they rely on the arm of flesh. He relieves others' oppression but they cause others' oppression. He does God's will but they go against God's will. He has a learned tongue but they have a perverse tongue. He praises God but they vilify him.

Figure 61 **Opposite Responses to the Servant**

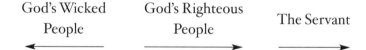

The servant draws near to God but the wicked forsake him. He follows God's counsel but they follow their own. He speaks God's word but they rely on empty words. He teaches the law of God but they observe commandments of men. He is a "light" to God's people but they choose darkness. He works justice but they work injustice. He is an example of righteousness but they refuse to learn righteousness. He increases people's joy but they heap sorrows on themselves. He releases God's people from bondage but they are taken captive. He puts his enemies to flight but their enemies put *them* to flight. He apportions God's people's inheritances in the Promised Land but they are dispossessed.

God hears his servant but he doesn't hear them. God fulfills his servant's predictions but he exposes theirs as false. God calls him by name but he deals with them namelessly. God vindicates him but he condemns them to die. God heals him of his wounds but he smites them with disease. God creates him anew but he makes chaos of them. God strengthens him against his enemies but he strengthens their enemies against *them*. God lends him his power but he strips them of strength. God enables him to turn nations into "dust" and "chaff" but he enables nations to turn *them* into "dust" and "chaff." God exalts him but he abases them. God gives him a new name but he cuts their names off.

These and similar linking ideas show that as we ascend the ladder we may follow persons higher than ourselves whom God imbues with power and appoints over his people. Also illustrated is the role a righteous leader plays in delivering God's people: to get where the servant is, God's people must do as he does. That follows a divine pattern and ultimately centers on God himself. To the degree that we keep the terms of God's covenant we experience upward momentum. A downward slide, on the other hand, is the result of "disloyalty" and "rebellion" when we live contrary to God's law. In short, God doesn't push us up the ladder but he arranges things so that our optimum course is to ascend.

People Pass or Fail the Three Tests of Loyalty

To ascend the spiritual ladder at the end of the world we must deal with three evil forces. These seek to prevent our progress, blocking us from attaining heaven. But they also provide tests of loyalty to God that all must pass who ascend to Zion/Jerusalem and levels higher. They illustrate the nature of ascent as overcoming opposition, showing that surmounting evils in the world is a necessary part of our growth. Those who pass the tests receive all the blessings of God's covenant: an endowment of God's Spirit, divine protection against enemies, permanent lands of inheritance, and enduring offspring. Those who fail the tests pass out of this life, perhaps to await a future opportunity to ascend.

Isaiah's three tests resemble those of Greek legend and appear also in the literature of ancient Mesopotamia. Odysseus, on his return home from Troy, for example, faces three similar such tests, each of which he passes. Cyclops, the angry one-eyed giant, does battle with him, intent on killing him. The Sirens, sensuous females on a "pleasure island," seek to seduce and capture him. And false suitors woo his wife in his absence and wantonly squander his inheritance. Isaiah's version of these tests are the king of Assyria/Babylon, idolaters or idolatry, and false brethren (see Figure 62). By passing the tests, God's people ascend to Zion/Jerusalem, but by failing them they descend to Babylon.

Figure 62   **Three Tests of Loyalty to God**

The King of Assyria/Babylon—
A Political Dictatorship

Idolaters/Idolatry—Materialism
and Sensual Gratification

False Brethren—Ostracism by
Ecclesiastical Authorities

The three tests don't necessarily follow a particular order yet constitute trials of God's people in every sense. Each attempts to divert their loyalty away from the true God to a counterfeit—to itself. The king of Assyria/Babylon represents a political dictatorship that pressures people under pain of death to submit to its control. Idolaters seduce people by selling them Babylon's standard of materialism and sensual gratification. And false brethren abuse their ecclesiastical authority and in God's name ostracize persons who don't subscribe to their current religious paradigm. Additionally, the three tests incorporate temptations such as envy, jealousy, lust, hate, anger, pride, and personal ambition.

In Isaiah's endtime scenario the archtyrant rises to prominence as a political power in direct proportion to God's people's spiritual decline. An external form of worship hides an internal emptiness. Thus, Paul predicts that there will "occur a falling away first" before the "man of sin is revealed, the Son of Perdition, who opposes and exalts himself above all that is called God, or that is worshiped, so that he as God sits in the temple of God, showing himself to be God." Concerning this usurper's false claims Paul adds that God will send the wicked a "powerful delusion, so that they will believe a lie" (2 Thessalonians 2:3–4, 9–11). Having rejected God's truth, they buy into false convictions.

The king of Assyria/Babylon not only pretends to be divine, he wields unprecedented political power. Possessing the military capacity to realize his self-serving ambitions, he wreaks havoc and disaster wherever he strikes. As evil as he is, his seemingly invincible strength sweeps many people off their feet, persuading them to submit to his control. The temptation to "go over to the winning side" will sway the masses as it swayed the German people and other nationals during World War II. By giving the archtyrant their allegiance, however, they dissolve their allegiance to Israel's God. Just as those who love darkness can't comprehend light, so what is evil is incompatible with what is good.

The archtyrant's charisma, too, influences multitudes to go along with his agenda. Isaiah depicts him figuratively as a "mouth," "tongue," and "lips," alluding to his power of speech and oratory. Daniel describes him as "a *mouth* speaking great things" (Daniel 7:8, 20; emphasis added). Isaiah further characterizes him as a "rod," "staff," and "scourge," reflecting his ability to enforce his rule (see Figure 63). Ezekiel predicts mass destruction in a day when violence springs up as a *"rod* of wickedness" (Ezekiel 7:11; emphasis added). If we would resist the most powerful force for evil the world has ever known, we must believe that "this too will pass"—that God will deliver those who wait for him.

Figure 63   **Figurative Representations of the Archtyrant**

"mouth"—"tongue"—"lips"—"rod"—"staff"

"scourge"—"anger"—"wrath"—"rage"

The evil influence idolaters have on God's people may be subtler than the two other challenges but it is equally deadly. Isaiah represents idolatry as "harlotry"—unfaithfulness to God's covenant. People become complacent and forget about God as they immerse themselves in the pleasures of Babylon. According to Isaiah, their loving and coveting material possessions *is* idolatry, and the effect of idolatry is spiritual blindness. When they are "blind" and "deaf" people perceive truth as falsehood and falsehood as truth. Even though an entire society engages in idolatry, God's people aren't justified in doing so. No matter how entrenched Babylon is, all who would ascend must learn to rise above it.

John predicts that many in the world will worship the image of the "Beast." Those who refuse to accept the Beast's "mark" will be unable to buy or sell (Revelation 13:11–17). For those who belong to Babylon, worshiping this idol will simply be more of what they are already doing. To escape Babylon's net when it is cast over everyone, therefore, we must determine beforehand how we will survive. Although Isaiah doesn't go into detail, he shows what a tight hold idolatry will have on God's people and that economic collapse follows. In God's

Day of Judgment, he declares, when the wicked suffer famine and destitution, the righteous "will eat the fruits of their own labors" (Isaiah 3:10).

They must choose between him and "gods that cannot save."

God warns his people to "come to their senses" and forsake their idols (Isaiah 46:8). He forgives them when they grind them to powder, "leaving no idols of prosperity and shining images standing" (Isaiah 27:9). Moses had required this of those who worshiped the Golden Calf. God asks his people to "turn to me and save yourselves" (Isaiah 45:22). He has chosen them to be his "witnesses," to testify that without him there is no "salvation," that apart from him there is no God (Isaiah 43:10–12). It is God's will that his people "magnify the law and become illustrious," enjoying all the blessings of the covenant (Isaiah 42:21). They must choose between him and "gods that cannot save" (Isaiah 45:20).

Another trial God's people face is the tendency by some to control others' spiritual lives. Driven by an ungodly loathing of those more zealous for God than themselves, certain "brethren"—religious leaders—misuse their authority by acting "holier than thou." Contrary to Jesus' counsel they pull out the wheat with the tares, excommunicating and blacklisting those whom they cannot bear (Isaiah 66:5). These suffer the misfortune of being social outcasts, of being treated as heretics and apostates. They must deal with the paradox of so-called men of God—"shepherds" of the people—making a pretense of mediating God's covenant while, in fact, persecuting them in his name (Isaiah 56:10–12; 61:7).

Ezekiel, too, describes false brethren as "shepherds," who instead of feeding the flock scatter and drive it away. They feed themselves off the fattest. They don't care for the sick to bind them up nor rescue those astray. The sheep wander where they can, becoming prey to "wild beasts"—forces alien and hostile to God. God responds by raising up his servant, who gathers the outcasts from whence they are scattered. God appoints his servant as his people's "prince" and "shepherd," establishing his covenant with those whom he gathers (Ezekiel 34). Ezekiel's scenario thus parallels Isaiah's, except that Ezekiel emphasizes the shepherds' abuses whereas Isaiah highlights how people deal with them.

In the end, those who claim God's authority in support of their unrighteous leadership see their worst fears realized—they lose their place in the kingdom of God. God brings them to judgment and releases them as shepherds. They themselves become prey to "wild beasts." The shame they brought on others comes on themselves in full. Isaiah likens persecution by false brethren to the Woman Zion—God's spouse—going into labor, also called the "Birthpangs of the Messiah." She gives birth to God's "son" or servant and to a "nation" of God's children (see Figure 64). That *nation* consists of those whom the servant gathers, who ascend the spiritual ladder (Isaiah 55:4–5, 12; 56:8–11; 66:5–9).

Figure 64   **The "Birthpangs of the Messiah"**

Such challenges can present huge difficulties for God's people. Through these trials they learn to let God fight their battles while they maintain their personal integrity. As they repudiate every power that rivals God's, they conquer their fear of death, deprivation, and rejection. They face the worst and realize that God sustains them, thus passing his test of their loyalty. To those who fear him—who loathe to offend him—God is a "sanctuary" in the midst of trouble. As they overcome opposition

God transforms their state of weakness into one of strength. The adversity they endure for being loyal to God—for taking a different stand than the rest of society—is the very thing that propels them upward.

Persons who fail these tests suffer a similar fate as those who challenge them (see Figure 65). Siding with evil may momentarily satisfy worldly lusts or personal ambition but it may permanently distance a person from God. At the last, all that was gained is lost. God's justice requires that he brings the wicked to judgment. The archtyrant makes an end of idolaters and false brethren, but God's servant makes an end of the archtyrant. The oppressors' anti-God attitude causes God to intervene. Those who seize God's power, who ingratiate themselves into his position, end up disinherited and humiliated. Those who unjustly suffer humiliation at the hands of evil authorities, ascend the ladder.

Figure 65   **Consequences of Passing and Failing the Tests**

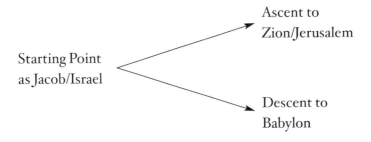

So simply calling ourselves God's covenant people doesn't decide our destiny at the end of the world. A person may confess that he is committed to God but at the same time pursue antichrist policies. He may claim to be a Jew, Christian, or Moslem but in reality be an idolater. He may be a professor of religion but irreligiously tyrannize God's people, believing that they are in error. What people do and what they desire in their hearts determines what level of the ladder they are on. Do they trust in God or the arm of flesh? Do they love God or the lusts of Babylon? Do they observe God's law and word or the commandments of men? Do they release others from oppression or oppress others?

People of Zion/Jerusalem accept all that goes with allegiance to God, including things that are disagreeable. They know life is a test, a sometimes grueling mortal probation for a glorious immortal destiny. They keep a long-term versus short-term perspective on life. They are willing to pay the price of a better life, of rewards that cannot be calculated in worldly terms. In the end, God turns their sorrows into joy. He reverses their adverse circumstances, answering their loyalty with a multitude of blessings. Those who wait for God's salvation, perhaps seemingly forever, ultimately see it unfold before their eyes. Those who hope in God against all odds, he fills with a full measure of his love.

People at Home and Abroad Face the Archtyrant

Isaiah deals with two geographically separate groups of God's people who live at the end of the world: those at home and those abroad. Each represents a cross section of levels on the spiritual ladder. Those who live in the *place* Zion or Jerusalem—whatever category they may be—belong to the "at home" group. Those who live among the nations of the world belong to the "abroad" group. Isaiah thus distinguishes between the *place* Zion or Jerusalem and *people* on the Zion/Jerusalem level (see Figure 66). In the interim before God destroys the wicked from the earth, persons on levels other than Zion/Jerusalem may dwell among his people "at home" just as they dwell among them "abroad."

Before God's Day of Judgment overtakes the world, different spiritual categories live alongside one another. Persons who belong to Babylon and Jacob/Israel, for example, may reside in the *place* Zion or Jerusalem but not be a part of the *people* Zion/ Jerusalem. Just as God cleanses the earth at the end of the world, so he cleanses the *place* Zion or Jerusalem before God's people reinherit it. Similarly, just as different categories live side by side before the three lowest pass away, so higher categories may advance up the ladder simultaneously. Some people, for instance, may be ascending from Jacob/Israel to Zion/Jerusalem at the same time others are ascending from Zion/Jerusalem to sons/servants.

Figure 66   **God's People at Home and Abroad**

The *People* of Zion/Jerusalem among All Nations

People on All Levels in the *Place* Zion or Jerusalem

Because they live under dissimilar conditions, God's people at home and abroad experience tests of loyalty differently. And yet, to ascend to a particular level God's people must pass equally challenging tests. Everyone who ascends endures similar trials, although God tailors these to fit people's individual circumstances. Ultimately, those at home welcome back from abroad those who return from among the nations, who come out of Greater Babylon on the eve of its desolation. Living "at home," however, is no guarantee that one will remain there. In the end, only the *people* of Zion/Jerusalem and above live in the *place* Zion or Jerusalem. The rest, of their own choosing, exit this world.

In Isaiah's endtime scenario the archtyrant attacks both those at home and those abroad. God gives him power over the wicked of God's people throughout the world because they have "transgressed the laws, changed the ordinances, and set at nought the everlasting covenant" (Isaiah 24:5). By violating its terms, they invalidate God's covenant. When they turn to evil, wherever they live, they forfeit the blessings and suffer the curses. Lost privileges, such as lands of inheritance and divine protection, are won back by keeping the terms of God's covenant on at least the Zion/Jerusalem level. When God's people repent of evil and prove loyal through times of trial, God reverses their circumstances.

By violating its terms, they invalidate God's covenant.

The general wickedness of God's people at the end of the world causes God's righteous people also to come under attack, although God delivers them. After conquering and laying waste the nations of the world, the king of Assyria/Babylon seeks to eliminate God's people who live in the *place* Zion or Jerusalem. As the apex of his ambitions, he wants to vanquish Zion/Jerusalem, signaling that his world rule is absolute. Because he seeks to displace God, he considers the best way to do so is to annihilate God's people or at least to enslave them. He seeks to destroy them because they keep the memory of Israel's God alive. Their testifying that he is real implies that the archtyrant is a fraud.

Many of Jacob/Israel thus ascend to Zion/Jerusalem at the time the king of Assyria/Babylon lays siege to the *place* Zion or Jerusalem. The type of that event is the Assyrian siege of Jerusalem in the days of King Hezekiah (Isaiah 36–37). After conquering the nations of the world the archtyrant's huge army surrounds God's people "at home," giving them an ultimatum: either they surrender or the Assyrian army wipes them out. Although vastly outnumbered, God's people follow the king's counsel and trust in Israel's God to deliver them. By so doing, they pass his test of loyalty and ascend the ladder. Henceforth Isaiah calls them "Zion" and "Jerusalem," a blessed category of God's people.

As anciently, God delivers his besieged people by annihilating the Assyrian army, which itself belongs to Isaiah's Babylon category. The angel of God smites it with a plague so that in one night all die (Isaiah 37:36). By such miraculous means one of two major endtime Assyrian armies disappears from the earth. The other army perishes when many of Jacob/Israel "abroad" rally against the Assyrian power (see Figure 67). God's people who mobilize did not go in the exodus out of Babylon under divine protection but prove loyal to God through that time. When they challenge the Assyrian army in mortal combat, God strengthens them and gives them the victory (Isaiah 30:30–32; 41:2, 15).

Figure 67   **Jacob/Israel's "Holy War"**

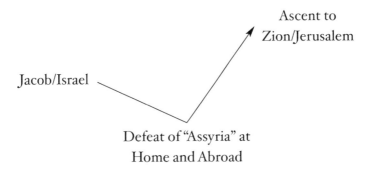

Ascent to Zion/Jerusalem

Jacob/Israel

Defeat of "Assyria" at Home and Abroad

Types of this second success against Assyria are the armies of ancient Israel. Before and after reaching the Promised Land they fought unfriendly forces that sought to destroy them. In each case, with God's help, they conquered their enemies. Led by Moses, Joshua, Israel's judges, and King David, they overthrew armies far superior in numbers. When they kept the terms of his covenant God protected them from adversaries at home and abroad. Just as he strengthened his people in the past, so he will strengthen them in the future. Physically defending God's people against the forces of evil—which constitutes an integral part of covenant keeping—helps qualify Jacob/Israel for ascent to a higher level.

The Israelites under Moses briefly attained the Zion/ Jerusalem level when they inherited the Promised Land. Those who didn't perished in the wilderness. The latter became a type of God's wicked people who fail to ascend at the end of the world. Those who *did* ascend in Moses' day forsook their false gods in favor of the true God and kept the terms of his covenant. Because the Promised Land, divine protection, and enduring offspring comprise the chief blessings of the covenant (see Figure 68), God's people could not inherit the land any other way. As noted, it wasn't enough that God had promised the land to their ancestors. He required that they themselves should qualify for it by living his law.

Figure 68   **Three Principal Blessings of God's Covenant**

Promised Land

Divine Protection

Enduring Offspring

At the end of the world the catastrophe the Assyrians suffer constitutes a direct consequence of their oppressing God's people. Under the terms of his covenant God blesses his people when they keep his law and word and curses them when they don't, as we have seen. But he also curses those who infringe on the rights of his people who prove loyal to him. When God's people faithfully observe the terms of the covenant and someone threatens them, then the curses of the covenant fall on the aggressor. All who fight against Zion/Jerusalem thus invite God's plagues on themselves. Knowingly or unknowingly they suffer divine justice as if they themselves were transgressors of his covenant.

That is why only Zion/Jerusalem and levels higher survive this scenario. All categories below Zion/Jerusalem are subject to God's justice and must unavoidably perish. Unless they repent they can't enjoy his mercy. In a day when all humanity takes sides—by choosing a "Covenant of Life" or a "Covenant with Death"—it is hazardous to belong to Babylon. Attacking God's righteous people turns out to be a big mistake for the Assyrian army, which knows nothing of the curses of God's covenant. God turns its hostility to the advantage of those it attacks. Assyria's assault on God's people forms the catalyst for many of Jacob/Israel to attain Zion/Jerusalem and for Assyria's armies to perish.

Led by the servant, God's people reconquer the earth from the Assyrian power when its two main armies suffer defeat (Isaiah 41:2–16). Because Assyria's forces will then be dispersed throughout the earth, it will virtually be a mopping-up exercise followed by a restoration of peace. Cyrus' military victories in Babylon, in which he rapidly seized local garrisons, are a type of that conquest and restoration. After taking the Babylonian empire Cyrus established his righteous rule over all nations. God approved of Cyrus, who ordered the rebuilding of the temple in Jerusalem. So too, at the end of the world, the servant rebuilds the temple in Jerusalem in anticipation of Jehovah's coming to the earth.

Zion/Jerusalem Assumes a Paradisiacal Glory

God's people inherit a new Paradise in the millennial age of peace. The basic covenant blessing of a land of inheritance turns into a land that God glorifies. The *place* where his people live—Zion or Jerusalem—becomes as the Garden of Eden: God "will open up streams in barren hill country, springs in the midst of the plains; [he] will turn the desert into lakes, parched lands into fountains of water" (Isaiah 41:18); "Wilderness and arid lands will be jubilant; the desert will rejoice when it blossoms as the crocus. . . . The glory of Jehovah and the splendor of our God they will see [there]" (Isaiah 35:1–2). He will make Zion's "wilderness like Eden, her desert as the garden of Jehovah" (Isaiah 51:3).

Enmity will pass away from the animal kingdom.

The land will produce bountifully for its inhabitants: "Then will he water with rain the seed you sow in the ground, that the land's increase of food may be rich and abundant" (Isaiah 30:23). Enmity will pass away from the animal kingdom: "The wolf and the lamb will graze alike; and the lion will eat straw like the ox" (Isaiah 65:25). On a nonliteral level Isaiah uses animals to symbolize people. Allegorically, therefore, clean animals according to the Law of Moses represent God's covenant people while unclean animals represent assimilated or non-covenantal lineages. In Isaiah's endtime scenario *both* come under God's covenant umbrella as many ascend from Jacob/Israel to Zion/Jerusalem.

Wherever God's covenant people spread abroad the earth turns into Paradise. God's new creation of the earth at the beginning of the millennial age raises the earth to the spiritual level of his people (see Figure 69). The curses of the covenant disappear as only its blessings prevail. Where no one violates the terms of the covenant, no evil effects follow. Sickness and disease, famine and plagues, poverty and deprivation will be no more: "They will not build so that others may dwell, or plant so that others may eat. . . . They will not exert themselves in vain, or bear children doomed for calamity. . . . The troubles of the past will be forgotten" (Isaiah 65:16, 22–23). All the earth will be at peace.

Persons who live into the age of peace will enjoy the privilege of God's presence. Of that time, Jehovah says, "I will delight in Jerusalem, rejoice in my people; no more will be heard there the sound of weeping or the cry of distress. No more will there be infants alive but a few days, or the aged who do not live out their years. . . . Before they call I will reply; while they are yet speaking I will respond" (Isaiah 65:19–20, 24); "I will extend peace to her like a river, the bounty of the nations like a stream in flood. Then will you nurse and be carried upon the hip and dandled on the knees. As one who is comforted by his mother I will comfort you; for Jerusalem you will be comforted" (Isaiah 66:12–13).

Figure 69 **Paradise a Re-Creation of the Earth**

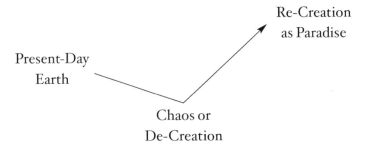

Even death, which was a consequence of Adam's and Eve's transgression, disappears. Death—called "the veil that veils all peoples, the shroud that shrouds all nations"—God abolishes forever (Isaiah 25:7–8). The righteous dead come back to life "when their bodies arise"; God will say to them "Awake and sing for joy you who abide in the dust, your dew is the dew of sunrise! For the earth will cast up its dead" (Isaiah 26:19). When God reverses the curse of death together with *all* covenant curses, people will be known for who they are and will see as they are seen. God "will wipe away the tears from all faces" and "remove the reproach of his people from throughout the earth" (Isaiah 25:8).

The "Fall" of Adam and Eve—their descent to a lower level—was never meant to be permanent. As shown in Chapter 8, God's covenant with his people provides the means for humanity to overcome the curse of death. We ascend to heaven by rising above *every* evil as we adhere to the terms of God's covenant. Of those who live during the millennial age, God says, "The lifetime of my people will be as the lifetime of a tree; my elect will outlast the work of their hands" (Isaiah 65:22). Types of God's people living an entire millennium are humanity's progenitors before the Flood. Even after living such a long time, however, they don't die, but, like Elijah, change in an instant to an immortal state.

The "Fall" of Adam and Eve was never meant to be permanent.

Because the earth becomes a new Paradise in the millennial age—God's kingdom on earth—that doesn't mean it was so once. Although the Garden of Eden is a type, it didn't cover the entire earth. When Adam and Eve transgressed his law God exiled them from the Garden. In much the same way, when the Israelites transgressed God exiled them from the Promised Land. Each *physical* exile reflected a spiritual descent. Because a paradisiacal glory pertains to the Zion/Jerusalem level, "Paradise lost" implies descent to a lower level. For the ancient Israelites, losing the "land flowing with milk and honey"—with its clusters of grapes only two men could carry—signified a similar descent.

Such descents, however, create the means for those who are born as Jacob/Israel to ascend to Zion/Jerusalem. In other words, the permanent ascent of *many*—as they overcome inherited covenant curses—would more than compensate for the temporary descent of relatively *few* (see Figure 70). What Adam and Eve lost in the short term, their posterity wins back for the long term. What the Israelites gave up, their descendants regain. Isaiah shows that in the millennial age Paradise and the Promised Land become one—as the Promised Land ultimately encompasses the entire earth, so the entire earth becomes a new Paradise. In that way God turns evil to good for all who prove loyal to him.

Figure 70 **Humanity's Descent and Ascent**

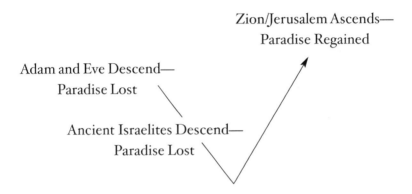

Because no way existed for Adam's and Eve's descendants to qualify for Paradise without they *themselves* ascending to Zion/ Jerusalem, we learn that the Fall was, in fact, a premeditated part of God's plan. There *had* to be a temporary descent to a lower level so that a permanent ascent could usher in the millennial age of peace. Zion/Jerusalem's rising "from the dust" at the dawning of the millennial age, moreover, implies not just the re-creation of God's covenant people as a nation but also their resurrection of the dead—the physical "rebirth" of *all* who, by that time, have ascended to higher levels. Such souls, too, inherit Paradise on the earth "when their bodies arise" (Isaiah 26:19).

For God's covenant people and levels higher—for all who ascend to Zion/Jerusalem and above—not only does "Paradise regained" endure an entire millennium, but millennial time on the Zion/Jerusalem level differs dramatically from present time on the Jacob/Israel level. Just as a thousand years to us is "as one day" to God (2 Peter 3:8), so time on levels between God's and ours can be calculated as multiples of present time.

A "millennium" on the Zion/Jerusalem level, in other word, may last many thousands of years as we now know time, not just a thousand years. Persons with Near-Death Experiences observe the slowing of "time" on lower spiritual levels and its speeding up on higher ones.

Postscript: People who have been in space and orbited the earth all say the same thing: what a supernal sense of peace they feel looking down on our world from above. Somehow, that "celestial" vantage point cures human enmity, making people's squabbles down below seem irrelevant. A feeling of God's love pervades their experience, perhaps in small part resembling the vision of Isaiah, who describes the earth's "sphere" in cosmic terms and identifies God as its loving Creator.

Astronauts, in effect, have been able to steal a glance at something transcendent, getting a sneak preview of what most humans haven't yet seen or felt. But Isaiah has seen in vision what astronauts have seen, and much more. God, he says, has created this earth as home to his covenant people. And God continues to "stretch out [the heavens] as a tent to dwell in" (Isaiah 40:22). That expansive view—of the earth's connectedness to other habitable spheres—is the privilege of seraphim.

It is indeed hard to imagine "the things God has prepared for those who love him." We don't see them until we get there, and we don't get there until we have believed and acted on our faith. God has built that way of doing things into his program. But he sends prophets like Isaiah, who are his spokesmen, to show how that works. He even sends astronauts as a backup to tell us what *they* see that the prophets have seen. And what have they seen? "Peace beyond all understanding."

6

GOD'S SONS/SERVANTS,
PROXY DELIVERERS

God's sons/servants keep the terms of individual covenants and live a higher law. They prove loyal under all conditions and see God. Individual covenants parallel ancient Near Eastern emperor–vassal relationships. Suffering and humiliation precede salvation and exaltation. Israel's God re-creates his elect in his image and likeness as his sons and daughters.

Rising above the Zion/Jerusalem level on the ladder to heaven are persons to whom God refers in familial terms as his "sons" and "daughters," who assume a greater role on behalf of his people. These choose to serve God by serving their fellow human beings. They minister spiritually to levels below their own, while they themselves are ministered to by ones above. God makes a covenant with his "sons" and "daughters" individually, not just collectively as he does with those of Zion/Jerusalem. That *individual* covenant is first conditional—dependent on the person's fulfilling its terms—then unconditional. When it becomes unconditional God himself ministers to his "sons" and "daughters."

Although the role of ministering to others applies equally to men and women, in the Hebrew worldview God addresses men specifically because they take the leading role in providing for and protecting his people and in governing their affairs. Perhaps on that account God also singles them out for censure and reproof more than women. In the Garden of Eden God commands Adam to keep his law and word. Eve follows suit without the need of being named (Genesis 2:16–17; 3:3, 11). A similar pattern prevails in Judaism's observing the Law of Moses to this day. Traditionally, God's law and word—the terms of his covenant—have applied explicitly to men and implicitly to women.

There exist instances in the Book of Isaiah and in the Bible as a whole, however, when words such as "sons" and "servants" are used as *legal* terms in a covenantal sense. In that case they refer to men explicitly and I identify them as such. God assigns different though complementary roles to men and women, and we learn about these from observing how God addresses and relates to each gender individually. Still, to allow for both general and specific meanings of these terms, I refer to Isaiah's second level of blessedness as the "son/servant" category, or, simply, as "sons/servants." That eliminates the need to use the cumbersome expression "sons and daughters/servants and handmaidens."

Once cleared of sin, they become serviceable to God.

As we have seen, people ascending to Zion/Jerusalem are primarily concerned with "repenting" of transgression and "returning" to God. They deal with the basic issues of life as they establish a covenant relationship with him and keep its terms.

By passing tests of loyalty, which God orchestrates for them, they show their allegiance to him. They reach a critical point in their journey up the ladder when they know God has forgiven them their sins. Their repentance is realized when, with God's help, they cease to do evil and learn to do good. Once cleared of the burden of sin, they become serviceable to God. Having ascended to the Zion/Jerusalem level, they are ready to help others do the same.

Persons who ascend to the son/servant level, on the other hand, are primarily concerned with things *beyond* the forgiveness of their sins. By tending to the spiritual and material needs of others, they follow God's example, developing his attributes and character traits. Although all too aware of how far they fall short, as they lean on God he strengthens them in their struggles. They become examples of righteousness by serving as God's agents of "deliverance" and "salvation" to those less fortunate than themselves. In the course of performing these roles, their relationship with God grows to fruition. Thus, they "go on to perfection," to "sanctifying" their lives in the service of God (see Figure 71).

Figure 71   **Successive Spiritual Objectives**

Sons/Servants—Perfection/Sanctification

Zion/Jerusalem—Forgiveness of Sins

Types of God's endtime sons/servants are those who fulfilled the role of deliverers and saviors to God's people anciently such as Israel's judges Othniel, Deborah, and Gideon, and Judah's King Hezekiah. They were instrumental in delivering God's people at a time when the nations around them sought to subject them (Judges 3:9, 15; Isaiah 38:6). Others, too, fulfilled savior roles just as important. During the conquest of the Land of Canaan, Joshua commanded the sun to stand still over the

Valley of Ajalon until the Israelites had slain their enemies (Joshua 10:1–14). Esther was instrumental in delivering the exiled Jews living in Persia from Haman's plot to kill them (Esther 11–13).

The great type of a deliverer, however, in whom all ancient savior roles converged, was King David (see Figure 72). The Davidic Covenant—the covenant God made individually with Israel's king—became a legal framework in which the savior role was acknowledged by God and people alike as filling the need for Israel's protection. Before that time, although God made individual covenants with Abraham, Isaac, Jacob, and others, such covenants didn't specify kingship of God's people as the Davidic Covenant did. All who ascend to the son/servant level and above ultimately follow the model of King David and his righteous heirs, the savior-kings who were types of Israel's future Messiah.

Figure 72   **Types of King David as a Deliverer**

At the time God's people asked the prophet Samuel to anoint them a king, the Philistines were on the verge of overpowering Israel. Samuel gave the politically correct response by saying that Jehovah was their King. In other words, if they kept his law he would bless them and strengthen them against their enemies. However, even Samuel saw that Israel had sunk so low spiritually that new measures were needed to protect God's people. When Samuel anointed Saul, human kingship was instituted in which the king served as an intermediary between God and his people (1 Samuel 8–9). After Saul fell from grace, Samuel anointed David, who subdued the Philistines and expanded Israel's dominions.

God's sons/servants follow the type of King David by demonstrating "loyalty" to God and "compliance" with his will in keeping the terms of his individual covenants. By honoring his covenant relationship with God, David became his "son" and "servant" (Psalms 2:6–7; 89:3, 20). So do all who ascend to the second level of blessedness. Like King David, and also earlier types, God's endtime sons/servants obtain divine protection for those to whom God calls them to minister. They intercede on behalf of his people as they face threats of various kinds in the "last days." God can't refuse the intercession of his sons/servants to deliver his people when they prove loyal and comply with his will.

The individual covenants God makes with his sons/servants are thus patterned after his covenant with King David. Keeping the terms of the Davidic Covenant, in fact, forms the essence of living God's higher law. It takes to the limit loving God with one's whole heart, might, mind, and strength and one's neighbor as oneself. God appears to his sons/servants and ministers to them personally as they pass through "descent before ascent." As they grow more *like* God by ministering to others, he blesses them with eternal blessings of promised lands, thrones, dominions, and so forth as he did his elect in the past. Their fulfilling the role of deliverers to God's people wins them everlasting glory.

God's Sons/Servants Overcome Sin and Iniquity

Those who attain this second level of blessedness are freed from iniquity as well as sin. While we often lump "sins and iniquities" together as though they are the same thing, there exists a significant difference between the two. Persons on the Zion/Jerusalem level, for example, receive God's forgiveness of their sins but must still overcome their iniquities (see Figure 73).

Once, when I was learning Hebrew, a teacher on an Israeli kibbutz defended her atheism to the class with the argument, "Ezekiel says a person isn't guilty of his father's sins, but Moses says the iniquity of the fathers is on the heads of their children to the third and fourth generation. So you see, the Bible contradicts itself!"

I raised my hand in defense of the Bible but for a moment didn't know how to respond. I finally blurted out that Ezekiel spoke of wrongs a person does, for which he alone is responsible. But Moses spoke of the consequences of wrongdoing on succeeding generations—residual effects children may inherit from their parents. I had seen the evil effects of World War II in my childhood and the fear and confusion it caused in the rising generation. Like my good Hebrew teacher, many Jews had become alienated and had abandoned Judaism. I had also seen a teenage friend devastated by his father's suicide and families with young children wrecked by the repercussions of their parents' divorce.

In response to my teacher's statement I would now say that covenant curses follow breaking God's law, perhaps long after we have repented and gained forgiveness for personal wrongs. Such curses continue down the generations until finally reversed through righteous living. Who can calculate the spiritual and emotional ripple effects of war, violence, abuse, molestation, drugs, divorce, teen pregnancies, and so forth on victims and their descendants and how those things distort people's attitudes towards each other? Such are a curse indeed on human society. For the sake of convenience I will refer to individual wrongdoing as "sins" and to the evil aftereffects of wrongdoing as "iniquities."

As a parallel example, Adam's and Eve's transgression of God's law brought the curse of death on us their descendants. While God may forgive us our personal sins, we have all still inherited our mortal condition. Although the Bible mentions no covenant in connection with Adam and Eve, we one must have existed as *all* relationships with God on any level are covenantal in nature. God's law and word in every instance that God reveals them constitute the terms of his covenant with his people and with individuals. Adam's and Eve's descendants may do their part by keeping his law and word and thereby qualify for immortality. But immortality still depends on Jehovah fulfilling his role of Savior.

Figure 73   **Different Degrees of Forgiveness**

Sons/Servants—Forgiveness of Sins and Iniquities

Zion/Jerusalem—Forgiveness of Sins

Jacob/Israel—No Forgiveness

God's endtime sons/servants resemble Israel's ancestors Abraham, Isaac, and Jacob by going a long way toward reversing covenant curses for others, notably their descendants. Abraham turned around the cursed condition of idolatry and famine from which he came into a blessed one, creating a new starting point in life for his son Isaac and his entire household. By his own loyalty to God, Isaac increased God's blessings on himself and his descendants. So did his son Jacob. To Jacob's son Joseph, for example, his father said, "Your father's blessings have exceeded the blessings of my progenitors to the utmost bounds of the ancient hills. They will rest on the head of Joseph . . ." (Genesis 49:26).

Each generation of Israel's righteous ancestors thus added to God's blessings on their descendants. Instead of being cursed to the third and fourth generation, as were Abraham's immediate ancestors, from Abraham and on they were blessed (see Figure 74). That was because Abraham dealt in a proper way with the curses afflicting his generation. In so doing he "paid off" the debt of iniquity he had inherited from his fathers. In modern terms we might say that Abraham overcame the dysfunctional patterns passed on to him by his progenitors, passing none to his own posterity. Abraham took ownership of them in his life by replacing inappropriate with appropriate behavior through living God's law.

Figure 74 **Abraham as a Transitional Figure**

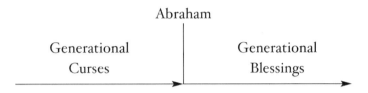

Just as Isaiah equates cleansing from sin with healing, so he does cleansing from iniquity. This secondary healing—of a person's whole soul—involves turning curses into blessings not just for oneself but also for others. Covenant curses are the cumulative, generational effects of sin, the result of transgressing God's law and word on the offender and his offspring. Through a process similar to "repenting" of wrongdoing and "returning" to God, individuals come to terms with their iniquities—with inherited dysfunctional patterns—and clean up their lives. Then, having progressed that far in overcoming evil, they inspire others to do the same. By such means they ascend to the son/servant level.

Those who make this transition completely change their thought processes. As they open themselves to the influence of God's Spirit, God enlightens them to his truth, to things as they really are—different from their former imperfect perception of the truth. They become aware of and discard fixed beliefs about themselves and others that have bound them to patterns of living below their potential. Their "emotional clearing," or rather, their spiritual purification, involves forgiving themselves and others their inappropriate behaviors and loving themselves and others unconditionally. An internal compass guides them. In the end, they find themselves by losing themselves in the service of God.

Jehovah Ministers Personally to His Sons/Servants

As we seek to be who we really are—children of God—God empowers us by his Spirit to conform our lives to his will until "his thoughts become our thoughts and his ways our ways" on our own spiritual level. He has put into us the divine gene that makes becoming godlike an intrinsic part of being human. Moreover, God has placed us in an earthly environment where growing in godliness can most readily occur. He teaches us the terms of his covenant that enable us to "repent" and "return," not just to the Promised Land, but, ultimately, to our heavenly home. In effect, Israel's return from exile among the nations is but an allegory of humanity's return from exile in this mortal state (see Figure 75).

Figure 75   **Israel's Return from Exile an Allegory of Humanity**

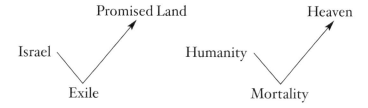

As a foretaste of their return "home" to dwell in his presence, Jehovah manifests himself to his sons/servants on the earth and ministers to them. Just as they had ministered to others spiritually and physically, and as they had been ministered to by angels to prepare them for this moment, so Israel's God personally ministers to them and they receive his promise of eternal blessedness. As that promise depended on their demonstrating "loyalty" to God and "compliance" with his will—on living the higher law of their individual covenants and serving him at all costs—so they have now come to know him. They thus have no more need to *believe* God lives; they *know* he lives and loves them.

After they thus prove loyal under all conditions, God blesses his sons/servants unconditionally as he did Abraham, Isaac, Jacob, and others to whom he appeared and ministered in person. Husbands, wives, and children become an integral part of a "family of God." Living a higher law involved seeking God's blessings for both themselves and their offspring, which blessings God now lovingly grants. As they sought others' welfare, so God seeks theirs. Their seeing God in such circumstances means they have attained a level of perfection and sanctification sufficient to live in his presence. God chooses them as his "elect," whereas before this their chosen or elect status was provisional.

> They find themselves by losing themselves in the service of God.

There is an important difference between obtaining God's blessings for oneself and obtaining them for others. We notice that distinction in two ancient types. The first demonstrates a blessing on the Zion/Jerusalem level while the second demonstrates the same blessing on the son/servant level (see Figure 76). The Israelites in the time of Moses and Joshua inherited the Promised Land as a people after they had learned to keep God's law and word. As they observed the terms of the Sinai Covenant, they overcame their sins but not their iniquities. Thus, many of their immediate descendants lapsed into an idolatrous lifestyle, jeopardizing the land their fathers had recently obtained (Judges 2:10–15).

Abraham, Isaac, and Jacob, on the other hand, obtained the Promised Land for themselves and their descendants as a *permanent* blessing. God promised it to them unconditionally as an "everlasting inheritance." He required only that in order to live in the Promised Land their descendants would have to keep the terms of the Sinai Covenant. Failing to do so would forfeit their right to it—the blessing would turn into a curse. Although Moses worked hard to raise God's people to the son/ servant level, only seventy elders did so when they saw God on Mount Sinai. The Israelites as a whole barely attained the Zion/ Jerusalem level. They thus had no guarantee of permanence in the Promised Land.

Figure 76   **The Promised Land as a Covenant Blessing**

Sons/Servants—An Unconditional Blessing

Zion/Jerusalem—A Conditional Blessing

Isaiah serves as a perfect example of ascent to the son/ servant level. When he sees Jehovah his God, the seraph who ministers to him declares "Your iniquities are taken away and your sins atoned for" (Isaiah 6:7). Isaiah has rejected the ways of his people and accepted God's ways (Isaiah 8:11–18). Like Abraham, Isaac, and Jacob, he has an individual covenant relationship with his God. As Jehovah ministers to Isaiah, so Isaiah ministers to King Hezekiah and others of his people. Going on from there and attaining the seraph level, Isaiah and others became types of an even higher category. Their lives show that we, too, can ascend and inherit every blessing, conditional and unconditional.

According to these ancient types, God blesses people differently, depending on which law they live. For example, God forgave the Israelites their sins, but he forgave their ancestors their iniquities. The Israelites kept God's law under the terms of the Sinai Covenant, but their ancestors kept a higher law. God's sons/servants resemble Israel's ancestors by living God's law and word on a higher level. God, therefore, cannot withhold additional blessings. Like Israel's ancestors, sons/servants receive *permanent* lands—"everlasting inheritances"—for themselves and their descendants in the millennial age. God grants these inheritances unconditionally after they prove loyal to him under all conditions.

"Son" and "Servant" Imply a Covenant Relationship

The prophets use the terms "son" and "servant" in both a general and specific sense. Against the ancient Near Eastern background of the Bible, these terms express a covenant relationship as between an emperor and a vassal king. When seeking to establish such a covenant relationship with the Assyrian emperor Tiglath-Pileser, for example, the Jewish King Ahaz says to him "I am your servant and your son" (2 Kings 16:7). In that sense the words "servant" and "son" are legal terms that reflect an agreement between a superior and inferior party. By making that statement, Ahaz assumes the role of a vassal king to Tiglath-Pileser, thereby turning his back on his covenant relationship with Israel's God.

The Old Testament uses the terms "son" and "servant" to define such a covenant between Israel's God and persons like Abraham, Moses, and King David, whom he assigns certain tasks. Jehovah's role parallels an emperor's and the individual's role a vassal's (see Figure 77). Blessings such as a Promised Land and divine protection have their counterpart in ancient Near Eastern covenants: so long as the vassal king is loyal to the emperor, the emperor allots the vassal a part of his empire as a *provisional* inheritance. That inheritance constitutes a "Promised Land." The emperor also protects the vassal in case of mortal danger, mustering his "hosts"—his armed forces—to come to the aid of the vassal.

After a vassal king proves exceedingly loyal to an emperor, however, the emperor grants the vassal and his heirs a part of his empire as an *everlasting* inheritance. The Promised Land then becomes an inherited right. At that point the nature of the relationship between the emperor and the vassal changes from being conditional to unconditional. That also affects the descendants of the vassal to all generations, as they benefit from their ancestor's loyalty to the emperor. Anciently, God made just such a covenant with Abraham, Isaac, and Jacob, each in turn. After God had tried and tested them, and they had shown themselves loyal to him under all conditions, their blessings became unconditional.

Figure 77   **Ancient Near Eastern Parallels of God's Individual Covenant**

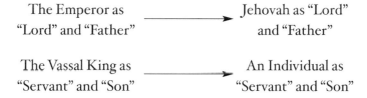

| The Emperor as "Lord" and "Father" | ⟶ | Jehovah as "Lord" and "Father" |
| The Vassal King as "Servant" and "Son" | ⟶ | An Individual as "Servant" and "Son" |

With the change from a conditional to an unconditional covenant, the vassal's status changed from "servant" to "son" and the emperor's from "lord" to "father." By formally adopting the vassal as his "son," the emperor created a legal basis for him and his heirs to permanently inherit their Promised Land. Coupled with this, the emperor assured his protection of the vassal in the event of a mortal threat. Just so, in Isaiah's endtime scenario those who attain the son/servant level obtain "everlasting inheritances"—Promised Lands—for themselves and their descendants. In addition, God promises to protect his sons/servants against the king of Assyria/Babylon and others seeking to destroy them.

Concepts familiar from the Bible, such as God's relationship with his servants as of a "Father" to his "sons," Jehovah's titles of "King of Kings" and "Lord of Lords," "Jehovah of Hosts," and so forth are thus not an innovation in the Bible but have ancient Near Eastern parallels. Although the ideas of a Promised Land, of a covenant between an "emperor" and his "vassals," and of a people's "salvation" aren't unique to sacred history, they are *made* sacred by the way they define spiritual realities. Indeed, a key to our fuller understanding of all such ideas is found within their *continuity* from earliest times into the Old Testament and from there into the New Testament and beyond (see Figure 78).

Figure 78   **Continuum of Spiritual and Political Concepts**

A second legal meaning of the term "son" is "heir." The Bible further uses the idea of sonship against its ancient Near Eastern background to imply heirship. Like the "sons" of an emperor, God's sons/servants, as they ascend the ladder, inherit divine powers. People understood that ancient Near Eastern emperors were human, not divine. But their claims to divinity, by providing a pattern of ascent to heaven, had a legitimate basis. The covenant between an emperor and a vassal conveyed the idea of advancing levels, culminating with heirship to the gods. The phrase "You are gods and all of you *sons* of the Most High [God]" (*běnê 'elyôn*) reflects that idea (Psalm 82:6; emphasis added).

Two types of such heirship—and of persons inheriting divine powers—are Moses and Elijah, both of whom attained the seraph level. Each prophet exercised the very powers the Canaanites attributed to their god Baal. In ancient Canaanite religion, Baal, the storm god, conquered Yamm/Nahar and Mot, two rival gods whose names mean *Sea/River* and *Death*. By dividing the Red Sea and leading his people safely through the waters and through the desert, Moses demonstrated abilities claimed for Baal. By bringing fire out of heaven and rain in the drought, Elijah would have been to the Canaanites as Baal himself. All seraphs possess these powers, which they employ in the service of God.

The Bible further uses the idea of sonship to imply heirship.

In Isaiah's endtime scenario God's servant and his associates demonstrate such abilities on behalf of God's covenant people when leading them safely to Zion or Jerusalem. In that context Isaiah describes the king of Assyria/Babylon as a personification of the false god *Sea/River*. Like Moses, the servant exercises divine powers in putting down the archtyrant and subduing the forces of chaos. Empowered by God, he and his seraph-associates lead God's people through seas, rivers, deserts, and fire to the Promised Land. In the process, they illustrate not just servanthood but also sonship, particularly in its highest sense of heirship. For that heirship, persons on the son/servant level are candidates.

The Promised Lands God grants unconditionally to his sons/servants and their descendants may extend to different parts of his "empire." As in the ancient Near East, Promised Lands aren't limited to one place, such as Palestine, but may include many places. God's dominions, for example, expand worldwide after God's servant and his fellow-servants reclaim the earth from the Assyrian power. The earth becomes God's at the end of the world when taken back from the forces of chaos that overrun it. After Babylon and all who belong to it perish, only Zion and levels higher remain. The elect inherit the new Paradise—which ultimately extends to the entire earth—as an "everlasting inheritance."

God's sons/servants, in effect, identify with those whom Jesus says will "inherit the earth." In his Sermon on the Mount Jesus cites the spiritual attributes of those who live into the

millennial age. Jacob's birthright blessing of his son Joseph—
that his inheritance would extend "to the utmost bounds of
the ancient hills"—similarly anticipates the worldwide scope
of God's kingdom (Genesis 49:26). Daniel predicts that God's
"saints" or "holy ones" will "inherit the kingdom" after the beast
that devours the whole earth is destroyed (Daniel 7:18–27). As
mentioned, Isaiah draws on Cyrus as a type of the universal
institution of righteous rule following the demise of an oppressive
world power.

The empire of David and Solomon provides a type of the
expansion of God's dominions. David and Solomon ruled
as emperors—as "fathers" and "lords"—of vassal kings of
the ancient Near East. Their empire followed the model of
the Hittite empire, except that David and Solomon were
themselves vassals—"sons" and "servants"—of Israel's God.
Vassal kings who were subject to *them*, on the other hand,
served as "fathers" and "lords" to their own peoples. An entire
hierarchy of father–son/lord–servant relationships thus existed
anciently, as on Isaiah's ladder to heaven (see Figure 79). That
pattern of ministering and being ministered to characterizes
God's people in an ascending mode.

Figure 79   **A Hierarchy of Father–Son Relationships**

Father
_____

Son

Father
_____

Son

Father
_____

Son

It is possible that covenants between ancient Near Eastern emperors and their vassals had their origins in, and sought to duplicate, covenants God made with individuals from the beginning of time. Or vice versa: perhaps Moses, Isaiah, and other prophets simply likened God's covenants with individuals to ancient Near Eastern ones. In any event, we must understand these covenants' terms and ideology if we are to comprehend the relationship between God and his servants in any age, especially ours. Persons who wish to ascend to the son/servant level can do so only as they become familiar with these relationships. Their *individual* covenant with God is the thing that makes such ascent possible.

God's Sons/Servants Secure Divine Protection

The role of "savior" or "deliverer" that God's sons/servants assume is thus likewise grounded in the covenant Israel's God makes with individuals and resembles the role of ancient Near Eastern vassal kings. That role reached its full development when Israel became a monarchy. With King David, God first made a conditional, then an unconditional covenant. After David (God's "vassal") proved exceedingly loyal, God (David's "emperor") confirmed his covenant with David and blessed him unconditionally with land and offspring (see Figure 80). God's individual covenant with David, called the Davidic Covenant, parallels the covenants ancient Near Eastern emperors made with vassals kings.

Figure 80   **Blessings of the Davidic Covenant**

Land and Offspring as Conditional Blessings	$\longrightarrow$	Land and Offspring as Unconditional Blessings

A conditional clause in these covenants, however, states that the emperor undertakes to protect not only the vassal king but

185

also the *people* of the vassal, provided the vassal proves loyal to the emperor. Under that arrangement, the people's protection depends on whether the current ruler keeps the terms of his covenant with the emperor. So long as the vassal king is loyal to him, the emperor protects them. But if he proves disloyal, the emperor does not. In that sense, the king (the emperor's vassal) serves as a "deliverer" to his people. The people rely on him for their protection because of his *individual* covenant with the emperor. When that covenant breaks down, the emperor cannot protect them.

In Isaiah's endtime scenario God's sons/servants assume this "deliverer" role in seeking God's protection of those who face danger. They do so wherever they minister, at home or abroad. Even as they follow the example of God's servant, the servant follows the example of Israel's God. Isaiah defines the deliverer's role when describing God's servant: "Because of his knowledge, and by bearing their iniquities, shall my servant, the righteous one, vindicate many" (Isaiah 53:11). God's ideal vassal—as a model for other vassals—"vindicates" or "justifies" many of God's people. As a result, instead of perishing in Babylon God's people come out from among the wicked in a new exodus to Zion.

It is again important to consider the *continuum* of these concepts against their ancient Near Eastern background. Moses, Isaiah, and other prophets utilize political realities common in their day to define spiritual principles. But that understanding has been compromised by the failure of Bible interpreters to distinguish between passages in Isaiah 52:13–53:12—in which Israel's God is speaking of his "servant" (Isaiah 52:13–15; 53:11–12)—and a passage in which a spokesman for God's people (possibly the servant) is speaking about Jehovah, Israel's suffering Savior (Isaiah 53:1–10). It helps to discern that both the emperor *and* his vassals perform savior roles, one spiritual and the others temporal.

While the servant fulfills his mission on the seraph level, obtaining God's intervention in among his people, sons/servants obtain God's protection on *their* level on behalf of those to whom they minister. All savior roles, however, follow the same pattern, for which Israel's God sets the example (see Figure 81). That is why the subject changes back and forth between Jehovah and his servant in the Servant–Tyrant Parallelism. In that structure both serve as deliverers, though on different spiritual levels, and so both are contrasted with the archtyrant. Whether Jehovah fulfills the function of Savior, or whether seraphs or sons/servants function as saviors, each answers for the transgressions of others.

In that context the "knowledge" the servant possesses (Isaiah 53:11) consists of the terms of God's covenant. In ancient Near Eastern covenant language, the term "knowledge" is a synonym of "covenant." The servant's "knowledge," therefore, refers to his individual covenant with God that is patterned after God's covenant with King David. Under the terms of that covenant God protects the people of the vassal *for the sake of* the vassal, their king. As in ancient Near Eastern covenants, the emperor protects the people of the vassal so long as the vassal proves loyal to the emperor. When assuming his surrogate role, the vassal answers to the emperor for his people's loyalties to the emperor.

Figure 81   **Saviors/Deliverers on the Model of King David**

Jehovah

God's Servant

God's Sons/Servants

Just so, according to the terms of God's covenant with King David, the servant answers for his people's loyalties to God in order to obtain their protection from a mortal threat. In Isaiah's endtime context that threat occurs when the king of Assyria/ Babylon sets out to conquer and destroy the world. Should some of God's people transgress, God will still protect them so long as the servant answers for their transgressions. In that case, the servant (God's vassal) "bears their iniquities" and thus "vindicates" or "justifies" his people before God. By paralleling the two phrases—"because of his knowledge" and "by bearing their iniquities"—Isaiah lets us know they are synonymous and inseparable ideas.

Based on his "knowledge" of the terms of agreement between God and himself, the servant thus fulfills a *proxy* role on behalf of God's people, confident that God will do his part. A proxy's function is to "stand in" for someone else, as in a legal proceeding or contract between two parties. On the model of King David (who, in turn, follows the pattern of ancient Near Eastern vassal kings), God's servant "stands in" for God's people, contracting with God in a legal agreement to purchase their protection against the threat to their lives that the archtyrant poses. Through his individual covenant with the emperor the servant thus *ransoms* God's people from the mortal danger that threatens them.

All savior roles follow the same pattern.

The servant's "righteousness," therefore, consists of his willingness, under the terms of God's covenant, to answer for his people's loyalties to God in order to obtain their protection against the king of Assyria/Babylon. That savior function forms the essence of living God's higher law. The servant "knows" that that is why such a covenant exists—that the individual covenant God makes with him operates precisely in that manner. He further "knows" that it is his role to seek God's protection or the archtyrant will destroy them. On that same model all sons/

servants "know" the terms of God's individual covenants with them that legitimize their role as deliverers of those to whom they minister.

Regarding the servant's role, Isaiah adds, "He bore the sins of many, and made intercession for the transgressors" (Isaiah 53:12). By again pairing these phrases he shows that God's servant—or any servant on the same covenant model— intercedes for those who are disloyal to God *by* making amends for their transgressions. The servant knows that under God's law of *justice* people are responsible for their own sins in order to obtain God's forgiveness. But in limited circumstances—as when death threatens—God creates another basis for judging some under the law of *mercy*. So long as they are loyal to the vassal and the vassal is loyal to God, God protects both the vassal and his people.

Proxy Salvation Proceeds from the Highest Levels

In Isaiah's covenant theology such proxy salvation occurs on the three highest levels of the spiritual ladder, depending on the *kind* of "salvation." When answering for his people's loyalties to God, a righteous proxy may fulfill the law of justice on their behalf. But the *degree* of salvation determines what price must be paid and on what level. Is salvation limited to delivering people physically from mortal danger? Does it additionally entail overpowering the forces of chaos, dispossessing the Babylon and Perdition categories? Does it involve reversing all covenant curses, including deliverance from mortality to immortality? The nature of the "salvation" dictates who pays the price (see Figure 82).

Isaiah's reference to the servant's bearing other people's "iniquities" identifies those who haven't yet been healed of dysfunctional patterns though they may have obtained forgiveness of their sins—that is, Zion/Jerusalem. Such persons, for example, may still suffer generational covenant curses even after having repented of personal wrongs. On the other hand, Isaiah's reference to the servant's bearing people's "sins" identifies a second category—Jacob/Israel, those who haven't yet received forgiveness. Nevertheless, although a servant bears others' transgressions, that doesn't mean God forgives them. Rather, the servant answers for them in order to obtain their physical protection, that is all.

Figure 82   **Different Degrees of Proxy Salvation**

A Complete Reversal of Covenant Curses

Dispossession and Despoliation of Enemies

Physical Deliverance from Mortal Danger

Even if some of Jacob/Israel initially experience proxy deliverance because a righteous vassal intercedes with God on their behalf by bearing their sins, that is still no guarantee they will survive into the millennial age. The Israelites whom Moses released from bondage in Egypt similarly had no guarantee they would enter the Promised Land. After experiencing proxy deliverance from Egypt when they slew the Passover Lamb, all who kept sinning perished in the wilderness. Just as will happen at the end of the world, their time of probation ran out. Because God is just as well as merciful, he ultimately holds people responsible for themselves. No one can cast his or her burden on another forever.

Although God makes allowance for people to repent when they transgress, time is a key factor in our lives on the earth. God took into account that the Israelites who came out of Egypt had lived as slaves and were only newly converted to him. Yet, he put a limit on how long they could continue doing evil. God's people who inherited the Promised Land were on two levels: (1) those who ascended Mount Sinai—a son/servant category; and (2) those who kept the terms of the Sinai Covenant—

a Zion/Jerusalem category. Both categories qualified for God's blessings. So long as they kept his law and word, God delivered them from death in the wilderness and from the nations who threatened them.

Moses stood as a proxy deliverer when Israel battled the Amalekites during its wandering in the wilderness. When Moses raised his hands, the Israelites won; when he let down his hands, the Amalekites won (Exodus 17:8–13). Raising both hands, however, symbolizes a holy man's prayer of intercession with God. If Moses hadn't lifted up his hands Israel would have lost the battle to the Amalekites. God honored Moses in the sight of his people because he kept God's law and word on the seraph level of the ladder. Later, God gave the same power to Jeremiah, appointing him "over nations and kingdoms to uproot and pull down, to destroy and overthrow, to build and to plant" (Jeremiah 1:10).

His loyalty to God's people reflected his loyalty to God.

Behind Moses' influence with God was his commitment to pay any price for his people's deliverance. His loyalty to God expressed itself in his loyalty to God's people. Note how he intercedes on their behalf when God is about to destroy them after they worship the Golden Calf. He passes up God's offer to make of *him* "a great nation" instead of them, the same blessing God had bestowed on Israel's ancestors Abraham, Isaac, and Jacob. Instead, Moses offers to have his name blotted out of the Book of Life (Exodus 32:11–13, 30–33). In other words, he is willing to die and give up the spiritual levels he had attained *for the sake of* saving God's people alive. God relents and refrains from slaying them.

In Isaiah's endtime scenario several simultaneous such intercessions occur, preventing God's people from perishing. Together, these lead to the "salvation" of those who live into the millennial age (see Figure 83). God's servant fulfills the role of Moses in different new versions of ancient events: release from bondage, exodus out of Babylon, victory over enemies, and "disinheritance" of the powers of chaos (Isaiah 41:2, 25; 42:1, 7; 45:1, 13; 49:5–12; 51:9–11). God's sons/servants, meanwhile, obtain "deliverance" from mortal danger for many of God's people. Like ancient Near Eastern vassal kings, they serve as "fathers" and "lords"—as proxy deliverers—to those to whom they minister.

Figure 83   **Simultaneous Endtime Intercessions**

God's Seraph-Servant—

Victory over Evil Powers

God's Sons/Servants—

Deliverance from Mortal Danger

Thus, when destruction stares them in the face God's people appeal to God to "relent *for the sake of* your servants" and refrain from slaying them. God responds, "So will I do *for the sake of* my servants, by not destroying all [my people]" (Isaiah 63:17; 65:8; emphasis added). In the very hour that God wipes out the wicked he delivers the righteous in an exodus resembling the exodus out of Egypt. He blesses his sons/servants and their dependents even as he curses idolaters, the one category dispossessing the other (Isaiah 63:1–6, 11–14; 65:11–23). Different levels of intercession with God—whether by sons/servants or seraphs—account for God's people experiencing "deliverance" and "salvation."

All such intercessions fulfill the terms of the covenant God makes with individuals on the son/servant level and above. On whichever level intercession occurs, each follows the model of the Davidic Covenant, in which the vassal answers for his people's loyalties to the emperor. Such intercession is in vain, however, unless the proxy deliverer backs up his mediation with "loyalty" to God and "compliance" with his will in keeping the terms of the covenant. Abraham, Moses, David, and others followed the same pattern of pleading with God for his people's deliverance by honoring the covenant's terms each on his own level. The *level* of intercession thus determines the *degree* of deliverance.

> The level of intercession determines the degree of deliverance.

Isaiah teaches that intercessory roles on behalf of God's people pertain particularly to men—God's sons/servants and levels higher. Men are deliverers, but women give them birth. The Woman Zion—God's spouse or covenant people—for example, gives birth to God's endtime servant (Isaiah 66:7). A type of that scenario is Deborah, who served as a prophetess and judge when the Canaanites oppressed Israel. She inspired and empowered Barak to overthrow Sisera's hosts and to deliver Israel from bondage to its enemies (Judges 4–5). Deborah referred to herself as a "mother in Israel" in a classic example of the power and influence a woman has with a man to live up to his role of savior.

As noted, another type of God's endtime salvation were the people of King Hezekiah. When Hezekiah pleaded with God to deliver them from the king of Assyria, God responded by destroying the Assyrian host (Isaiah 37:14–36). But Isaiah's intercession on the seraph level—"on behalf of the remnant that is left"—was a part of the picture (Isaiah 37:4). It worked together with Hezekiah's to bring about God's intervention. In those events Isaiah was a type of God's servant and Hezekiah a type of God's sons/servants. Isaiah identifies the endtime

"remnant that is left" as God's repentant people who return to
Zion in an exodus from the four directions of the earth (Isaiah
11:11–12, 15–16; 12:1–6).

In summing up, God's "salvation" consists of *proxy* salvation,
which individuals on higher levels obtain for those lower.
Ultimately, however, one qualifies for "salvation" by keeping
God's law and word on one's own level. Because father–son
relationships govern every level of the ladder, such compliance
includes loyalty to those higher. God delivered the Israelites
who were loyal to Moses and the Jews who were loyal to
Hezekiah. In effect, "deliverance" and "salvation" are the
combined result of persons on higher and lower levels acting
in concert within the terms of God's covenants. All salvation
is God's salvation, but God chooses those on higher levels to
assist in bringing it about.

God's "salvation" consists of proxy salvation.

As God's sons/servants fulfill their proxy roles, they
themselves ascend to the next level, at which point new father–
son relationships come into play. These extend also in the
opposite direction. Just as Israel's God is "Lord" and "Father" to
the highest levels, so the archtyrant is "lord" and "father" to the
Babylon level. A big difference is that Jehovah is preeminently
the Savior of all whereas the archtyrant is preeminently the
Destroyer of all (see Figure 84). God seeks to elevate his vassals
to the highest levels, but the archtyrant drags his lackeys to the
lowest. King Ahaz' allegiance to the king of Assyria, for example,
led to God's rejection of Ahaz and the failure of divine protection
in his day.

We find a further type of father–son relationships in the
ancient communities of "sons" of the prophets. Those "sons"
were disciples of the prophets, but they also relied on them
for protection, calling them "lord" and "father" (2 Kings 2:1–12;

4:38–44). The prophet Elisha became the *heir* of Elijah—a prophet on the seraph level—when Elijah's mantle fell on him (2 Kings 2:1–15). Similarly, before David became king in Israel he addressed King Saul as "lord" and "father" while Saul called him "son" (1 Samuel 24:10–11, 16). In an opposite sense—on the bottom rungs of the ladder—we find "sons" of Belial, and Judas, a "son" of Perdition (1 Kings 21:10–13; John 17:12; 2 Corinthians 6:15–18).

Figure 84   **Opposite Connotations of "Lord" and "Father"**

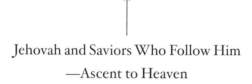

Jehovah and Saviors Who Follow Him
—Ascent to Heaven

The Archtyrant and Tyrants like Him
—Descent to Hell

To the Israelites it was important to appoint righteous military leaders who would not compromise God's protection by living evil lives. Whenever David led them in battle, for example, the Israelites proved victorious (1 Samuel 17:1–52; 23:1–5; 30:1–19). Leading to King Saul's jealousy of David was a song voiced abroad in Israel that "Saul slays his thousands but David his tens of thousands" (1 Samuel 18:7). After Saul fell from grace the Philistines made sport of the Israelites until David became king (1 Samuel 31; 2 Samuel 8). Henceforward, the covenant God made with David became the type and model of proxy salvation among God's people (Psalm 89:19–37; Isaiah 37:14–36).

We see a type of the "disinheritance" of wicked nations at Israel's conquest of the Promised Land from the Canaanites. Those idolatrous inhabitants of the land God had promised Abraham, Isaac, and Jacob disqualified themselves from occupying it by becoming utterly depraved. In the endtime version of these events Isaiah includes the wicked of God's people among those who are dispossessed. In particular, Isaiah draws a stark contrast between God's sons/servants—persons who honor their individual covenants with God—and those who "forsake" God who were once his covenant people. These apostates, who finally turn anti-God, form a significant portion of Isaiah's Greater Babylon.

On the other hand, God renews his covenant with those who repent and return, who receive a millennial "inheritance": "You will spread abroad to the right hand and to the left; your offspring will dispossess the nations and resettle the desolate cities. . . . For he who espouses you is your Maker, whose name is Jehovah of Hosts; he who redeems you is the Holy One of Israel, who is called the God of all the earth. 'Jehovah calls you back as a spouse forsaken and forlorn, a wife married in youth only to be rejected,' says your God. . . . 'In a fleeting surge of anger I hid my face from you, but with everlasting charity I will have compassion on you,' says Jehovah who redeems you" (Isaiah 54:3, 5–6, 8).

Service and Suffering Qualify God's Chosen Ones

As we have seen, God's sons/servants who intercede for God's people pay the price of justice on their behalf. In such cases God temporarily judges those for whom they intercede under the law of mercy. But he judges his sons/servants who intercede under the law of justice. He saves his people from threatening situations *"for the sake of* his servants." In order to obtain God's protection of his people, his sons/servants must answer to God for the sins or disloyalties of those whose cause they plead.

Such intercession on behalf of others fulfills the terms of the covenant God makes with individuals. Their "knowledge" of what is required of them leads them to confidently perform their proxy roles.

When God's sons/servants fulfill these proxy functions, however, they may end up making extraordinary sacrifices. At the time the Assyrians besieged Jerusalem King Hezekiah suffered to the point of death. Just as his people were in mortal danger from the Assyrians, so was he from a terrible illness. During his descent phase Hezekiah "poured out his soul unto death," not expecting to recover. Only at that point did God heal him and answer his plea for his people's protection. When he passed the test, ascending to the son/servant level, God said "I will add fifteen years to your life. And I will deliver you and this city out of the hand of the king of Assyria; I will protect this city" (Isaiah 38:1–6, 16).

Hezekiah's proxy role on behalf of his people parallels the ancient Near Eastern practice of the "arrested sacrifice" of the king, a yearly rite that sought to ensure the renewed fertility of the land. That springtime ritual in non-Israelite cultures consisted of the symbolic slaying of the king followed by his recovery to new life. The king experienced personally the plight of his people as they faced starvation should the land not revive. By ritually reenacting the cyclical pattern of the seasons, he sought the blessings of the gods on his people for the coming year. A Mesopotamian king, a contemporary of Hezekiah, was so impressed by Hezekiah's real-life version of this ritual that he sent him gifts (Isaiah 39:1).

> The degree of his "suffering" was equal to the "salvation."

Hezekiah's proxy role on behalf of his people further resembles animal sacrifice. Under the Law of Moses ritually clean beasts served as *proxies* for persons who had sinned.

Priests slew the animals in place of transgressors in symbolic fulfillment of God's justice. Although Hezekiah didn't die, his afflictions were nonetheless "unto death." The degree of his "suffering" was equal to the "salvation" that followed. His "punishment" secured his people's "deliverance." As Isaiah shows, that deliverance and salvation stemmed directly from Hezekiah's humbly enduring his illness in which he yielded his life to God (Isaiah 38). Animal sacrifice has additional meanings, as discussed in Chapter 8.

Suffering for others' sake often poses hardships for God's sons/servants. The "punishment" they endure during their descent phase brings "deliverance" to those for whom they intercede. As God's elect, they face frequent persecution from persons on the lowest levels who take out on them the guilt of their unrepented sins. On mere "hearsay" they "judge a man guilty," although he is innocent (Isaiah 29:21). The zeal of God's holy ones amuses them as they "open wide the mouth [at them] and stick out the tongue" (Isaiah 57:4). They get satisfaction from "tormenting" and "reviling" the righteous (Isaiah 60:14). They detest those who are zealous for God's law and vigilant for his word (Isaiah 66:5).

In his Sermon on the Mount Jesus warns that we must expect persecution as we develop spiritually, although one might suppose the opposite would be the case. Jesus' teaching on that occasion moves climactically from simple principle, such as "Blessed are the poor in spirit," to weighty precept: "Blessed are the peacemakers." Finally, Jesus addresses those who are singled out for maltreatment for being different for God's sake: "Blessed are you when people revile you and persecute you and speak all manner of evil against you falsely for my sake." Jesus puts such persons on the spiritual level of prophets: "For in like manner persecuted they the prophets who were before you" (Matthew 5:3–12).

Typically, God reveals himself to his sons/servants *after* he tries their trust in him through tribulation. His ministering to them under such conditions is thus as much a comfort to them in their distress as it is a part of their ascent on the ladder (see Figure 85). It is after they descend into adversity and wade through afflictions that sons/servants see God (Isaiah 30:20). All who ascend to enjoy the privilege of God's presence, from ancient times to today, do so by keeping the terms of their *individual* covenants. Not only does their "suffering" win God's mercy on behalf of those for whom they intercede, but it purifies them from their own and generational iniquities and sanctifies them to see God.

Figure 85   **God as a Comforter in Distress**

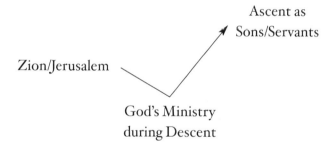

Just as people on the Zion/Jerusalem level pass tests of "loyalty" and "compliance" while keeping the terms of God's covenant, so do God's sons/servants and all who ascend. As noted, the severity of those tests intensifies from level to level while God's blessings increase accordingly. Blessings become unconditional or "everlasting" both in this life and the next from the son/servant level on up. The trials and tribulations sons/servants pass through have the effect of softening their hearts, of generating compassion for their fellow human beings. Resembling God's love for us, their love becomes unconditional.

In their descent phase they offer God "the sacrifice of a broken heart" (Psalm 51:17).

God answers the "suffering" and "humiliation" of his sons/ servants with promises of "salvation" and "exaltation": "Because their shame was twofold, and shouted insults were their lot, therefore in their land shall their inheritance be twofold and everlasting joy be theirs" (Isaiah 61:7). After their humbling, God "endows those who mourn in Zion, bestowing upon them a priestly headpiece in place of ashes, the festal anointing in place of mourning, a resplendent robe in place of a downcast spirit" (Isaiah 61:3). When the full weight of God's judgments falls upon the wicked, God will "charge my holy ones" and "call out my valiant ones" and reverse their adverse circumstances (Isaiah 13:3).

> They offer God "the sacrifice of a broken heart."

Ascending to the son/servant level, or any other level, further involves letting things go, though they may have been a big part of our lives. "Rebirth" on a higher level may mean "ruin" on a lower one. Persons willing to enter this unknown do so trusting that their "latter end"—like Job's—will be greater than their beginning. They die to their lower selves in order to live up to their higher selves. They make a paradigm shift, espousing a nobler cause (see Figure 86). If we are to suffer for transgressions not our own we must have uncommon personal integrity. The lines of distinction between "punishment" for one's own and others' sins and iniquities fade before God finally sends "deliverance."

As can be seen, a progressively higher law pertains to each spiritual level. Because transgression is possible at any point, no one can say he is immune from sin. Moses sinned by smiting the rock a second time with his rod instead of speaking to it to bring forth water for God's people (Numbers 20:7–12). Yet

Moses served God on the seraph level more faithfully than all. What constitutes a sin on one level, moreover, may not be a sin on another. It would be a serious transgression for someone to try to sacrifice his own son, but it would have been a serious transgression for Abraham not to have done so. God adapts his law and word to different categories and circumstances of his people.

Figure 86   **Degrees of Commitment as Paradigm Shifts**

Sons/Servants—Willing to Suffer and Die

Zion/Jerusalem—Committed to Doing Good

Jacob/Israel—Ambivalent about Choosing Right

Experiences intensify before persons reach "chosen" or "elect" status. Those who become sons/servants may expect increasing challenges. Before God exalted him as Israel's deliverer, David endured persecution and humbling as an outcast of society. Before Hezekiah was born a savior of his people, he underwent severe suffering. Yet, in no instance did God choose to deliver his people by some other means. Only under the terms of his covenant, using proxy deliverers on different spiritual levels, does God ordain salvation. Under certain circumstances people lower may lean on those higher. Amazingly, God weaves together the fates of nations and individuals into a single covenantal tapestry.

Outside of these covenant agreements, wherever life exists, there exists no salvation. In other words, "deliverance" and "salvation" don't just happen when we try to be good. Just as there are different *kinds* of salvation—from the many predicaments we find ourselves in—so there are different *requirements* for salvation, depending on the spiritual level. Covenant blessings increase exponentially as we ascend the ladder, one being divine protection. As the need for deliverance grows greater, persons on higher levels meet with escalating challenges. To deliver or save others, however, itself aids a person's ascent. Thus, those already delivered deliver others, who deliver others, and so forth.

Outside of these covenant agreements there exists no salvation.

The wonder of this divine design is how God orchestrates the minutest aspects of his children's existence everywhere at once. He manages the lives of masses of people in places far and wide so that they blend perfectly into one another whether they align themselves with his purposes or not. Even powers of opposition serve a crucial role in this interacting hive of humanity, aiding the ascent of those who serve God. What appears to some as the random and chaotic course of history is in reality a truly purposeful creation still in progress. The earth and not all, but *many*, of its inhabitants—all who prove loyal to God—are in the process of becoming more than we can possibly conceive.

Sons/Servants Have Male and Female Dimensions

The role of proxy savior forms a basis for patriarchy and kingship. God establishes this male paradigm within the framework of his covenants. Patriarchy and kingship consist of a person serving as "father" and "lord" according to a celestial pattern. Accordingly, Israel's God functions as the highest ideal of a proxy Savior—as "Father" and "Lord"—on the same covenant model. We call Abraham, Isaac, and Jacob "patriarchs" not just because they fathered the people of Israel but because they sought and obtained God's eternal blessings for their descendants. We call David a "king" not just because he exercised political office but because he sought and obtained God's protection of his people.

In matriarchy the savior role assumes a different but complementary form. In a literal sense a woman pays with her blood to renew her fertility, to nourish her offspring during pregnancy, and to give them birth into the world. She sacrifices herself on behalf of her children in nurturing them through childhood. Those things, however, are also an allegory of a larger, spiritual role. As a spouse to her husband, a woman may function as "mother" and "mistress" to many children—her own and others whom she gathers under her wings. By God's heavenly design she is the *complement* of her husband. He begets and she gives birth—physically and spiritually—thereby aiding others to ascend.

Isaiah calls those who serve as proxy saviors "foster fathers" and "nursing mothers." These minister to lower levels, acting as kings and queens first in a spiritual sense—by ministering salvation to God's people—and second in a political sense, in the millennial age. Each gender is unique and indispensable; neither duplicates the other. People often depict a woman's role in terms of the phases of the moon. Much of it, such as nurturing and extending comfort, is hidden and unseen. A man's role resembles the phases of the sun. In his descent he dies so that he might rise again and beget new life. Reflecting that idea, ancient Near Eastern kings were called the "sun" of their peoples.

Those who attain the son/servant level fulfill male and female functions first by ministering to each other. The man serves the woman and her children as their proxy savior by seeking and obtaining God's protection. The woman's love sees the man through his descent phase. In the midst of the disintegration of the old paradigm, when support systems come crashing down, far from "wanting out" and rejecting him as a "loser," she sees past the hard times and sustains him until the new paradigm is in place. His "suffering" is her suffering and his "ruin" her ruin until he ascends again like the sun. Loyalty to God entails loyalty to one another, otherwise one's ministry amounts to hypocrisy.

Literal birth, which comes after hard labor, typifies spiritual birth. Just as the child emerges from the darkness and confinement of the womb into the light, so a person emerges from the darkness of his descent into the greater light. The Hebrew day, which lasts from evening to evening, coincides with the sun's going down before it rises again. That parallels Isaiah's pattern of chaos before creation, "humiliation" before "exaltation," etc. The ancient Maya incorporated the idea of *descent before ascent* into their very worship structures. A seven-part series of valleys and plateaus, for example, appears at Teotihuacán, Mexico, as a person ascends, by degrees, towards the Temple of the Sun.

Literal birth—after hard labor—typifies spiritual birth.

The idea of "male and female" first appearing on the son/servant level means that persons who attain that level do so within male–female relationships not as single individuals. It further implies that male–female relationships *below* the son/servant level have no permanence (see Figure 87). People may contract marriages on lower levels but they are temporary. God can't validate such marriages beyond this life except where people ascend to the son/servant level. To do so they must keep the terms of God's individual covenants. That includes fulfilling marriage obligations in conjunction with proxy functions. Isaiah, for example, served as a "prophet" but his wife as a "prophetess" (Isaiah 8:3).

Male–female relationships become permanent as sons/servants fulfill patriarchal and matriarchal roles according to God's pattern. When we ascend God "creates" or "re-creates" us in his image and likeness. As the Book of Genesis asserts, that image is male and female: "God created man in his own image; in the image of God he created him: *male and female* he created them" (Genesis 1:27; emphasis added); "When God created man, he made him in the likeness of God: *male and female* he created them" (Genesis 5:1–2; emphasis added). On the son/servant level and above, therefore, "What God has joined together, let not man separate," neither in this life nor the next (Matthew 19:6).

Figure 87   **Marital Status of Persons Who Ascend**

Seraphim—Male and Female

Sons/Servants—Male and Female

Zion/Jerusalem—Male or Female

Jacob/Israel—Male or Female

From Isaiah's pattern of ascent we learn that "creation" or "re-creation" on a higher level occurs only after a person proves loyal to God by fulfilling covenantal requirements. By including marriage as a condition for ascent to the son/servant level Isaiah shows it to be an integral part of God's higher law and one of the terms of God's individual covenant. Judaism has thus emphasized marriage from its beginning. Traditionally, only a married man qualifies to serve as a rabbi. In orthodox Christianity crowns are placed on the heads of the bride and bridegroom at their marriage ceremony, symbolizing the couple's potentiality for "salvation" *and* "exaltation" as a king and queen in the kingdom of God.

Like divine–human relationships, the only male–female relationships that God legitimizes are covenant relationships. Men and women enter into a *covenant* to love and serve one another through all of life's challenges, just as sons/servants love and serve God in their individual covenants. That commitment between a husband and wife is, in fact, an inherent part of the *same* covenant between a "son/servant" and his "Father/ Lord," as no one ascends to that level alone. In other words, when God confirms his individual covenant with his sons/ servants and it becomes unconditional or "everlasting," so do the covenant relationships themselves. Eternal life in its fullest sense, therefore, is married life.

Isaiah shows marriage to be an integral part of God's higher law.

In a parallel example, when covenants become unconditional or "everlasting," so do inheritances of Promised Lands and other aspects of the covenant. Anciently God granted the Promised Land unconditionally not only to Abraham, Isaac, and Jacob, but equally to their wives, Sarah, Rebecca, Leah, and Rachel, who are *still* their wives. From Isaiah's perspective, for a "vassal" to prove exceedingly loyal to the "emperor" thus means demonstrating "loyalty" to God and "compliance" with his will by fulfilling all the terms of his individual covenant, including the marriage covenant. When every covenant relationship, divine–human and human–human, has been honored, ascent occurs.

Israel's God, on whom all who ascend model themselves, himself honors the marriage covenant. As an example, he "marries" the Woman Zion—his covenant people—with "everlasting love" (Isaiah 54:5, 8). "Jehovah will delight in you, and your land will be espoused. As a young man weds a virgin, so will your *sons* wed you; as the bridegroom rejoices over the bride, so will your God rejoice over you" (Isaiah 62:4–5; emphasis added). In order to ascend to the son/servant level, "sons" must marry their own "woman Zion"—their spouse—

among the "daughters" of God's people. With them God makes an "everlasting covenant" when they keep their individual covenants (Isaiah 55:3; 61:8).

In short, Isaiah never alludes to the idea that God intended a covenant relationship to be temporary, whether that relationship is with God or with a spouse. Rather, God's design for the "salvation" and "exaltation" of his children is that their relationship with him and with each other should be on the highest level possible and should be permanent or "everlasting" (see Figure 88). The very purpose of any covenant God makes is to enable a person to ascend from living a lesser law to living a higher law pertaining to a higher covenant. That means that eternal life and everlasting happiness are based on *eternal* covenant relationships, extending from this earth life into the millennial age and beyond.

Figure 88   **Covenant Relationships of Persons Who Ascend**

Seraphim—Permanent

Sons/Servants—Permanent

Zion/Jerusalem—Provisional

Jacob/Israel—Provisional

Jesus' statement that "at the resurrection they will neither marry nor be given in marriage" but will be "like the angels of God in heaven" (Matthew 22:30) thus refers to those who fail to make sure their "chosen" or "elect" status during their lifetime. Such souls did not ascend to the son/servant level as male and female while on this earth. Any individual covenant God may have made with them would thus have remained conditional. As it never became "everlasting" or unconditional those persons assume life in the next world as "angels" who minister on lower levels. Had they lived a higher law their relationship as husband and wife would have become permanent, on earth and in heaven.

Adam and Eve's relationship must therefore have been made permanent *before* their descent from a higher level. To have inherited Paradise as an "everlasting inheritance" Adam and Eve must have ascended to at least the son/servant level, which is attained in part by honoring the marriage covenant. That they later fell to a lower level doesn't take away from the fact that any couple may, by keeping God's covenant on the son/servant level, inherit Paradise. As God is an impartial God who loves his children equally, he would have blessed Adam and Eve with that privilege only after they had lived a higher law. One blessing of that law is to receive a Promised Land regenerated to a new Paradise.

Moreover, just as Paradise anciently didn't cover the entire earth, so God didn't create Adam *in* the Garden of Eden but placed him there afterwards. In other words, Adam and Eve didn't inherit the Garden of Eden at their creation or re-creation but later on when God "planted" it (Genesis 2:8, 15). So also may sons/servants inherit Paradise as an "everlasting inheritance" when the earth regenerates in the millennial age (Isaiah 35:1–2; 51:1–3). In sum, to permanently attain Paradise all must live God's higher law and that includes loyalty to the marriage covenant. Although people on the Zion/Jerusalem level also inherit Paradise in the millennial age, their inheritance is *provisional* not "everlasting."

Sons/Servants Become New "Adams" and "Eves"

Because God's creation is continually evolving, the creation of Adam and Eve literally occurred on a continuum with parallel creations. For example, God also "creates" or "re-creates" the heavens and the earth, Jacob/Israel, Zion/Jerusalem, sons/servants, his seraph-servant, and all who *ascend* the ladder

(Isaiah 45:18; 43:1, 6–7; 49:8; 65:17–18). In effect, "rebirth" on every level constitutes "re-creation," as the person assumes a new role and new identity. God even re-creates, or rather "de-creates," those who *descend*, because they are no longer what they used to be (see Figure 89). They don't conform to the "image of God." By their own choice they fall short of what they potentially can be.

Figure 89   **Creation, Re-Creation, and De-Creation**

Seraphim—Re-created

Sons/Servants—Re-created

Zion/Jerusalem—Re-created

Jacob/Israel—Created

Babylon—De-created

Perdition—De-created

Although we play a vital part in our "rebirth" or "re-creation"— by living God's law and developing his character traits—it is actually God who does the creating. What we become when we are reborn and ascend is his doing, not ours. When God says he "creates" Jerusalem, or "creates" his servant, therefore, he is saying that they have attained the next level, graduating from what they used to be to something new, closer to their divine potential. As the creation of Adam and Eve is an integral part of God's ongoing creation, and as their inheriting Paradise isn't unique in Isaiah's context of ascent, their creation, too, must have followed God's pattern of "re-creation" on ascending levels of the ladder.

Thus, God continues to "create" us spiritually, some male and others female, until we become like him—until we grow into his *image* and *likeness*. Just as God "creates" or "re-creates" us physically when we are born or resurrected, so he creates us spiritually when we are reborn and ascend. As that is a cyclical process, God continues to be our Creator. When we co-create with God and raise children, for example, we don't just give them birth and leave them alone. We care for them, sacrifice for them, and do all we can to help them achieve their full stature. We want them to be all they can be as they become adults—like us. In that sense, we continue to be co-creators with God of our children.

Only on the second level of blessedness and above does Isaiah call such persons God's "sons" and "daughters," implying they are potential heirs of God. These terms don't take away from the purely legal meaning of "sons" as "vassals" but rather confirm it. Yet, they allow for levels within levels on the ladder, such as Jacob and Israel, or servant and son. Several spiritual levels may even coexist within a single family, as was the case with Abraham and his sons Isaac and Ishmael, and with Isaac and his sons Jacob and Esau. Heirship by virtue of sonship thus has a twofold aspect: (1) it is a person's inherited right as a child of God; and (2) he or she qualifies as an heir by ascending the ladder to heaven.

God continues to "create" us spiritually until we become like him.

God's creation of a man and woman on the son/servant level resembles God's creation of Adam and Eve because as a "son" and "daughter" of God they obtain "everlasting inheritances" for themselves and their descendants on the earth in the millennial age. But that age, as we have seen, consists of the earth's transformation into a new Paradise, which event completes a key cycle in God's creation. Paradise regained constitutes salvation from the Fall, having produced new Adams and Eves. Or, rather, God grants new "Adams" and "Eves" (persons who attain the son/servant level or higher) Paradise for their inheritance. The new Paradise is *their* Promised Land, just as the old was Adam's and Eve's.

Adam's and Eve's willingness to leave Paradise thus served a greater good than their own immediate happiness. That they descended does not mean they couldn't ascend again to where they had been, so long as they didn't go past the "point of no return." Rather, their descent, by providing others the means to ascend, resembles more a prelude to ascent. Their descent *for the sake of* their descendants—who would thereby be enabled to attain the level they were on—would take Adam and Eve to an even higher place than before. Moses was similarly willing to have his name "blotted out of the Book of Life"—to descend for a time to a lower level—*for the sake of* the greater good of God's people.

When God banished Adam and Eve from Paradise they thus experienced "ruin," "disinheritance," "punishment," "suffering," and "humiliation" as part of a *descent phase* (see Figure 90). Their "latter end"—their "rebirth," "inheritance," "deliverance," "salvation," and "exaltation" on a higher level—would be greater than their beginning. For a time, instead of eating fruit in Paradise, Adam had to till the ground God had cursed "for his sake," but also, as a consequence, for the sake of Adam's sons. Eve and her daughters would bring forth children in sorrow (Genesis 3:16–17). Only under those conditions could their descendants ascend by living God's law and overcoming covenant curses.

Figure 90   **Adam's and Eve's Descent and Ascent**

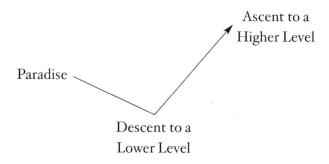

To show us that Adam was literally God's "son," Moses uses identical terms to describe Adam's son Seth as he does God's son Adam: "This is the record of the genealogy of Adam. When God created man [Adam], he made him in the *likeness* of God: male and female he created them; and he blessed them and called their name man [Adam], when they were created. And Adam lived a hundred and thirty years and begot a son in his own *likeness*, in his own *image*, and he called his name Seth" (Genesis 5:1–3; emphasis added). As a rhetorical device these terms establish the idea that the one is a son like the other. Isaiah, too, uses the words "create" and "beget" interchangeably in his writings.

People on the Zion/Jerusalem level inherit the new Paradise *for the sake of* God's sons/servants, the new "Adams" and "Eves" to whom it rightly belongs. They receive God's blessings provisionally, depending on their continued loyalty to God. With them God has not yet made an unconditional covenant as he has with his "sons" and "daughters." He hasn't yet "created" them in the *image* of God—male and female—because they haven't exemplified manhood and womanhood in their fullest sense by serving as patriarch and matriarch. According to Isaiah, a "man" is a protector and intercessor (Isaiah 32:2; 59:16). A "woman" is one who gives birth, physically and spiritually (Isaiah 45:10; 66:8).

Isaiah combines marriage imagery and priestly functions to describe those who assume male and female roles: "I rejoice exceedingly in Jehovah; my soul delights in my God. For he clothes me in the garments of salvation, he arrays me in a robe of righteousness—like a bridegroom dressed in priestly attire, or a bride adorned with her jewels" (Isaiah 61:10). In the millennial age "The least of them will become a clan, the youngest a mighty nation" (Isaiah 60:22). Of such proxy saviors, Isaiah says "Their offspring will be renowned among the nations, their posterity in the midst of peoples; all who see them will acknowledge that they are the lineage Jehovah has blessed" (Isaiah 61:9).

The "priestly" role of sons/servants is to teach God's law and "make atonement" for his people as priests did anciently. They do so, however, by serving as proxy saviors, answering for people's loyalties to God, not by sacrificing animals. As is shown in Chapter 8, animal sacrifice was a type of Jehovah's atonement for transgression. Ultimately, in the millennial age, *all* killing of beasts comes to an end: "Whoever slaughters an ox is as one who kills a man, and whoever sacrifices a lamb, as one who breaks a dog's neck" (Isaiah 66:3). God appoints his sons/servants as kings (vassals) and priests (ministers) just as he appointed David as a king and Aaron as a priest (Exodus 40:13; 1 Samuel 16:13).

The Son/Servant Level Defines a Female Paradigm

Just as Isaiah speaks of endtime "kings" and "queens" who minister to God's people, so one might expect him to speak of "priests" and "priestesses." However, that isn't the case. Neither Isaiah nor the Bible mentions a woman's role of "priestess" (not that such doesn't exist). The closest reference to it, in fact, comes from the passage cited above—of "a bridegroom dressed in priestly attire" and the parallel idea of "a bride adorned with her jewels" (Isaiah 61:10). While the priest's role, as noted, is preeminently to "make atonement" on behalf of God's people, its complementary role for a woman, according to Isaiah, has to do with "adorning herself with jewels." What does such imagery signify?

For the answer we return to the female paradigm of giving birth physically and spiritually. Like other prophets, Isaiah uses the imagery of precious metals and stones—"gold" and "jewels"—to define an elect or son/servant category of

God's people (Isaiah 13:12; 49:18). By contrast, semi-precious metals and stones represent Zion/Jerusalem and common ones Jacob/Israel. The lowest categories compare to "alloys" and "dross" (Isaiah 1:21–25). (See Figure 91.) In the millennial age God brings "gold in place of copper, silver in place of iron . . . copper in place of wood, iron in place of stones" (Isaiah 60:17). In other words, all lower levels disappear, while people on higher levels ascend.

Figure 91   **Figurative Representations of Spiritual Categories**

Sons/Servants—Precious Metals and Stones

Zion/Jerusalem—Semi-precious Metals and Stones

Jacob/Israel—Common Metals and Stones

Babylon—Alloys

Perdition—Dross

By implication, the woman's role that parallels the man's role of priest involves adorning herself with God's elect *people.* When figuratively portraying God's people whose ancestors were exiled—who repent and return home in the "last days"— God says to the Woman Zion, "You will adorn yourself with them all as with jewels, bind them on you as does a bride." These same "jewels," however, are the woman's "*children* born in the time of your bereavement" (Isaiah 49:18; emphasis added). As obtaining "jewels" means paying a price—in this instance, a descent phase of "bereavement"—it implies a savior role on behalf of those to whom the woman ministers, who become her "children."

In fact, Isaiah's ideal *woman*—who exemplifies womanhood, matriarchy, and the roles of "bride" and "queen"—*is* the Woman Zion. Her attributes are those of every woman who ascends to the son/servant level and above. Although she represents the Zion/Jerusalem level as a *category* of people, Isaiah describes her in an ascending mode as a role model for the individual woman: she repents of her sins, expiates her iniquity, marries God by an everlasting covenant, brings joy to her husband, gives birth to offspring, heralds the "good news," and ascends her throne (Isaiah 1:27; 40:2, 9; 52:1–2; 54:5–10; 62:5; 66:8). Her adorning herself with "jewels" thus crowns an entire course of action.

These female roles raise the lingering question of an elect woman's relationship to her husband as he fulfills *his* roles according to the divine model. Because "rebirth" or "re-creation" on the son/servant level is possible only as male and female, what are the dynamics that make that feasible, assuming a husband and wife have the desire to comply with the pattern God has revealed? In answering that question we may first observe that each relies on the other to provide an *environment* in which they can fulfill the roles God has designed that enable them to attain eternal happiness. Just as both go through roughly the same steps in ascending the ladder, so also in some instances their roles overlap.

Adorning herself with "jewels" crowns an entire course of action.

A woman looks to her husband to provide basic survival in the form of food, clothing, shelter, and protection for herself and her children. She benefits from her husband's creating the environment in which she can safely raise and nurture her children, enabling her to give birth to them spiritually as well as physically. She shares in teaching them God's law and word and providing a tangible example of an elect family. Her husband looks to her for support, counsel, comfort, and inspiration as he meets the challenges of the outside world.

For her part she creates the environment for him to measure up to God's pattern of patriarchy and manhood, as without her he might not be so motivated.

It is also a woman's drive for spiritual knowledge and a sense of fulfillment that requires a man to rise to her expectations. If not, he might be just as happy to pass through life playing golf or watching football, especially if friends admire him. Paradoxically, because a woman's role in this world isn't always comfortable or fulfilling, she may likewise go all the way into the world and assume roles traditionally associated with men, as she is as capable as they are. Or she may focus her attention solely on her family. Isaiah, however, validates her desire to minister to *others* of God's children besides her own—even while still nurturing them—provided her own take precedence (see Figure 92).

Figure 92   **Matriarchal Roles of the Ideal Woman**

Physical and Spiritual   Spiritual Birth of
Birth of Children   Additional "Children"

In a real sense a woman gives birth spiritually to her husband as her deliverer. Just as the Woman Zion gives birth to God's servant in the coming Time of Trouble, so a wife's challenge is to inspire her spouse to come into his own during his descent phase when the going gets rough. Current needs and changing circumstances additionally demand much give and take between husband and wife as they fulfill their respective ministering functions. On attaining the son/servant level both see God. Isaiah's wife, for example, was a prophetess, not just by virtue of being Isaiah's wife, but in her own right. Together, a husband and wife become *heirs* of God because of the husband's legal sonship to God.

Patriarchy and matriarchy are thus partly expressed in the husband's and wife's covenant relationship with each other. He serves as "father" and "lord" to her and her children by obtaining their divine protection under the terms of his individual covenant with God. She is "mother" and "mistress" to all her household, immeasurably influencing her husband's development as he grows into his role of vassal/savior. She directly participates in his "rebirth" or "re-creation," sanctifying him as he sanctifies her. The word for "marriage" in Hebrew (*qidûšîn*) means "sanctification," denoting a process through which two people become "holy." The woman's role of *helpmeet* reflects this "power of two."

In the marriage covenant a wife gives herself *to* her husband, but the husband gives himself *for* his wife, willing to endure all things for her sake in order to ensure her happiness and protection and that of her children. When two fulfill that divine pattern the blessings of the covenant are theirs, including eternal life and "exaltation." If one or both fall short, however, so do their blessings. Still, as God is just he cannot deprive one of such blessings in the next life who fulfills his or her part in this life. When two are "unevenly yoked," they still serve one another by each giving the other opportunities for growth. The believing spouse "sanctifies" the unbelieving one (1 Corinthians 7:12–14).

The woman's role of *helpmeet* reflects the "power of two."

Persons with whom God makes individual covenants who are *unable* to enter into a covenant relationship with a spouse aren't damned but may await a future chance to do so. Although earth-life sometimes seems the sum total of our existence, life continues far beyond. God loves the disadvantaged no less than others—perhaps more so: "Let not the eunuch say, 'I am but a barren tree.' For thus says Jehovah: 'As for the eunuchs who keep my Sabbaths and choose to do what I will—holding fast to my covenant—them I will give a handclasp and a name within the walls of my house that is better than sons and daughters'" (Isaiah 56:4–5). Their "salvation" and "exaltation," too, are assured.

Other such questions may remain on hold until God's entire plan plays itself out in the millennial age. Many paradoxes surrounding these issues no doubt have to do with the nature of our present world and its perversion of things sacred, particularly matters relating to women. While Western society vulgarizes female attributes in the media, shamelessly debasing a woman's character and divine potential, Eastern societies often conceal women under veils and coverings that demean their persons and render them subservient. A sure indicator of a people's religious and cultural refinement is how it treats women. Are women depreciated and suppressed, or are they honored and beloved?

In the purer environment of the millennial age we may expect to see both men and women in their true colors without the need of social movements to remind us where we fall short. When we follow God's paradigm for humanity's happiness, the enriching influence women have on society and the strength men lend in leadership inevitably beget a state of blessedness. The status and dignity each gender deserves, and their appreciation and esteem for one another, flow spontaneously from men and women leading out in their God-given roles. But when we disavow God and knowingly or unknowingly deviate from his plan, to that degree we must deal with chaos and confusion about who we are.

Postscript: Looking at the lives of Old Testament personalities who attain son/servant status, we observe striking commonalities. By exercising faith in God through severe trials, they influence for good a much broader category than their own—like a war hero or heroine who turns the tide of battle, or a peacemaker who stands in the breach. They fill a need within the larger community in the act of pursuing their own course in life. Paradoxically, their individuality blends perfectly into the whole so long as they surrender their will to God.

A problem many of us have with "taking on added responsibilities" is a fear of losing our personal freedoms. But that attitude generates societal disparity. It breeds spiritual dwarfs on the one hand and spiritual giants on the other—people who, by filling the gap, become more than they believed they were capable of. Another paradox is that we become free, we gain autonomy, precisely by becoming a "slave" to God—by obeying his law and word. The opposite is to become a slave of self and selfish passions and live in a spiritual vacuum.

But isn't it OK, we ask, to "take time out" from life? Jonah tried that and couldn't do it. At what point, then, *do* we finish our spiritual journey? The answer is never. This paradox, that in giving we receive and in serving we are served, surely explains our divine destiny: "You have made man a little less than the gods [Hebrew *'ĕlōhîm*] and crowned him with glory and honor" (Psalm 8:5); "I said, 'You are gods [Hebrew *'ĕlōhîm*] and all of you sons of the Most High'" (Psalm 82:6). Are not gods the most serving and yet the most free?

7

SERAPHIM, GOD'S ANGELIC MESSENGERS

*Seraphim overcome death and see the end from the beginning.
Their worldwide ministry is characterized by divine
intervention. They gather God's elect from throughout the earth.
John's 144,000 servants of God correspond with Isaiah's seraphs/
saviors. The servant's descent and ascent open the way for Israel's
God to intervene and deliver his people.*

As we have seen, God's sons/servants assist in bringing
to pass the endtime "salvation" of God's people—their
"deliverance" from the threat of death into the millennial
age. They do this by serving as proxy saviors or deliverers to
others of God's people to whom they minister. God makes
individual covenants with them patterned after his covenant
with King David. Their proving loyal to God and complying
with his will as they keep the terms of his covenant forms
the essence of living God's higher law. Their descent into

"suffering" and "humiliation"—as they intercede for those less blessed than themselves—leads to their "exaltation" as they and their spouses ascend to see God.

Persons on the seraph level follow the same pattern by keeping the terms of the covenant God makes with them individually that is similarly patterned after the Davidic Covenant and its protection clause. The emperor delivers those who are loyal to the vassal provided the vassal is loyal to the emperor and answers for their loyalties to him. Like sons/servants, seraphs "vindicate" or "justify" those to whom they minister by bearing their iniquities so that they may escape death at the hands of the king of Assyria/Babylon. Seraphs, however, take covenant keeping to the next level. They physically bring many of God's people *out* of destruction at the time God cleanses the earth of wickedness.

Those who ascend to this third level of blessedness compare in stature to gods. Their scope of vision and ministering functions encompass heaven and earth. Isaiah introduces seraphim in Isaiah 6 and parallels their role with his own in Isaiah 40. Through a series of linking terms and ideas, Isaiah's Seven-Part Structure traces Isaiah's ascent from son/servant to seraph. The structure shows that just as God empowers the seraphs so he empowers Isaiah. After more than forty years of serving as a prophet of God Isaiah receives a new commission. "The Ascension of Isaiah," which book exists in four ancient languages, describes Isaiah's ascent to heaven and compares him as a prophet to Moses.

Seraphs take covenant keeping to the next level.

From his Seven-Part Structure we learn that Isaiah ultimately does what the seraphs do: As the seraphs stand in God's council, so does Isaiah. As the seraphs have a "cosmic" vision, so does Isaiah. As the seraphs are witnesses of God's glory, so is

Isaiah. As a seraph declares the forgiveness of Isaiah's sins and iniquities, so Isaiah declares the forgiveness of the sins and iniquities of God's people who repent. As a seraph heals Isaiah, so Isaiah heals Hezekiah. Plural verbs in Isaiah 40 suggest that other persons besides Isaiah receive this angelic commission. That chapter's endtime context implies that it is seraphs whom Isaiah says will "*ascend* as on eagles' wings" (Isaiah 40:31; emphasis added).

Isaiah's ascent to the seraph level, moreover is a type of the ascent of God's servant. The servant, in turn, is a model for all who attain seraph status at the end of the world (see Figure 93). They declare the deliverance of God's people and help bring it about. When Jesus said "He will send his *angels* . . . and they will gather together his elect from the four winds" (Matthew 24:31; emphasis added), he surely meant those who would attain the seraph level. In Isaiah's endtime scenario gathering the elect is precisely the mission of God's servant and his seraph-associates. They bring God's "sons" and "daughters" to the place Zion or Jerusalem in a new exodus from the four directions of the earth.

Figure 93

**Isaiah's Ascent to the Seraph Level
a Type of Endtime Ascent**

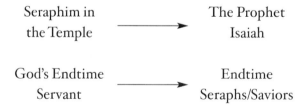

From the way Isaiah traces his own ascent to the seraph level we can conclude that the seraphim he saw in the temple, too, had at some point ascended the ladder. God didn't create them seraphs all at once, but they advanced sufficiently to dwell in his presence yet minister to persons on earth. Angels, in other words, aren't a different species than we are, as some have supposed, but they too are children of God on different spiritual levels, whose category of "translated beings" ministers between heaven and earth. Like Moses, Elijah, and Isaiah, however, those who serve on earth on the seraph level are as the angels of God because he imbues them with extraordinary divine powers.

We gain such an understanding from the word "angel" (*mal'āk*) itself, which means "messenger"—one whom God sends to minister in his name. Daniel, who spoke with the angel Gabriel, calls him "the *man* Gabriel" and describes other angels as having "the appearance of a *man*" (Daniel 9:21; 10:16, 18; 12:6–7; emphasis added). The "angel" who addresses John is none other than "your fellow-servant and of your *brethren* the prophets" (Revelation 19:10; 22:9; emphasis added). The "angels" who saved Lot from Sodom were "men" on an errand from God (Genesis 19:1, 16). Even Jehovah and two angels who informed Abraham that Sarah would have a son are called "men" (Genesis 18:1–16).

Of course angels also minister to us from the world of spirits *without* our seeing them—inspiring, protecting, comforting— as they receive "assignments" from higher up the ladder. In fact, they are often more concerned for our wellbeing than we are. Our intercession with God on behalf of others greatly influences their ministry, as they may intervene in the lives of those for whom we pray when we are unable to assist them. As we ascend the ladder angels on ever higher levels help us. Such a "change of guard" of those who minister to us is consistent with what happens on all rungs of the ladder: those above minister to those below but are themselves ministered to by ones above them.

God has kept seraphs in reserve as a power for good.

As noted, seraphs minister on the earth within the parameters of God's individual covenant. Although their role resembles that of angels, it consists of more than serving as "messengers." As kings and priests to God—as proxy saviors on the seraph level—they are more effectual in their ministry than all others of God's children. Their earthly roles are central to God's endtime redemption of his people. Together with God's servant, they labor against evils greater than God's people are able to overcome of themselves. God has kept seraphs in reserve as a power for good to all who rely on him. The "deliverance" and "salvation" they obtain for others is second only to that of Israel's God.

God grants those who attain the seraph level a vision of his glory and of the end from the beginning. He renews their strength as he did that of Moses and Elijah, who didn't die in the usual sense. Many of these seraphs overcome death at a feast God prepares for people of all nations who ascend to higher levels at the end of the world. God's glory covers these holy ones as it covered Moses in the tabernacle in the wilderness when God spoke with him face to face. Just as God came to Mount Sinai, so he comes to Mount Zion (Isaiah 4:5; 24:23; 25:6–8; 31:4). In the same way he commissioned Isaiah as a seraph, so he commissions others. As Enoch and Elijah ascended to heaven, so do they.

Seraphim Serve as God's Angelic Emissaries

While the word *seraph* (from the root *'sārap*, "to burn") means "fiery/burning one," it also means "serpent," which creature serves as a messianic symbol in Hebrew prophecy and in Maya culture. Fiery serpents, whose poisonous bites felt like a burning fire, attacked the Israelites who had sinned in the Sinai wilderness. When God instructed Moses to make a brass seraph and lift it up on a pole like an ensign, all who looked at it were healed while those who didn't died (Numbers

21:6–9). That act symbolized the role of proxy Savior that Israel's God would perform in delivering his people from death. All who looked to him would be healed or saved, while those who didn't would not.

To a lesser extent that incident also symbolizes the role of proxy savior that seraphs fulfill by following the pattern of Jehovah himself. As a "fiery flying serpent"—a flying seraph—for example, God's servant assists in establishing Zion as a place of safety for God's covenant people when calamities fall upon the nations (Isaiah 14:29–32). The servant's personifying *light*, too, reflects his power as a seraph. The archtyrant, on the other hand, personifies *darkness*, which the servant counteracts. As Moses exercised power over the elements to bring God's people out of Egypt, so the servant and other seraphs/saviors exercise power over the elements to bring them out of Greater Babylon.

The ability to "fly" or move about at will accompanies this level of the ladder. Isaiah describes the seraphs he sees in the temple as having six "wings." He says "With two they could veil their presence, with two hide their location, and with two fly about" (Isaiah 6:2). The "wings" of the seraphim, therefore, are in the nature of energy fields that lend them the power of teleportation—the ability to move with complete freedom—and, if they wish, to act unseen. They demonstrate mastery over fire and all the elements. With their voice they can shake the earth. They serve as God's angelic emissaries—God ministers to them in person, but they minister to levels immediately below their own.

Having seen the end from the beginning, they "see eye to eye."

Persons on the seraph level serve as "watchmen." They stand on duty on the "walls" and "watchtower" and report what they see and hear. Having seen the end from the beginning, they "see eye to eye" in everything pertaining to God's people as Jehovah's coming to the earth draws near. They warn of Greater Babylon's fall and call on people everywhere to repent. They "raise their voice" mightily to herald Jehovah's coming to reign as King. They call on God day and night to deliver his people as they intercede with him on their behalf. They work alongside the servant to teach God's people a higher law, to sanctify and prepare them to enter into God's presence (Isaiah 21:6–12; 52:7–8; 62:6–7).

The ability to *convince* others of God's law and word and of the urgency of their situation marks the ministry of seraphs. As Elijah convinced people about who was God and who wasn't, so do the servant and his seraph-associates. As the angels persuaded Lot to flee from Sodom, so they gather God's elect out of Greater Babylon before its destruction (see Figure 94). As Moses persuaded Pharaoh to let Israel go, so God sends them as deliverers to "Say to the north, 'Give up!' and to the south, 'Withhold not!' Bring my *sons* from afar, and my *daughters* from the end of the earth—all who are called by my name, whom I have created, molded, and wrought for my glory" (Isaiah 43:6; emphasis added).

Figure 94   **The Role of Seraphim Then and Now**

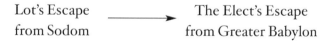

Lot's Escape   ———▶   The Elect's Escape
from Sodom   from Greater Babylon

Like God's sons/servants, from which level they ascend, seraphs/saviors fulfill endtime missions when God's people are sliding into apostasy. After lifting higher spiritually as many as they can, they also rescue them physically by gathering them from among the wicked. When the wicked are "all diverted to their own way, every one after his own advantage" (Isaiah 56:11), then, Isaiah says, "the righteous disappear, and no man gives it a thought; the godly are gathered out, but no one perceives that from impending calamity the righteous are withdrawn" (Isaiah 57:1). When good and evil reach their apogee, God sends his seraphs to deliver one category of people from the fate of the other.

As proxy saviors, seraphs purchase a salvation somewhere between physical deliverance from mortal danger—as obtained by sons/servants—and spiritual salvation from sin wrought by Israel's God. Seraphs' ministry is marked by *divine intervention* accompanied by miracles (see Figure 95). Elijah had the power of teleportation, opening or closing the heavens, dividing the waters, bringing fire from heaven, enlisting heavenly armies, multiplying provisions, healing the sick, raising the dead—all the kinds of things that seraphs do. Just as the earth swallowed transgressors in Moses' time, or as fire leaped forth and consumed them, so signs from God follow God's endtime seraphs/saviors.

Figure 95   **Agents of Proxy Salvation**

Jehovah—Spiritual Salvation from Sin and Iniquity

Seraphs—Divine Intervention Accompanied by Miracles

God's Sons/Servants—Physical Protection against Enemies

The service seraphs perform and the "suffering" they endure—in paying the price of justice on behalf of others—is proportionate to the "salvation" they obtain. Moses was an outcast from Egypt, settling in the land of Midian until God called him to deliver Israel from bondage. He suffered endless hardships and setbacks as even those whom he delivered turned against him. Elijah became a fugitive when Jezebel, King Ahab's Canaanite wife, put all the prophets of God to death. Ravens fed him before he escaped to Sidon. Finally, he wandered to

Mount Sinai until God imbued him with power and appointed him over kings. Anyone who attains seraph status may expect to experience the worst.

The afflictions these prophets suffered and the ministry in which they served created a reservoir of "merit" that backed up their intercession with God. When they appealed to God for anything, he could not deny them because they had made every sacrifice a person could make. They kept his law and word on the highest human level possible. Nor did they ask anything for themselves, their whole concern being for the welfare of God's people. They were "beloved" of God because they did his will to the exclusion of all else. They thus received powers and privileges well beyond others'. Their blessedness surpassed all. These seraphs were the "firstfruits" of those who ascended to heaven.

Seraphs/Saviors Minister among All Nations

In contrast to sons/servants—who obtain the *local* deliverance of God's people—the mission of seraphs/saviors is *international* in scope (see Figure 96). Moses exercised power over Egyptians, Amalekites, and Canaanites on behalf of God's people. God sent Elijah to Syria and Israel to anoint kings. Isaiah prophesied against Babylon, Assyria, Egypt, Cush, Syria, Ammon, Moab, Edom, Philistia, Tyre, and Sidon. At the end of the world God appoints his servant as a "light to the nations" to gather his people from the four parts of the earth. God sends him to Greater Babylon to persuade them to "repent" and "return." His seraph-associates assist him in ministering to the nations of the world.

Although seraphs/saviors ascend from the son/servant category and are also called God's "servants" (Isaiah 54:17; 66:14), linking ideas identify them with the "kings" and "queens" of the Gentiles, the nations among whom God scattered his people (Isaiah 49:22–23a; 60:3–4, 10–11). That doesn't mean, however, that seraphs/saviors originate with non-Israelites. (As noted, God anciently exiled his people into Assyria and Babylon from whence they dispersed and assimilated into the nations of the world.) Their serving as "kings" and "queens" likewise needn't imply political office. Rather, their role stems from serving as proxy saviors of God's people at the time they return from exile.

Figure 96   **The Scope of Proxy Salvation Agents Render**

Jehovah—Universal

Seraphs—International

God's Sons/Servants—Local

Because the role of savior exists solely within God's individual covenants, seraphs, like sons/servants, serve as "kings" and "queens" of God's people on the model of God's covenant with King David. Word links in the Book of Isaiah additionally identify servants of God on the seraph level with the tribes of Israel (Isaiah 49:6; 63:17). The seraphs' Gentile identity, therefore, reflects their origin and ministry among assimilated Israelites, while their tribal identity denotes their lineage. In the end, however, both sons/servants and seraphs/ saviors assume political office over those to whom they minister, serving as "judges" and "rulers" of God's people in the millennial age (Isaiah 1:26; 32:1).

Isaiah's seraphs resemble the "saints" of whom Daniel says, "The saints of the Most High will take the kingdom and possess the kingdom forever" (Daniel 7:18). They also fit Obadiah's description of "saviors" who *ascend* on Mount Zion," where God delivers his people (Obadiah 1:17, 21; emphasis added). John's vision of 144,000 "servants" of God, twelve thousand of each tribe, too, describes Isaiah's seraph category. These stand with the Lamb on Mount Zion and are called the "firstfruits" of all the earth (Revelation 7:1–8; 14:1, 4). As God's "watchmen" (Isaiah 52:8; 62:6), they parallel Enoch's "watchers" (1 Enoch 12:2), angels who minister between heaven and earth (see Figure 97).

All who fulfill the role of proxy saviors on any level are God's "sons" and "servants." In covenant language these terms simply imply vassal status. Even Jehovah, when fulfilling his role as his people's Savior, assumes vassal status, as discussed in Chapter 8. The sealing of 144,000 "servants" with the name of God on their foreheads immediately before the destruction of the wicked reflects their ascent from sons/servants to seraphs. As proxy saviors, they plead with God and labor incessantly on behalf of his people until their endtime deliverance is accomplished (Isaiah 62:6–7). Their models are Jehovah and his servant as they offer themselves as a ransom for those to whom they minister.

Figure 97   **Prophetic Parallels of Seraphs/Saviors**

Isaiah—"Kings" and "Queens"

Daniel—"Saints/Holy Ones"

Obadiah—"Saviors" on Mount Zion   Seraphs/Saviors

John—144,000 "Servants" of God

Enoch—"Watchers"/Angels

We find a type of the "sealing" of God's servants at the Babylonian destruction of Judea. Elect persons, who wept for the wickedness of God's people, received the "mark" of God on their foreheads. When the Babylonians invaded the land, they "passed over" those with the mark, killing the rest—men, women, and children—beginning at the temple (Ezekiel 9:4–7). While that event resembles God's endtime deliverance and destruction only in part, the type of a "mark" as protection holds true. Isaiah predicts that some who receive such a "mark" gather God's people from among the nations and bring them home in a pilgrimage to Jerusalem at the time Jehovah comes in glory (Isaiah 66:18–20).

John's "angel from the east" corresponds with Isaiah's servant, who also hails from the east (Isaiah 41:2, 25; 46:11). That "angel" oversees the sealing of the 144,000 servants of God with the name of God on their foreheads. In Isaiah's version of that event the servant anoints and empowers persons who "mourn in Zion" on account of the wickedness of God's people. That event precedes the "day of vengeance of our God" that is the prelude to the millennial age (Isaiah 61:1–3, 6). A type of those whom the servant anoints is Aaron, whom Moses anointed and empowered as a high priest in Israel. Word links in the Book of Isaiah identify the servant as the "angel" of God's "presence" (Isaiah 63:9).

The Hebrew Prophets Corroborate One Another

Tying Isaiah's scenario into other prophetic writings helps piece together a fuller picture of endtime events. Isaiah doesn't spell everything out for all to see. Instead, he develops his theology by means of literary devices that illustrate every archetype of good and evil. He then shows that theology being acted out in the "last days." Other prophets do similar kinds of things, building on what God had revealed before. The remarkable thing is that their words harmonize so completely as if composed by a single author, though they may have been written centuries apart. Each prophet provides pieces of a larger puzzle. By matching up the pieces we obtain a composite image of the end of the world.

Hosea, Jeremiah, and Ezekiel all predict an endtime "David." While many people apply such prophecies to Jesus, no evidence exists for doing so. The prophets' own descriptions identify two distinct individuals with different but complementary roles. Judaism and Christianity have tended to force one individual into the mold of the other, causing disparity between these faiths and preventing each from honestly viewing the other. Isaiah's Seven-Part Structure and Servant–Tyrant Parallelism show that both religions have a portion of the truth but neither one the whole. These literary structures identify the suffering Savior as Israel's God and the "David" of Hebrew prophecy as his "servant."

Isaiah describes God's "servant" as a descendant of David, the son of Jesse, who gathers God's people from exile and prepares them to meet Israel's God Jehovah. Hosea predicts that "the people of Israel will live many days without a king or prince and without sacrifice." Finally, they will *return and seek Jehovah their God and David their king*, and they will fear Jehovah and his goodness in the last days." He adds "The people of Judah and the people of Israel will be gathered together and appoint themselves one leader." They will *ascend* out of the earth" in a new wandering in the wilderness to the Promised Land as at the exodus out of Egypt (Hosea 1:11; 2:14–15; 3:4–5; emphasis added).

Each prophet provides pieces of a larger puzzle.

From Jeremiah: "'The days are coming,' says Jehovah, 'that I will bring my people Judah and Israel back from exile . . . and restore them to the land I gave their fathers, and they will inherit it.'" In a time of trouble like no other, God will deliver his people from bondage to enemies. In that day they will *serve Jehovah their God and David their king whom I will raise up unto them*." He adds "Though I make a complete end of all nations among whom I have scattered you, yet I will not make a complete end of you." Instead, "I will save you from afar and your descendants from the land of their captivity." These events, moreover, occur "in the last days" (Jeremiah 30:3, 7–11, 24; emphasis added).

In response to unrighteous shepherds abusing the flock Ezekiel says Israel's God will "look for those who are lost and bring back those driven away. I will bind up the injured and strengthen the weak." Jehovah will *"place one shepherd over them—my servant David—and he will feed them. . . . And I, Jehovah, will be their God and my servant David will be a prince among them."* At that time Jehovah will "search for [his] sheep and deliver them out of all the places where they were scattered in a cloudy and dark day." He "will bring them out from among the nations and gather them from the countries and bring them into their own land" (Ezekiel 34:12–13, 16, 23–24; emphasis added).

In that day Jehovah reunites the two houses of Israel: "I will take the people of Israel from among the nations, where they have gone, and I will gather them from every direction and bring them into their own land. And I will make them one nation in the land on the mountains of Israel, and one king will be king to them all. And they will never again be two nations nor will they be divided into two kingdoms any more." He adds *"My servant David will be king over them and they will all have one shepherd. . . .* They will live in the land I gave my servant Jacob, where your fathers lived . . . they and their children and their children's children forever" (Ezekiel 37:21–22, 24–25; emphasis added).

The Jewish idea of the Messiah comes from these prophecies and from Isaiah's description of God's "servant" (see Figure 98). They paint a scenario in which Israel's God gathers and reunites his scattered people at the time calamities fall upon the nations. That gathering of God's people—which the servant and his seraph-associates bring to pass—precedes Jehovah's coming to reign on the earth that begins the millennial age. We can thus see that prophecies of the servant do *not* refer to Jesus, though their roles parallel each other on adjacent levels of the ladder. They refer to one who heralds Jesus' second coming, who prepares the way before him as John the Baptist did at his first coming.

Zechariah describes "a man whose name is the *branch*. . . . He will build the temple of Jehovah, and he will be glorious and sit and rule on His throne. He will be a priest on His throne, and there will be a covenant of peace between them both" (Zechariah 6:12–13; emphasis added). Malachi adds "I will send *my messenger* [Hebrew *mal'āki*, also 'my angel'], who will prepare the way before me. Then, suddenly, the Lord whom you seek will come to his temple. As for the *messenger* of the covenant whom you desire, he is coming" (Malachi 3:1; emphasis added). The temple is thus built in the place Zion or Jerusalem so that when Jehovah comes to the earth he may govern his people from there.

Figure 98	**Jewish Expectations of the Messiah**

He Will Establish the Political Kingdom of God

He Will Gather the Twelve Tribes of Israel

He Will Build the Temple in Jerusalem

Zechariah's and Malachi's scenarios resemble Isaiah's in that they have both endtime as well as historical meaning. Like all proxy saviors, God's servant functions as a king and a priest. Addressing his servant under the codename "Cyrus," Jehovah says "He is my *shepherd*; he will perform all my will. He will say of Jerusalem that it must be rebuilt and its temple foundations relaid" (Isaiah 44:28; emphasis added). Jehovah calls him "my anointed" or "my messiah" (*měšîḥî*), the title of Israel's kings (Isaiah 45:1). Before Jehovah's coming the servant rebuilds

Jerusalem and its temple. Jehovah comes when his people return to the place Zion or Jerusalem and build the temple from which he reigns.

According to Isaiah, God's servant, not Jehovah himself, fulfills these preparatory messianic prophecies, whereas Jehovah fulfills the role of suffering Savior. While Christians apply Isaiah 53 to Jesus (which chapter for the most part depicts the suffering Savior), Jews apply it to themselves. In other words, in their view *they* are the ones who, through many centuries of persecution, have endured heinous "suffering" and "humiliation" on behalf of the rest of humanity, thereby helping to redeem the nations of the world. We may ask whether the Jews, who know their own scriptures best, might possibly be right. Based on the prophetic idea of "the one and the many," they are partly right.

As mentioned, the principle of "the one and the many" in practicality means that God's people experience in their lives or history things similar to what a prominent figure in Israel experiences. They—*as a nation*—thus pass through the same kinds of things that a king or ancestor passes through. As a type of Israel's exile and return, for example, Jacob was forced to flee to the land of Haran, though he afterwards returned to the Promised Land. In the New Testament Matthew uses that same principle in reverse: he applies the prophet Hosea's statement "I have called my son out of Egypt" to Jesus, whereas Hosea was speaking about *Israel's* coming out of Egypt (Hosea 11:1; Matthew 2:15).

God's Seraph/Servant Fulfills an Endtime Mission

Metaphorical pseudonyms throw light on the servant's mission of gathering God's people. Isaiah describes the servant using terms such as "ensign" and "hand" that define his ministry (see Figure 99): "In that day the *sprig* of Jesse, who stands for an *ensign* to the peoples, will be sought by the nations, and his rest will be glorious. In that day Jehovah will again raise his *hand* to reclaim the remnant of his people—those who will be left out of Assyria, Egypt, Pathros, Cush, Elam, Shinar, Hamath, and the islands of the sea. He will raise the *ensign* to the nations and assemble the exiled of Israel; he will gather the scattered of Judah from the four directions of the earth" (Isaiah 11:10–12; emphasis added).

Figure 99   **Figurative Representations of God's Servant**

"ensign"—"hand"—"arm"—"covenant"—"light"

"mouth"—"rod"—"staff"—"whip"

In the above passage a "sprig"—a young descendant—of David the son of Jesse acts as an "ensign" or rallying point to God's dispersed people. Just as a flag-bearer unites a group of people, so God's servant, on attaining seraph status, unites God's people and leads them home from among the nations. By paralleling the raising of God's "hand" with the raising of the "ensign" Isaiah further establishes the idea that this person is both God's "ensign" to the nations and his "hand" of deliverance. Thus, when God "raises" his servant—when he exalts and empowers him—descendants of the northern kingdom of Israel and southern kingdom of Judah gather out of all lands to Zion or Jerusalem.

Just as ancient Assyria exiled Israel's Ten Tribes, so their descendants return from endtime "Assyria" (see Figure 100): "Jehovah will dry up the tongue of the Egyptian *Sea* by his mighty wind; he will extend his *hand* over the *River* and smite it into seven streams to provide a way on foot. And there will be a pathway out of Assyria for the remnant of his people who will be left, as there was for Israel when it came up from the land of Egypt" Isaiah 11:15–16; emphasis added); "In that day a loud trumpet will sound, and they who were lost in the land of Assyria and they who were outcasts in the land of Egypt will come and bow down to Jehovah in the holy mountain at Jerusalem" (Isaiah 27:13).

Just as Moses sang a Song of Salvation at Israel's exodus out of Egypt, so those return sing a Song of Salvation at the new exodus: "In that day you will say 'Give thanks to Jehovah; invoke his name. Make known his deeds among the nations; commemorate his exalted name. Sing in praise of Jehovah, who has performed wonders; let it be acknowledged throughout the earth! Shout and sing for joy, O inhabitants of Zion, for renowned among you is the Holy One of Israel'" (Isaiah 12:4–6). Jeremiah predicts that the new exodus—"from the land of the North and from all countries where [God] had banished them"—will so surpass the old that thereafter they celebrate only the new (Jeremiah 16:15).

Figure 100   **Exile and Return of the Lost Ten Tribes**

In a restatement of these events Isaiah again depicts God's raising his "hand" and "ensign" to bring about his people's return from dispersion: "I will lift my *hand* to the nations, raise my *ensign* to the peoples, and they will bring your sons in their bosoms and carry your daughters on their shoulders. Kings will be your foster fathers and queens your nursing mothers" (Isaiah 49:22–23; emphasis added). When God raises his "hand" and "ensign" (when he empowers his servant) certain "kings" and "queens" among the nations (proxy saviors on the seraph level) assist the servant to gather from exile the "sons" and "daughters" among God's people (God's sons/servants and their dependents).

Those events take place in a time of tyranny when formidable forces too great for God's people are tightening their grip: "Can the warrior's spoil be taken from him, or the tyrant's captives escape free? Yet, thus says Jehovah: 'The warrior's spoil will indeed be taken from him and the tyrant's captives escape free. I will contend with your contenders and I will deliver your children'" (Isaiah 49:25). Through word links in his writings Isaiah identifies the "warrior" and "tyrant" who "spoils" God's people as the king of Assyria/Babylon whose "captives" the servant releases. Many of the captives consist of God's people of Israel's Ten Tribes who come out of endtime "Assyria" in the new exodus.

God's empowerment of his "arm"—his servant on the seraph level—leads directly to the new exodus: "Awake, arise; clothe yourself with power, O *arm* of Jehovah! Bestir yourself, as in ancient times, as in generations of old. Was it not you who carved up Rahab, you who slew the dragon? Was it not you who dried up the sea, the waters of the mighty deep, and made of ocean depths a way by which the redeemed might pass? Let the ransomed of Jehovah return. Let them come singing to Zion, their heads crowned with everlasting joy" (Isaiah 51:9–11; emphasis added). The metaphor of God's "arm," as at the former exodus, signifies divine *intervention* and the servant's role as God's deliverer.

The metaphor of God's "arm" signifies divine intervention.

God calls him: "I create you and appoint you to be a *covenant* of the people, to restore the land and reapportion the desolate estates, to say to the captives, 'Come forth!' and to those in darkness, 'Show yourselves!' They will feed along the way and find pasture on all barren heights; they will not hunger or thirst, nor be smitten by oppressive heat or by the sun: he who has mercy on them will guide them; he will lead them by springs of water. . . . See these, coming from afar, these, from the northwest, and these, from the land of Sinim" (Isaiah 49:9–10, 12; emphasis added). The servant thus frees God's people from the archtyrant, leads their new exodus, and restores them to lands of inheritance.

In another description of the servant, one that emphasizes his spiritual ministry, God says "My servant whom I sustain, my chosen one in whom I delight, him I have endowed with my Spirit; he will dispense justice to the nations. . . . I Jehovah rightfully call you and grasp you by the hand; I create you and appoint you to be a *covenant* of the people, a *light* to the nations, to open eyes that are blind, to free captives from confinement and from prison those who sit in darkness" (Isaiah 42:1, 6–7; emphasis added). The servant thus first fulfills a spiritual mission—to God's people who are spiritually "blind," "captive," and "in darkness"—before he physically delivers them (see Figure 101).

The metaphors "covenant" and "light" nuance the servant's spiritual ministry. They depict him figuratively as mediator of God's covenant—particularly in his intercessory role of proxy savior—and as a source of light to which the nations may look when the world enters its darkest hour. Types of these roles are Moses, who mediated the Sinai Covenant, and King David, who served as a "lamp" to God's people. God's "calling," "grasping by the hand," "creating," and "appointing" his servant all signify his commission as a priest-king on the seraph level. After he fulfills the spiritual part of his ministry during his "servant" mode, God empowers him to fulfill the physical part as his exalted "son."

At that point God says to his servant "You will summon a nation you did not know, and nations who did not know you will hasten to you, because of Jehovah your God who gloriously endows you" (Isaiah 55:5). Just as God sustains his servant—at his passing tests of loyalty—so God sustains his people on their return from exile: "I will strengthen you . . . and uphold you with my righteous *right hand*" (Isaiah 41:10; emphasis added); "Do not fear, for I have redeemed you. I have called you by name and you are mine. When you cross the waters, I will be with you; [when you traverse] the rivers, you will not be overwhelmed. Though you walk through the fire, you will not be burned" (Isaiah 43:1–2).

Figure 101   **The Servant's Spiritual and Physical Missions**

Spiritual Mission   Physical Mission

during "Servant" Phase   during "Son" Phase

At their return God protects his people Zion/Jerusalem *for the sake of* his sons/servants, and he protects his sons/servants *for the sake of* seraphs/saviors. That follows the type of God's protecting Lot for Abraham's sake and Lot's daughters for Lot's sake when they flee Sodom. God's "redeeming" and "naming" his people means they have attained the Zion/Jerusalem level. By Isaiah's definition "redeeming" involves God's forgiveness of their sins, while "calling by name" affirms their new covenant status. After centuries of suffering generational covenant curses God's people qualify, by repenting of transgression, for the salvation that flows down the spiritual ladder from Israel's God.

"Redeeming" involves God's forgiveness of sins.

People whom the servant "did not know," who "did not know" him, represent the Jacob/Israel category. The servant and his associates begin their ministry among these to bring

241

as many as they can to the Zion/Jerusalem level and from there to the son/servant level. Because to "know" implies a covenant relationship, to "not know" means no such relationship exists at first. As mediator of God's covenant the servant brings people of all nations into a covenant relationship with Israel's God and gathers them from dispersion at the end of the world. Seeing the urgency of their situation on the eve of Babylon's destruction, they "hasten" to the servant, recognizing him as an agent of God's salvation.

The endtime exodus resembles Israel's divinely escorted exodus out of Egypt: "Go forth out of Babylon, flee from Chaldea! Make this announcement with resounding voice; broadcast it to the end of the earth. Say, 'Jehovah has redeemed his [collective] servant Jacob.' They thirsted not when he led them through arid places: he caused water to flow for them from the rock; he cleaved the rock and the water gushed out" (Isaiah 48:20–21); "Turn away, depart; touch nothing defiled as you leave there. Come out of her and be pure, you who bear Jehovah's *vessels*. But you will not leave in haste or go in flight: Jehovah will go before you, the God of Israel behind you" (Isaiah 52:11–12; emphasis added).

The pilgrimage of God's people to the Promised Land thus consists of a new wandering in the wilderness under divine protection. As God accompanied them in the past, so he will again, supplying their needs for the journey home. The term "vessels" figuratively describes God's elect, those whom the seraphs convey to Zion. As proxy saviors they "bear" or "carry" God's chosen ones with them just as the Israelites carried vessels of offerings to the temple in their ancient pilgrimage to Zion (Isaiah 66:20). Following the type of Lot's exit from Sodom, the new exodus and new wandering in the wilderness thus consist of both an escape from destruction as well as a return to the Promised Land.

The Servant Endures Suffering and Humiliation

God's "raising," "creating," and "gloriously endowing" his servant all express the servant's ascent to the seraph level. As with all ascent, however, he attains it after first experiencing a descent phase. The servant's "suffering" and "humiliation" are redemptive because they pay the price of justice on behalf of God's people so that they might obtain mercy. Alienated and captive, they can't deliver themselves but require a "savior" as Israel did anciently. The servant and his associates unlock the door that enables a fallen people to again enter God's good graces. They turn a spiritual dead end into an avenue of escape for those who still find themselves under the curse of a broken law.

Speaking of seraphs/saviors God says "I have appointed watchmen on your walls, O Jerusalem, who will not be silent day or night. You who call upon Jehovah, let not up nor give him respite till he reestablishes Jerusalem and makes it renowned in the earth" (Isaiah 62:6–7). As did Isaiah, so God's servant and his associates "offer up prayer on behalf of the remnant [of God's people] that is left" (Isaiah 37:4). When God's covenant people "cry out to Jehovah because of the oppressors, he will send them a savior who will take up their cause and deliver them" Isaiah 19:20). As at Assyria's siege of Jerusalem God delivers them "for my own sake and for the sake of my servant David" (Isaiah 37:35).

Before God responds to deliver his people his servant is "despised as a person" and "abhorred by his people" (Isaiah 49:7)—they reject him as the Jews rejected Jesus. Yet he serves God at all casts: "My Lord has endowed me with a learned tongue, that I may know how to preach to those grown weary a word to wake them up. Morning by morning he wakens my ear to hear, as at study; my Lord has opened my ear, and I rebel not, nor back away. I offered my back to smiters, my cheeks to those who plucked out the beard; I hid not my face from insult and spitting. Because my Lord helps me, I will not be disgraced; I have set my face like flint, knowing I will not be confounded" (Isaiah 50:4–7).

The servant's brutal "marring" pays the price of deliverance.

Because his mission at first seems ineffective the servant thinks "I have labored in vain, I have spent my strength for nothing and to no purpose. Yet my cause rested with Jehovah, my recompense with my God." Trusting in God in his descent phase, however, he can say in the end "I won honor in the eyes of Jehovah when my God became my strength" (Isaiah 49:4–5). As others similarly commit to serve they receive similar assurances in the face of opposition: "Those who gather into mobs are not of me; whoever masses against you will fall because of you. . . . Whatever weapon is devised against you, it will not succeed; every tongue that rises to accuse you, you will refute" (Isaiah 54:15, 17).

The servant's "suffering" and "humiliation" during his *servant* phase lead to his "salvation" and "exaltation" in his *son* phase when God miraculously heals him: "My servant, being astute, will be highly exalted; he will become exceedingly eminent: just as he appalled many—his appearance being marred beyond human likeness, his semblance unlike that of men—so will he yet astound many nations, kings shutting their mouths at him" (Isaiah 52:13–15). The servant's brutal "marring," as his enemies seek to destroy him, pays the price of deliverance for God's people and shows his loyalty to God. As he endures the law of justice on their behalf, he opens the heavens for himself and them.

When reversing his servant's circumstances, God says "Kings will rise up when they see you, princes will prostrate themselves, because Jehovah keeps faith with you, because the

Holy One of Israel has chosen you. . . . At a favorable time I have answered you; in the day of salvation I have come to your aid" (Isaiah 49:4, 7–8). As God strengthens him the servant confronts his enemies: "He who vindicates me is near. Who has a dispute with me? Let us face one another! Who will bring charges against me? Let him confront me with them! See, my Lord Jehovah sustains me. Who then will incriminate me?" (Isaiah 50:8–9). Like Pharaoh, who opposed Moses, no earthly power can prevent him.

When God's "watchmen" do as the servant does God blesses them as he blesses him: "How comely upon the mountains are the feet of the messenger announcing peace, who brings tidings of good, who heralds salvation, saying to Zion, 'Your God reigns!' Hark! Your watchmen lift up their voice; as one they cry out for joy, for they will see eye to eye when Jehovah returns [to] Zion" (Isaiah 52:7–8). In that day God reveals himself to his "elders" as he did on Mount Sinai (see Figure 102): "The moon will blush and the sun be put to shame, when Jehovah of Hosts manifests his reign in Mount Zion and in Jerusalem, and [his] glory in the presence of his elders" (Isaiah 24:23; cf. Exodus 24:9–11).

Figure 102   **Jehovah's Appearance on Mount Sinai and Mount Zion**

Seventy Ancient   Endtime Elders

Elders See God   See God's Glory

All things come together for God's people as they prove loyal at the end of the world. God defeats their foes and settles their debts, more than making up for what they had lost. He grants them far greater privileges than they had before. People in the lowest categories—causers of chaos—disappear from among them forever. Persons in higher categories know they may ascend yet further. Emulating those in the lead, they rise to new levels. Order and accord prevail throughout the earth as people on all levels minister to one another in a perfect pattern of love and peace. After every man-made system has been tried and has failed, humanity finally accepts God's plan—which had been there all along.

When Jehovah comes to reign on the earth he will not rule as a dictator whose every word his subjects jump to obey. He will reign partly through righteous servants who have given their all in his cause. Their experience and understanding qualify them in matters of judgment to implement and administer a theocratic form of government. Because God facilitates his people's growth, he manages the affairs of his kingdom in ways that encourage each person's ascent. That includes delegating power and authority to those who have proven capable of governing others who haven't come as far as themselves, who minister spiritually and politically after the pattern of Jehovah himself (see Figure 103).

Figure 103   **Delegation of Authority
in God's Millennial Government**

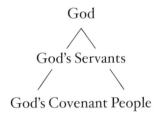

At that time God "will restore your judges as at the first and your counselors as in the beginning" (Isaiah 1:26). Jehovah "will be as a crown of beauty and wreath of glory to the remnant of his people: a spirit of justice to him who sits in judgment, a source of strength to those who repulse the attack at the gates" (Isaiah 28:5–6). Finally, "when oppressors are no more and violence has ceased, when tyrants are destroyed from the earth, then, in loving kindness, will a throne be set up in the abode of David, and in faithfulness a judge sit on it who will maintain justice and expedite righteousness" (Isaiah 16:4–5). In that day "a king will reign in righteousness and rulers rule with justice" (Isaiah 32:1).

Prominent among persons who govern under Jehovah in the millennial age is his servant. Isaiah's Seven-Part Structure names two reprobate counterparts whom the servant succeeds (see Figure 104). First, he replaces one who has acted as a "father" to God's people, a type being the exaltation of Eliakim and humiliation of Shebna. Jehovah appoints *"my servant* Eliakim" in the place of Shebna, the king's "steward," clothing him in the robes of Shebna's office. Eliakim serves as a "father"—a proxy savior—to God's people. Isaiah describes him figuratively as a *"nail* in a sure place." On him "hang" or "depend" many "vessels" who are his father's "offspring" (Isaiah 22:15–24; emphasis added).

Figure 104   **Two Reprobate Counterparts of God's Servant**

Ineffective	Alienated
Spiritual "Father"	Political "Son"
—a False Proxy Savior	—a False Proxy Savior

Second, Jehovah appoints his servant to succeed an apostate Davidic dynasty whose current ruler colludes with the archtyrant. A type of that event is King Ahaz, who relinquishes his father–son relationship with Jehovah, his emperor, in favor of the king of Assyria (2 Kings 16:7). Jehovah therefore declares that another "son" or vassal—Immanuel—will displace Ahaz. That successor will be a proxy savior to God's people at the time the king of Assyria invades the Promised Land (Isaiah 7:10–22; 8:6–8; 9:2–7). The servant's dual roles, like those of all persons on higher levels, thus coincide with his office as a king and a priest, being political and spiritual in conformity with God's government.

We can feel reassured about what occurs at the end of the world because there are *types* that aid our understanding. Although precedents of good and evil appear in the past, only the good apply to Jehovah's millennial reign. The government of Moses and the judges who ruled under him was one such type. The empire of David and Solomon was another. Cyrus's righteous world rule was a third (see Figure 105). All types combined, however, still fall short of God's perfect ministry. Formerly there existed much evil in the world, hindering people's best efforts at good government. As Jesus says of the existing order, "My kingdom is not of this world"—it is not of Babylon but of Zion/Jerusalem.

Figure 105 **Types of God's Ideal Millennial Government**

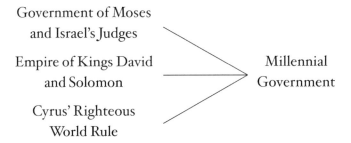

Government of Moses
and Israel's Judges

Empire of Kings David
and Solomon

Cyrus' Righteous
World Rule

Millennial
Government

Covenant Curses Turn into Covenant Blessings

When God reverses his people's circumstances at the beginning of the millennial age, seraphs/saviors assist in bringing about a marvelous transformation of human life. Persons on upper levels can now minister unopposed to improve the lot of God's people. God not merely reverses longstanding covenant curses, turning them into blessings, but those blessings far exceed former ones: "Though you had been forsaken and abhorred, with none passing through [your land], yet I will make you an everlasting pride, the joy of generation after generation. You will suck the milk of the nations, suckling at the breasts of kings. Then will you know that I, Jehovah, am your Savior" (Isaiah 60:15–16).

Persons serving God's people in the dark days before the millennial age must remind them that better times lie ahead. As in labor, the hardest phase is just before birth: "Wilderness and arid lands will be jubilant; the desert will rejoice when it blossoms as the crocus. Joyously it will break out in flower, singing with delight; it will be endowed with the glory of Lebanon, the splendor of Carmel and Sharon. The glory of Jehovah and the splendor of our God they will see. Strengthen the hands grown feeble, steady the failing knees. Say to those with fearful hearts, 'Take courage, be unafraid! See, your God is coming to avenge and to reward. God himself will come and deliver you'" (Isaiah 35:1–4).

A descent phase—a time of troubles and trials—separates those who give up, who abort their rebirth, from those who live the higher law, whom God receives into his presence: "Then will Jehovah delay [his coming], that he may favor you; out of mercy toward you he will remain aloof. For Jehovah is the God of justice; blessed are all who wait for him. O people of Zion, O inhabitants of Jerusalem, you will have no cause to weep. . . . Though my Lord give you the bread of adversity and the water of affliction, yet will your Teacher remain hidden no longer, but your eyes will behold the Master" (Isaiah 30:18–20). Unlike the wicked, whose descent is final, the righteous finally ascend to see God.

Miracles of healing occur of both God's covenant people and their lands of inheritance as seraphs/saviors escort God's people home (see Figure 106). Such miracles follow the types of Jesus, Moses, and Elijah: "Then will the eyes of the blind be opened and the ears of the deaf unstopped. Then will the

lame leap like deer, and the tongue of the dumb shout for joy.
Waters will break forth in the wilderness and streams [flow] in
the desert. The land of mirages will become one of lakes, the
thirsty place springs of water" (Isaiah 35:5–7). As God restores
his elect people and their lands, the survivors of the earth's
cleansing participate in the regeneration of the earth itself to
the Zion/Jerusalem level.

In the pattern of "the one and the many," God empowers
his people as he does his servant: "Awake, arise; clothe yourself
with power, O Zion! Put on your robes of glory, O Jerusalem,
holy city. No more will the uncircumcised and defiled enter
you. Shake yourself free, rise from the dust; sit enthroned, O
Jerusalem. Loose yourself from the bands around your neck,
O captive Daughter of Zion. Thus says Jehovah: 'You were
sold without price, and you will be redeemed without money'"
(Isaiah 52:1–3). As those who repent complete their descent
phase, the servant releases them from captivity. They ascend,
reconstituted as a spiritual and political nation of God's
people—Zion/Jerusalem.

Figure 106   **A Reversal of Covenant Curses**

The Blind See

The Deaf Hear

The Lame Walk

The Dumb Speak

The Land Regenerates

The Righteous Are Empowered

God's Land and People Are Protected

God endows his elect people with his Spirit and establishes
them in their lands of inheritance: "Then will a Spirit from on

high be poured out on us; the desert will become productive land and lands now productive be reckoned as forest. . . . And the effect of *justice* will be peace, and the result of *righteousness* an assured calm forever. My people will dwell in peaceful settlements, in safe neighborhoods, in comfortable dwellings. . . . Blessed are you, who will then sow by all waters, letting oxen and asses range free" (Isaiah 32:15, 17–18, 20; emphasis added). Besides its literal meaning, "righteousness" describes God's servant who pays the price of "justice" to obtain his people's deliverance.

Those who keep God's law and word, who walk in his "light," see a reversal of circumstances. They receive divine guidance, regenerate physically, and participate in a restoration of civilization: "Then will your *light* dawn amid darkness and your twilight become as the noonday. Jehovah will direct you continually; he will satisfy your needs in the dearth and bring vigor to your limbs. And you will become like a well-watered garden, like a spring of unfailing waters. They who came out of you will rebuild the ancient ruins; you will restore the foundations of generations ago. You will be called a rebuilder of fallen walls, a restorer of streets for resettlement" (Isaiah 58:10–12; emphasis added).

Those who live by God's law and word see a reversal of circumstances.

God transforms his people's abode: "Mountains will be removed and hills collapse with shaking, but my charity toward you will never be removed, nor my covenant of peace be shaken. . . . Poor wretch, tempest-tossed and disconsolate! I will lay antimony for your building stones and sapphires for your foundations; I will make your skylights of jacinth, your gates of carbuncle, and your entire boundary of precious stones. All your children will be taught by Jehovah, and great will be the peace of your posterity. You will be firmly established through *righteousness*; you will be far from oppression and have no cause to fear, far from ruin, for it will not approach you" (Isaiah 54:10–14; emphasis added).

Men and beasts will live in harmony (see Figure 107): "Then will the wolf dwell among lambs and the leopard lie down with young goats; calves and young lions will feed together, and a youngster will lead them [to pasture]. . . . A suckling infant will play near the adder's den, and the toddler reach his hand over the viper's nest. There will be no harm or injury done throughout my holy mountain, for the earth will be filled with the knowledge of Jehovah as the oceans are overspread with waters" (Isaiah 11:6–9). The "knowledge" of God filling the earth implies that all then alive will honor God's covenant. That "knowledge" increases as one ascends the ladder until one "knows" God face to face.

Figure 107   **Features of the New Paradise**

God's Spirit Is Poured Out

The Land Produces Abundance

Peace Is Restored to Humanity

Ancient Habitations Are Rebuilt

Dwelling Places Are Beautified

Men and Beasts Live in Harmony

The Knowledge of God Fills the Earth

Those who received the lesser "light" then receive the greater: "Arise, shine, your *light* has dawned; the glory of Jehovah has risen upon you! Though *darkness* covers the earth, and a thick mist the peoples, upon you Jehovah will shine; over you his glory will be visible. Nations will come to your *light*, their kings to the brightness of your dawn. . . . No longer will the sun be your light by day, nor the brightness of the moon your illumination at night: Jehovah will be your everlasting *Light* and your God your radiant glory. Your sun will set no more, nor your moon wane: to you Jehovah will be an endless *Light* when your days of mourning are fulfilled" (Isaiah 60:1–3, 19–20; emphasis added).

The ceaseless intercession of seraphs/saviors on behalf of God's people brings about a glorious blessedness: "For Zion's sake I will not keep silent; for Jerusalem's sake I will not keep still till her *righteousness* shines like a *light*, her *salvation* like a *flaming torch*. The nations will behold your *righteousness* and all their rulers your *glory*; you will be called by a new name, conferred by the *mouth* of Jehovah. Then will you be a crown of glory in the *hand* of Jehovah, a royal diadem in the palm of your God. You will no more be called the forsaken one, nor your land referred to as desolate; you will be known as she in whom I delight and your land considered espoused" (Isaiah 62:1–4; emphasis added).

Those who receive the lesser "light" will receive the greater "Light."

The work of God's servant and his seraph-associates thus comes to fruition at the dawning of the millennial age. As God's people repent and increase in righteousness they experience "salvation." The coming to the earth of Jehovah, who personifies "salvation," will be a tangible fulfillment of his people's expectations. All salvation will then be seen to flow from Israel's God. All will recognize him as the origin of every blessing, as the source of all good. Even proxy saviors on the highest levels can only *qualify* themselves and others for salvation. The power to save, and beyond that to exalt, comes from Jehovah. He, therefore, is the "gate of heaven" through whom all must pass who would enter.

Humanity Rediscovers the Path to Exaltation

The fact that God exalts his seraph/servant and all who ascend to upper levels has nothing to do with favoritism or elitism but forms an inherent part of how God deals with humanity as a whole. Exaltation doesn't come because he loves one person more than another, only as they live or fail to live a higher law. He himself keeps his law and word. Jehovah personifies the law—he *is* the law because he lives the law on its highest plane of observance. Jehovah also personifies his word—he *is* the word because he embodies the very eternal truths his word contains. He asks nothing of seraphs/saviors or sons/servants, such as paying the price of justice on behalf of others, that he doesn't ask of himself.

Isaiah teaches that Jehovah's exaltation on the highest level corresponds proportionately to his prior humiliation when treated by his creatures on earth as though he were the lowest. Jehovah consents to such "humiliation" in order that he might save his people from lesser levels. At the same time, by that very act, he establishes the pattern for "exaltation." As no one can fully accomplish what God does, we emulate persons on higher levels until we assimilate godlike traits. But to assume there is no place further to go when we are just halfway up the ladder, that only a select few "saints" can attain such a goal—as though somehow they are different from the rest of us—would be a tragedy indeed.

Exalted persons have discovered the key to heaven. Jesus said "Strait is the gate and narrow the way that leads to [eternal] life, and few there be who find it" (Matthew 7:14). The "few" who attain upper levels—who, based on certain "knowledge," sacrifice their all—have learned the nature of the journey. When we are willing to suffer *for the sake of* others, to pass through the refiner's fire and realize our nothingness before God, fear, pride, and other vagaries evaporate. Jesus may also have intended seraphs/saviors when he said "He who is greatest among you will be your servant" (Matthew 23:11). A "servant" describes the kind of being Jehovah/Jesus is and all whom he exalts above others.

Israel's God establishes the pattern for "exaltation."

For most of humanity, caught in Babylon's web, however, such a calling appears impractical, even preposterous. To people in the Babylon category the idea of ascending to heaven is euphoric—a fairytale. Many not only don't believe in God, few practice any religion at all let alone live out their lives in the service of God. Those who have done just that, in fact, still seem a long way from attaining anything like seraph/savior status. They evidence no special powers more than anyone else. Hometown preachers, media ministers, and cloistered monks alike are still very much human, fettered by all the frailties of mortality. Their best efforts fall far short of the celebrated feats of biblical heroes.

That state of affairs, however, reflects more today's world than the nonexistence of seraphs/saviors. Isaiah and Jesus compare the end of the world to the time before the Flood, when "all humanity had corrupted its way" and "the earth was full of violence" (Genesis 6:11–13). In other words, people in the "last days" will be mostly of Babylon, with billions abandoning even the Jacob/Israel level. When in a descending mode people hardly take seriously the idea of a ladder to heaven. Those on lower levels aren't just spiritually blind, ignorant of matters divine, they are also defiantly stubborn and unwilling to change. For that reason God has decreed the end of the world (see Figure 108).

And yet humanity's downward path sets the stage for the upward path of individuals to attain the seraph level, in part due to the added adversity. Jesus predicts that at the end of the world the love of many will "wax cold" and they will hate and betray one another (Matthew 24:10, 12). Considering themselves in the right, they will even put his followers to death, thinking they do God a service (John 16:2). Surely only those who tragically misjudge God's character would contest a true and winning cause. We cannot therefore confuse today's widespread intellectual enlightenment with widespread spirituality. Knowledge, or rather, information, can make clever devils as well as enlightened angels.

 Figure 108

The End of the World— Many Descend, Few Ascend

False and failed attempts to ascend to heaven, from the Tower of Babel to the endtime Antichrist, also don't refute true ascent. Humanity's collective memory has kept that hope alive in the cultures of Israel, Egypt, Greece, Arabia, and the Orient. Europe in the Middle Ages saw a preoccupation with the Holy Grail. The earliest threads of that tradition identify the Grail with an open vision of God. The Grail Castle, in which such events occurred, was considered a microcosm of the universe, with ministering angels ascending and descending (see Figure 109). The castle's seven chambers, as in a temple, led in an ascending order to the center, where the candidate gained his transcendent experience.

Those traditions all speak of the purity, faith, and courage of the initiate. In his quest for the Grail he defended the cause of the poor, fought off evil opponents, rescued damsels in distress whose virtue was threatened, and lived a life devoted to doing good without expecting reward. The true knight was a savior of his people who restored righteous kingship and reestablished

Paradise on earth. He had access to the Tree of Life and the Fountain of Living Waters in the inmost chamber of the castle. He and his wife were a part of the Grail "family," an elect group identified with the original Knights of the Round Table. Pilgrimages to the Grail Mountain expressed people's desire to attain the same.

Figure 109 **A Grail Castle**

In the light of Isaiah's theology the Grail Cup commemorates the suffering Savior who pays the price of justice for those who repent of their sins. He drinks the cup of the wrath of God in their stead, paying with his blood to obtain their "salvation" (see Chapter 8). For all who serve as proxy saviors, drinking from this cup follows the pattern of Israel's God. It forms a part of their descent before ascent, called by Jesus a new "baptism" (Matthew 20:22–23). Those who thus serve God by serving others are reborn on the highest levels of the ladder, receiving God's promise of immortality and eternal life. Those who become seraphs may, like Enoch and Elijah, assume immortality even on earth.

Out of the Grail tradition emerged the "nobility," a social class whose role was to bless the lives of those less blessed than itself. By providing lower classes with gainful employment and protecting their interests, feudal lords had the opportunity of being saviors of their people. Allegiance to "his majesty" the king was virtually equivalent with allegiance to God, as people trusted in their God (emperor) and king (vassal) to preserve the peace and administer the affairs of the kingdom. Even such a recent though often exploited social structure offers a type of ascending levels. The fairytale lives of royal families foreshadowed the prospect God holds out to his elect who live into the millennial age.

Biblical accounts of persons who attained seraph status, such as Enoch, Elijah, Isaiah, and John, reveal little of the internal struggles or personal wrestles they had along the way. If we fail today to attain the seraph level after devoting our lives to God, it means we have strayed from *his* path to exaltation, though our lives may be exemplary in other respects. The inability of modern "saints" to repeat the acts of the ancients is a sign that we, in spite of far greater numbers, have fallen far behind. God's response to this condition is to raise up his servant who endows with power all who heed God's call to repent. At the time Jehovah descends to the earth there are thus many who ascend to heaven.

God Manifests Himself to Humanity by Degrees

Isaiah ascends to heaven only after serving God with unwearying commitment over many years. Although God gives him a vision of the end from the beginning, rather than reveal it openly he encodes it. He uses literary tools both to conceal and to reveal its message. The experience of his ascent and what he perceives of the future isn't so much a secret as it is sacred. Isaiah sits in God's council but leaves unspoken that it was he who did so. His Seven-Part Structure alone identifies Isaiah as the visionary. Hiding his identity reflects the humility of persons on higher levels and the fact that we are no longer talking about the same "Isaiah" as before but of a person reborn as an angelic emissary.

Persons who attain the son/servant level see God but don't receive a cosmic vision. That was Isaiah's experience when God first appointed him as a prophet. In that instance Isaiah saw God in the confines of the temple, but later he saw him in the expanse of the cosmos. Like Isaiah, those who see God are healed of maladies. "The Ascension of Isaiah" relates how Hezekiah saw God at the time he fell ill and was healed by Isaiah. In short, we receive divine manifestations according to our place on the ladder. Because the degree of one's ascent is equal to one's prior descent, God's blessings and privileges correspond with the curses or misfortunes one is able to reverse, whether our own or others'.

> At the time Jehovah descends to the earth many ascend to heaven.

Spiritual blindness or impairment of vision as well as other impediments aren't confined to the lowest categories. As a person ascends his vision expands until it comprehends eternity. Seeing with the eyes, hearing with the ears, understanding with the heart, repenting, and being healed (Isaiah 6:10) consists of a *cyclical process* that continues unbroken until one passes through the "gate." The peeling away of layers of blindness we learn by our own experience as we ascend. As Paul says, "The things of God no one knows except the Spirit of God" (1

Corinthians 2:11). To qualify for increasing increments of that Spirit to enlighten us we must prove loyal to God and comply with his will.

People of Zion/Jerusalem experience no visions of great magnitude but receive guidance from God's Spirit. That is proof to them that God's love is real. God's Spirit comforts and directs them in their spiritual odyssey. As they covenant with God to keep his law and word, he blesses them in sublime ways and aids their attempts to ascend. They "know" God in the sense that they see his hand at work in their lives. God comes through for them when they call on him in their distress, and that is to know him in part. They also know him by being freed from sin, seeing the effects of God's merciful forgiveness. Having unburdened themselves of transgression, the load they carry is a lot lighter.

People of Jacob/Israel receive spiritual insights, though they are most often helped by persons on higher levels. While their experience of things divine isn't vast, they accept that God exists, that there is a divine Creator. But they rely largely on the testimony of others for their understanding, much of which may be in error. Their main challenge is to get a correct idea of God without which they progress very little. Laboring under false assumptions or misled by distorted truths, they stumble. In a society diffused with deceit, how can they covenant to keep God's law and word when it is preached by others than his servants? Endless variations on the theme of religion are just that—variations.

Levels below Jacob/Israel—Babylon and Perdition—receive manifestations from God of a different kind. People are under condemnation feel the judgment of an offended God. Instead of speaking to them through inspiration and revelation, he speaks to them through covenant curses—distress, deprivation, misery, dispossession, dearth. Misfortunes stalk them because they are unwilling to learn the ways of God. Such souls are past hearing his word and past feeling the impulses of his Spirit. A key difference between the two lowest levels lies in what happens beyond death. While it is possible for the one still to ascend, the other enters the Pit of Dissolution never to reemerge (see Figure 110).

What a contrast these souls make with the joyous souls who enter heaven! What a waste of this mortal probation, which itself constituted a descent and thus an opportunity for ascent! Whereas God, who resides on the highest rung of the ladder, invites the company of his children, his spiritual offspring, these reject him. Who indeed would forsake God's exalted fellowship in favor of the isolation of the Pit? Who would choose darkness over light, misery over joy, hate over love, and forfeit the chance of eternal happiness? All, however, are at liberty to decide. For that, we can be eternally grateful, as without humanity's agency to choose, God's plan to save and exalt his children could never work.

Figure 110   **Degrees of Divine Manifestation**

Seraphs/Saviors—A Cosmic Vision of the End from the Beginning

Sons/Servants—Local Vision of God as in a Temple or Mountain

Zion/Jerusalem—Comfort and Inspiration from God's Spirit

Jacob/Israel—External Testimony and Spiritual Promptings

Babylon—Plagues or Curses under the Law of Justice

Perdition—Annihilation in the Pit of Dissolution

Isaiah sees the effects of choices: "My servants will eat indeed, while you will hunger; my servants will drink indeed, while you will thirst; my servants will rejoice indeed, while you will be dismayed. My servants will shout indeed, for gladness of heart, while you will cry out with heartbreak, howling from brokenness of spirit. Your name will be left to serve my chosen ones as a curse when my Lord slays you. But his servants he will call by a different name. . . . See, I create new heavens and a new earth; former events will not be remembered or recalled to mind. Rejoice, then, and be glad in what I create. See, I create Jerusalem to be a delight and its people a joy" (Isaiah 65:13–15, 17–18).

Postscript: Absolute truth is something that is true whether we believe it or not. For me, God and angels fall in that category. My encounter with things divine, however, has come only after I have believed, and my certain knowledge has come only after I have believed and acted on what is true. From that, I know that God adapts what he reveals to each one's capacity, to one's personal frame of reference.

Still, modern technologies help us conceptualize what may soon be a common part of the human experience. A computer, for example, teaches us the concept of looking into "windows within windows." That resembles Isaiah's ladder, the final window being the portal to heaven. The privilege of seeing God, however, can never come cheaply but occurs when we access and utilize the encoded data.

Another technology is the laser. If we compare truth to light, then our spirits' capacities to acquire truth resemble a ruby's capacity to absorb light. As the light inside accumulates it becomes supercharged. It can then focus and penetrate in a manner that it couldn't before. Barring cracks in our rubies that leach away our light, we may absorb truth until our light can pierce heaven's deepest mysteries.

Whether we discover the truth in artifacts dug up in the Middle East or in ancient documents viewed in a new light, what we do with it is what counts. If "the truth will prevail" then it must become a vital part of us or *we* will not prevail. Using the truth to upgrade our spirituality—by placing God rather than ourselves at the center of our universe—divides the men from the boys, or rather, angels from men.

8

JEHOVAH, THE GOD OF ISRAEL, KING OF ZION

Jehovah conforms to the types of a Davidic king, firstborn son, and sacrificial victim in paying the price of justice on behalf of his people so that they might obtain mercy. He follows the emperor–vassal model, serving as both Father (emperor) and Son (vassal). The Son's descent as suffering Savior precedes his ascent as King of Zion.

Standing at the top of the ladder to heaven, on its highest rung, is Israel's God Jehovah. But far from being a remote and inaccessible God, like the false gods idolaters worship, he is intimately involved in the individual journeys of his children. While we are on the earth, however, that may not always seem evident. He leaves plenty of room for us to exercise faith in him or we couldn't complete the journey. Without being tested in our loyalty to him we could not ascend. Because Jehovah personally receives those who enter heaven, that is the only way we can get there. Our firsthand knowledge of God comes after he tries our faith to the fullest. On completing our quest we see him face to face.

As King of kings and Lord of lords—as "emperor" to his "vassals" in heaven and on earth—Jehovah rules supreme. Still, he doesn't rule capriciously or condescendingly like the gods of Greek mythology. His people determine their own fates—their "rebirth," "deliverance," "salvation," "exaltation," and "inheritance," or their "ruin," "punishment," "suffering," "humiliation," and "disinheritance." Jehovah stipulates the law of his kingdom, but whether his people keep the law and enjoy the blessings or break it and suffer the curses is on *their* heads. God reveals his word to them through his emissaries, but it is up to his people whether they comply and ascend or rebel and descend.

Although Israel's God is the greatest, he is willing to be judged the least. His paradigm consists of ministering and being ministered to, beginning at the top. But during the course of fulfilling his ministry, Jehovah, who represents the highest level on the ladder, voluntarily subjects himself to the lowest. Although he is the God of Israel, he, too, experiences a descent phase before being exalted as King of Zion. While serving as a proxy Savior to all—to pay the price of justice for all—he assumes vassal status following the types of human saviors. But because the price he pays is greater than theirs, Jehovah endures "suffering" and "humiliation" below all that deliverers on lower levels endure.

Isaiah's Seven-Part Structure makes clear that unless Jehovah assumes the role of Savior of his people, there can be no forgiveness of their sins no matter how much they repent. When one transgresses God's law he becomes subject to divine justice. A debt accrues that must be paid. Otherwise God would be unjust and no God at all. But to compensate a person who has been wronged one must do so on the level of the injured party—he must make "restitution in kind." Moreover, because one can't recompense God on *his* level it would remain forever impossible for anyone to ascend; one could only descend. Built into God's plan of salvation, therefore, is that Jehovah himself pays the debt.

In God's plan of salvation Jehovah himself pays the debt.

For making such complete amends no human type exists or can exist. We thus find none except incomplete parts of it such as the role Davidic kings assume in answering to God for the loyalties of their people. The price of justice Jehovah pays to bring about the salvation of his people has no human type because no one on a level below his can make full restitution. Instead, God chose animal sacrifice to symbolize his proxy sacrifice. Under the Law of Moses ritually clean beasts such as bullocks or lambs were slain in the place of transgressors. But because lower creatures can't fulfill justice on behalf of higher ones, sacrificial animals, unlike human proxies, served only as types, nothing more.

From the beginning, after Adam and Eve had descended to a lower level, all humanity required "salvation." Salvation had to include deliverance from death—the curse all inherited when Adam and Eve transgressed. As in ancient Near Eastern covenants between emperors and their vassal kings, God's covenant obliged God to deliver his people from a mortal threat so long as they kept the terms of his covenant. Ultimately, however, that threat would come not from the king of Assyria/Babylon or from any human oppressor but from death itself. At some point, therefore, when his vassals fully keep his law and word, God is obliged to reverse the curse of death. That is the only way it can happen.

As Creator of heaven and earth, God is not going to start something he can't finish. When Isaiah says God is "the first and the last" or is "at the first and at the last," for example, he means that God, who created all things in the beginning, will create or re-create all things at the end, and everything in between. Isaiah depicts God's measuring out cosmic "waters," gauging the expanse of the heavens, compiling the earth's "dust" by measure, weighing out mountains in scales, and positioning the earth's islands; but God also creates or re-creates the earth's inhabitants, the nations, his covenant people, and, in an endtime context, those who "ascend" (Isaiah 40:12, 15, 17, 22, 27, 31) (see Figure 111).

Figure 111   **God's Continuing Creation**

New Heavens, New Earth	Those Who Ascend to Glory
Paradise on the Earth	God's Covenant People
Premillennial Earth	Nations/Peoples
Primordial Earth	Humanity

From Isaiah's perspective, then, God's creation is by no means a one-time, all-inclusive endeavor, with everything starting and finishing according to his plan, in which everyone lucky enough to get into heaven is caught up in an unchanging hypostatic union with God—an endless vision of God, holding a person spellbound for eternity—while those unfortunate souls who go to hell burn in its fires in excruciating pain for all eternity without ever burning up. That isn't the God of the prophets who have seen him and testified of him from the beginning, but of medieval artisans who were less familiar with God's word than they were with torturing people for their beliefs and burning them at the stake.

Like God's creation of the cosmos, his creation of humanity is ever expanding and never-ending, just as our individual journeys are within it. The end of one cycle of creation is only the beginning of another. While we may be the *object* of God's creation, we aren't its center—God is. In other words, our lives revolve around God, not the reverse. To assume otherwise is like believing the sun revolves around the earth—which we often do when we impose our Sunday School ideas on God. That is why science and the Bible can *never* conflict. If we believe they do, it is we who haven't reconciled the two. One is not wrong and the other right, but the same God who created the cosmos, created us too.

Isaiah Defines the Nature of God as a "Father"

We solve much of the mystery of who God is from what Isaiah teaches through his Seven-Part Structure. Putting aside for a moment our vague notions of God as some "Great Heavenly Being" (which he nonetheless is), we first come down to earth and discover that we ourselves resemble God the higher we ascend the ladder. Recall that God created Adam and Eve "in his own image and likeness" and gave them Paradise for an inheritance. Remember also that God confirms all who ascend to the highest levels as his "sons" and "daughters," to whom he likewise gives Paradise for an inheritance. In short, one cannot separate the Creator from those he creates, whether Adam and Eve or ourselves.

Our very definition of God links us inseparably to him. Yes, he is the Creator of the cosmos—the heavens and the earth. But as Isaiah makes clear that cosmos exists solely for its occupants "as a tent to dwell in." God's "throne" is there (Isaiah 40:22). And as he continues to "stretch out the heavens" it would indeed be ethnocentric of us to assume that ours is the only "tent" God is concerned with. The Hubble Telescope's pictures of deep space show the existence of billions of galaxies stretching out in all directions as far as space can be detected. Obviously, God's creation has been going on since long before we arrived on the scene, and it will go on long after the millennial age is over.

And yet, in spite of this vital link between God as Creator and ourselves, in our present time and space God manifests himself to humanity by degrees, not all at once. Our ascent on the ladder through the "time warp" of mortality demands that God puts some distance between us so that we can learn about becoming like him. Thus, just as those on the periphery of a galaxy can't tell us what goes on in the inner circle, so a preacher can't pontificate about a God he has never seen. We may make guesses about the nature of God, but God has set things up so that only those who ascend can truly know him. And those who know him are the least likely to tell about it—except, like Isaiah, in encoded form.

God manifests himself by degrees, not all at once.

Isaiah first sees God in the temple "seated on a throne," while later he sees him enthroned in the cosmos (Isaiah 6:1; 40:22). That transition reflects Isaiah's ascent from son/servant to seraph. From that point on in his life Isaiah no longer prophesies in the usual manner—piecemeal—as he receives visions and revelations from God. Having seen the end from the beginning, he now writes lengthy prophetic discourses, integrating them and his earlier prophecies into a sophisticated literary framework. Isaiah requires his readers to unravel his literary devices to get at his message, which itself teaches us that the truth is to be found by searching, by unlayering and decoding what already exists.

Just as science doesn't yet have all the answers to the secrets of the universe, so we can't presume to know all the mysteries of God. God has never revealed everything about himself, but he makes his truth known as we show increased readiness to receive it. Enormous paradoxes face the seeker of the truth in both science and theology. But paradoxes aren't contradictions. Because one thing *appears* to contradict another doesn't mean that such is the case. Instead, we often learn more from resolving paradoxes—from sorting out *seeming* contradictions—than we can in any other way. Determining the nature of God has been a problem with God's people since the Israelites worshiped the Golden Calf.

Because the closer we get to God the more marked the paradoxes, it sometimes seems that God includes enough ambiguity in his revealed word to provide an "out" to those who resist his invitation to seek the truth. At virtually every level, in effect, God has built into the scriptures two ways you can interpret them: one for those who want to fall back on established views, right or wrong, that may have some element of truth but not the whole truth; the other for those who want to search out all God has revealed no matter how great the paradoxes (see Figure 112). God makes that a test for us—a "snare" for the self-righteous, but a path into his presence for his "disciples" (Isaiah 8:11–17; 28:9–13).

Figure 112   **Contrary Responses to Scriptural Anomalies**

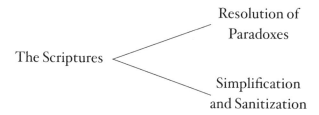

It is true that keeping the terms of God's covenant alone enables us to ascend and see God, yet Isaiah's literary devices are the bait that tempts us on. To those weaned of milk Isaiah offers meat, he himself having partaken of the same. Those who assimilate the "first principles" of God's law and word Isaiah beckons onward and upward—not into a mysterious unknown but into realms somehow familiar to our genetic memory as children of God. Indeed, the closer we get to God the more we feel "at home." Isaiah's imagery of "family" and the human life cycle in our relationship with God intensifies as we ascend. The gate of heaven leads to where God dwells, who is literally humanity's Father.

Isaiah asserts throughout his writings that we are the offspring of God. The idea of God as "Father" and his people as "sons" permeates the Book of Isaiah (Isaiah 1:2; 30:1, 9; 43:6; 45:11; 63:8, 16; 64:8). Apart from the covenantal meaning Isaiah assigns these terms—of "father" meaning emperor and "sons," vassals/heirs—most everything Isaiah says is first of all literal. By means of an a–b–a mini-structure, for example, Isaiah teaches that his people's "Maker" is also their "Father," he who has literally "begotten" them as his "sons" or "children" (Isaiah 45:9–11). In that sense, because we already have physical bodies, the God we worship is our own Ancestor, the Father of our spirits.

> Isaiah asserts that we are the offspring of God.

That would suggest, however, that we lived prior to being physically born on the earth. Just as Isaiah teaches that we continue our existence *after* our mortal experience, in fact, so he teaches that we existed *before* this life. An example of an afterlife is the archtyrant, whose spirit enters "Sheol" or Hell on its way to the "Pit": "Sheol below was in commotion because of you, anticipating your arrival; on your account it roused all the [departed] spirits of the world's leaders" (Isaiah 14:9). While for the Perdition category there is no resurrection (Isaiah 26:14), the spirits of the righteous will be reunited with their bodies "when their bodies arise . . . for the earth will cast up its dead" (Isaiah 26:19).

That we existed *before* our lives on the earth is evident from the idea that God appoints persons on higher levels prior to being born to come here and perform specific tasks. God's endtime servant declares "Jehovah called me before I was in the belly; before I was in my mother's womb, he named me" (Isaiah 49:1). The servant's "calling" and "naming" signify his ascent to a higher level and his commission to fulfill his earthly role. Jeremiah was similarly assigned his prophetic mission prior to being born on the earth: "Before I formed you in the belly, I *knew you*; before you came out of the womb, I *set you apart*. I *appointed you* as a prophet to the nations" (Jeremiah 1:5; emphasis added).

In other words, persons like Isaiah, Jeremiah, and God's servant, who begin their earth lives on levels higher than Jacob/Israel, attained those levels *before* birth (see Figure 113). God "calls" and "appoints" people to such key ministering roles only *after* they ascend to the highest levels. Thus, although they were born on the earth from parents who had descended from Adam and Eve, prior to that they (and each of us) had descended from God. Adam and Eve themselves fall in that category. If, as Isaiah teaches, our wisdom, understanding, power, and intelligence increase as we ascend, then there is no reason to believe that an impartial God would create anyone on the highest levels all at once.

Figure 113   **Attested Pre-Earth Spiritual Levels**

Sons/Servants

Zion/Jerusalem

Jacob/Israel

That idea accords with the New Testament teaching that God "foreknew" his elect people and also "predestined" them: "We know that all things work together for good to those who love God, who have been called according to his purpose. For those whom God foreknew, he also predestined to be conformed to the *image* of his Son, that he might be the firstborn among many *brethren*. And those whom he predestined, he also called; and those whom he called, he also justified; and those whom he justified, he also glorified" (Romans 8:28–30; emphasis added). In a real sense God's elect resemble Jesus, who was "foreordained before the foundation [or 'creation'] of the world" (1 Peter 1:20).

Jesus' "foreordination" *before* the earth was created to fulfill the role of suffering Savior means that God's plan for the "salvation" and "exaltation" of his children was conceived far in advance. As Jesus was to reverse the consequences of Adam's and Eve's transgression, we can know that the Fall was an integral part of God's design (see Figure 114). Otherwise there would have been no need of a savior. God's plan, however, would also involve the savior roles of "brethren" of Jesus (Romans 8:29). Saviors on levels below his would fulfill key ministering roles to assist God's children to ascend. For that purpose, therefore, such saviors, too, were "called," "named," and "appointed" beforehand.

Figure 114   **Humanity's Fall and Redemption Foreseen**

Foreordination $\longrightarrow$ Creation $\longrightarrow$ Fall

Fall $\longrightarrow$ Spiritual Growth $\longrightarrow$ Redemption

In the light of Isaiah's ladder to heaven, humanity's fallen state was thus not a "mistake" that we should regret, for which we should blame Adam and Eve, or God. Rather, it represented an occasion for Adam's and Eve's descendants to gain experience. It provided an opportunity for us to ascend above our present level by dealing appropriately with covenant curses such as illness, pain, and death, which are a consequence of transgression. On whatever level individuals are born on this earth, their mortal nature enables them to rise higher by overcoming evil. God's redemption would realize a reversal of the effects of the Fall for all who accepted his formula for saving and exalting his children.

Creation and Re-Creation Are a Cyclical Process

A key to understanding God's creation, and the whole of life—the nature of God and our relationship to him—is God's *re-creation* of us as we ascend to heaven. It explains how Adam and Eve came into being, why they could be called our first parents, and why there was a Fall. Re-creation accounts for the existence of lower life forms and how these increase in intelligence as they live out their lives. It puts the whole phenomenon of our permanence in a bigger context than just ourselves on this one earth in a sea of cosmic marvels. It makes sense of God's promise to Abraham that his descendants would be as numerous as the sands of the seashore and as the stars in the heavens (Genesis 22.17).

Because re-creation occurs on every level of the ladder, God's creation is an unbroken, *cyclical* process that ensures that those lower may ascend higher. The many cycles or sequences of creation going on simultaneously on different spiritual and physical planes enable those whom God has created to pass through different phases of ascent and descent. From Isaiah's perspective God's creation could not have started with Adam and Eve, nor can it end with the millennial age. Compared with the ever-expanding cosmos and its countless hosts that God has created, what he has revealed of this earth is but a detail of a much bigger picture, a brief "moment in time" within an endless continuum.

If God is indeed an impartial God then *our* descendants can ultimately be as many as the sands of the seashore and the stars in the heavens. What he promised Abraham was what God was himself—the Father of an innumerable earthly and heavenly posterity. We too can become kings and priests to God, the

King of kings and Lord of lords. We can become "Adams" and "Eves" and inherit Paradise as an "everlasting inheritance." We can become co-heirs with Jesus, as Paul teaches and Isaiah confirms. Why, then, should being a literal son of God be a more difficult doctrine to believe than being created from a ball of clay? Was Eve really made from a *rib*, or did Moses use a figure of speech?

Isaiah agrees with the Genesis account that describes Seth the son of Adam in the same terms as Adam the son of God, as previously mentioned. God "begets" his children as does man, whom the Psalmist depicts as "a little less than God/the Gods" (Psalm 8:5; *mĕ'at mē'ĕlōhîm*). Isaiah's Seven-Part Structure shows that the pattern of relationships between levels on the ladder is the same up or down. By including *God* in that pattern—as in proxy salvation, descent before ascent, and a father–son hierarchy—Isaiah lets us know implicitly that God's "begetting" of children is similar to ours. To grasp that point it helps to replace our Greek notions of a nebulous, amorphous God with a Hebrew one.

> When we pay the price of searching we *will* find.

If man's creation in the "image and likeness" of God is "male and female" as the Book of Genesis asserts, then we need to consider whether God is male and female. Without resorting to simplification and sanitization, let us face squarely what Moses, Isaiah, and others who have seen God say on this subject. As each of us is individually accountable for how we receive the gift of God's word, we can't fall back on others to tell us what a prophet means; we *ourselves* must study it out in our minds. It is a universal principle that when we pay the price of searching we *will* find—God guides us to the truth by his holy Spirit. Whether we believe a truth can't change it, but believing it can change us.

Isaiah's mini-structure depicts God as male and female (see Figure 115): "[a] Woe to those in conflict with their *Maker*, mere shards of earthenware pottery! As though the clay were to say to him who molds it, 'What are you doing? Your hands have no skill for the work.' [b] Woe to those who say to the *Father*, 'What have you begotten?' or to the *Woman* [or, *Wife*], 'What have you borne?' [a] Thus says Jehovah, the Holy One of Israel, their *Maker*: 'Will you ask me for signs concerning *my sons*, or dictate to me about the deeds of my hands? It is I who made the earth and created man upon it; I with my hand suspended the heavens, appointing all their host'" (Isaiah 45:9–12; emphasis added).

Figure 115   **Mini-Structure Defining God as Male and Female**

a—God as "Maker," even of those who rebel,

who question his work.

b—God as "Father" and "Woman/Wife,"

who "beget" and "give birth."

a—God as "Maker" of his "sons/children,"

whom he "creates/appoints."

This parallel structure teaches that humanity's Maker is the same God who gave them birth, who consists of Father and Mother. That is not to say that God is like us but rather that we are like God, or can become so as we adopt his/their divine attributes. The idea of God as Father *and* Mother also doesn't mean God is not one. As Moses solemnly reminds God's people, "Hear, O Israel, Jehovah our God, Jehovah is *one*" (Deuteronomy 6:4; emphasis added). Although the plurality of the name God/Gods in Hebrew (*elōhîm*) itself denotes a plural entity, yet God was, and will always be, "one." That paradox is less a contradiction in terms than it is a riddle that increases our understanding of God.

In addressing these and other such questions, the biggest stumbling to our understanding isn't the scripture itself, which has its own checks and balances, "second witnesses," different ways of saying the same thing, and so forth, but our own prior perceptions of God based on our assumptions or unwillingness to look deeper into the reality of spiritual things. When it comes to God, it seems only the broken-hearted can be penetrated by the truth. In this world the fear of man far outweighs the love of God. Those loudest in denouncing the truth are as empty vessels that make the most sound. Like Jesus and the prophets, persons who declare the truth may even be in danger of their very lives.

That "holy" and "valiant" persons anciently could have been killed or ill-treated at all shows that popular opinion in their day entirely negated what they taught. But popular opinion has never been a standard for understanding the Word of God, neither then nor now. Rather, servants of God in every age have been prepared to die as martyrs at the hands of self-righteous religionists so that their testimonies of the truth could stand as a witness against the wicked. As human nature hasn't changed, and as the "last days" are the most terrible time of blindness of all, that must happen once more. The truth of God will triumph when democracy gives way to theocracy in matters of God and religion.

Isaiah makes clear that those who rely on others rather than God for their spiritual understanding can't gain "exaltation"—the heavenly glory God holds up as humanity's goal. To ascend to the highest levels each person must learn on his or her own the true character of God (Isaiah 28:9; 40:25–26). That begins with processing through the scriptural evidences he has provided of his divine nature as our Creator—as the *One* who has "begotten" us and "given [us] birth"—and by keeping his law and word. When we blindly accept this or any elucidation of God's word without searching things out for ourselves and asking God to confirm their truth, we can't expect to be worthy of heavenly glory.

God's "Oneness" Implies Unity, Not Singleness

The question of God's oneness has been a vexing one for both Judaism and Christianity, causing unnecessary disparity between the two. One teaches the concept of a singular, nebulous "Being" whom we can never see. The other tries to force three separate persons—Father, Son, and Holy Ghost— into a single "essence." Those who have seen God, including Abraham, Moses, and Isaiah, tell a different story, be they patriarchs, prophets, or private individuals. In our day no less than in ancient times, false gods, false ideas of God, and false spokesmen for God far outnumber the true. In Elijah's day, for example, the ratio was eight hundred and fifty false prophets to one (1 Kings 18:19).

The Old Testament itself relates how two can be "one." According to Joseph, who interpreted dreams, the two dreams of Pharaoh in reality were "one," signifying what the future had in store for Egypt (Genesis 41:1–32). Ezekiel's two "trees" or sticks were "one" in his hand, symbolizing the future reunion of the two houses of Israel (Ezekiel 37:15–22). In an example closer to the point of our discussion, when God brought the "woman" (or "wife") to Adam they became "one flesh" (Genesis 2:22–24). Later, when Adam and Eve ate the forbidden fruit, they became "as God/Gods [*elōhîm*], knowing good and evil" (Genesis 3:5). Yet that same God or Gods whom *they* became like is "one."

Finally, Jesus' eloquent prayer for his disciples that they would be "one" with him as he was "one" with the Father affirms the idea of oneness as unity rather than singleness (John 17:6–23) (see Figure 116). That idea is not lost on John, who records Jesus' prayer in the context of the disciples' keeping Jesus' law and word even as Jesus keeps his Father's law and word. The oneness Jesus taught is grounded in the love of God, apart from whom no unity exists. The whole purpose of Jesus' last great discourse is that his disciples might be "in" him as he is "in" the Father (John 14:6–16:33). The oneness *of* God and oneness *with* God thus embodies the very plurality that the term "God" contains.

The setting in which Moses declares God's oneness to Israel is not at Sinai where God gave the law but just before Israel enters the Promised Land (Deuteronomy 4–7). Moses warns against the gods of the nations whose lands Israel inherits and against the gods of other nations: "Fear Jehovah your God; serve him and take oaths in his name. Don't go after other gods, the gods of the people around you" (Deuteronomy 6:13–14). Using that "teaching moment," Moses commands Israel to "love Jehovah your God with all your heart and with all your soul and with all your might" (Deuteronomy 6:5). By so doing God's people will be *one* with God as he is one, but also one with each other.

Figure 116   **Biblical Examples of "Oneness"**
in Multiple Entities

Two Dreams of Pharaoh

Two Houses of Israel

Adam and Eve

Jesus' Disciples

The Father and the Son

When God said "Let *us* make man in *our* own image, in *our* own likeness" he wasn't using the "royal plural" of European monarchs but correct grammar (Genesis 1:26; emphasis added). God's oneness, as expressed in his unity of purpose, loses nothing by the fact of God's plurality. Rather, God's plurality is the very thing that begets man's creation. If God had created Adam and Eve differently than any other creation, or procreation, he would have made sure we understood it. The physical processes governing all living persons testify that "multiplying and replenishing the earth" is the process through all have come into being, whether before or after Adam's and Eve's fall from a higher level.

Moses' allegory of Adam's and Eve's creation contains enough clues to help us figure this out, especially when we look for analogies. Zion/Jerusalem's awakening and rising "from the dust," for example, signifies creation or re-creation on a higher level. Adam's formation "from the dust" may thus similarly signify creation or re-creation (see Figure 117). The "serpent" as a messiah symbol in Hebrew prophecy alludes to the idea of a false savior (Satan) duping Adam and Eve into transgressing God's law and word. The Hebrew metaphor of "trees" representing people and their "fruit" words and deeds nuances Adam's and Eve's partaking of the tree of the "knowledge" of good and evil.

Death and resurrection are the best example of "ruin" and "rebirth," chaos and creation, etc., on a *physical* level. But rising "from the dust" doesn't mean a person didn't exist before—he did. At that point he simply enters a new phase of existence. Likewise, Adam's creation or re-creation "from the dust" doesn't mean he didn't exist before. Because God's law is the same for all, Adam *had* to exist previously in order to have inherited Paradise. To qualify for that kind of blessedness one must ascend to at least the son/servant level as both male and female. Aside from that, the idea of Adam's "creation" being a physical "rebirth" or *resurrection* in no way lessens the significance of the event.

Figure 117   **Physical Creation and Re-Creation
"from the Dust"**

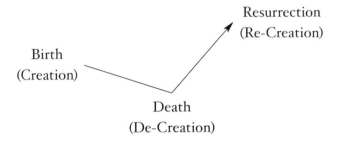

The fact that Adam and Eve "hid themselves from the presence of Jehovah" in the Garden of Eden after they had transgressed (Genesis 3:8) tells us, first, that they dwelt in God's presence before the Fall; and second, that one can't dwell in God's presence while in a state of transgression. To attain God's presence one must ascend the ladder by living God's higher law, as noted. Adam and Eve evidently attained that state *before* they transgressed. If not, they would have existed in a state similar to ours—with God's messengers ministering to them, not God himself. Their being banished from the Garden of Eden was thus a physical manifestation of a spiritual descent, as with all descent.

By the same token, resurrection is no guarantee of ascent to a higher level. Descent and ascent are a *spiritual* process, of which physical descent and ascent are a type. Isaiah likens mortality to a "veil that veils all peoples" (Isaiah 25:7). When God removes the veil all will be seen for who they are, in this life as in the next. So, too, at our resurrection our appearance will match our spiritual level. Our physical features may differ, not just because of our level on the ladder, but—as with the stars in the heavens—because of different character traits. The higher we ascend, the more we become like God, while the lower we descend, the less like him and more disparate from each other we are.

Just as the Creation is a reflection of the Creator, so the "heavens" (also a plural term) testify of God's unity and plurality. The cosmos as we now know it consists of many "heavens," each associated with a different galaxy. The "heavens" visible to the naked eye—the Milky Way—is but one of countless galaxies, all of which constitute "heavens" in parts of the cosmos not our own, but all of which, like God or Gods, exist in harmony as a unity. If, as Isaiah says, God created the heavens and the earth—the Milky Way and Planet Earth—does he mean that a single being created this galaxy, or that God/Gods as a plurality created it and possibly other galaxies as dwelling places for their children?

Resurrection is no guarantee of ascent to a higher level.

In fact, there is no reason to suppose ours is God's only creation of an earth as a place in which to live. Isaiah's cosmology and all reasoning remonstrate against it. Predictions of new heavens and a new earth themselves tell us we will inhabit another space and "time." Those who attain the seraph level already have one foot, so to speak, in another dimension as they come and go between the worlds. Those who haven't seen heaven don't know where it is, except that God and angels dwell there and that the heavens are God's "throne" (Isaiah 66:1). If those who ascend, too, inherit thrones and rule as kings and queens, will those thrones ultimately also be in heaven or are they only on the earth?

Isaiah's use of celestial imagery as a type of persons who ascend itself leads to interesting parallels of a ladder to heaven. When we think of smaller heavenly bodies that orbit larger ones in terms of the smaller keeping the "law" of the larger (whether of gravity or electrostatics), then the cosmos alludes to ascending levels. Moons orbiting planets, planets orbiting stars, and stars orbiting centers of galaxies parallel persons observing ever higher laws as they ascend (see Figure 118). The movement in unison of larger heavenly bodies and the lower nature of "rogue" entities, such as comets, asteroids, and dust, parallel the "oneness" of higher spiritual levels and the chaotic character of lower ones.

Figure 118   **An Ascending Order of Heavenly Bodies**

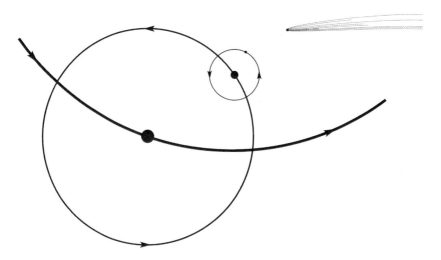

With galaxies, the pattern of orbiting bodies ends, although some galaxies merge and become one galaxy. In that case their billions of stars don't collide or harm one another but readjust their orbits within the larger entity. New stars are born—each with its planets, and they with their moons—out of the debris that breaks loose from novae or from stars' close encounters. Stars form when they accumulate enough mass to start fusion, at which point they begin to shine. Adam's formation "from the dust," as God breathes into him the "breath of life," parallels the birth of a star. Persons who haven't yet attained the level of Adam and Eve parallel bodies of lesser mass such as planets and moons.

In no account does God's creation of the heavens and the earth appear *ex nihilo*—out of nothing. As Genesis asserts and

Isaiah confirms, God created the heavens and the earth out of existing matter, namely cosmic "waters" and "dust," which at first existed in a dark and chaotic state (Genesis 1:1–10; Isaiah 40:12). Creation thus consists of the unifying of ununified elements, in cosmic and human bodies alike. Both develop through an organic process that has existed for billions of years. The "oneness" of God, of the cosmos, and of those who inhabit it, derives from their capacity to observe universal laws, even though in respect to all of them the truth sometimes appears stranger than fiction.

It is indeed time to put away theories of creation "out of nothing" and other conjectures concerning which science and the scriptures give clearer answers. Just as religionists have erred on the Creation, so they have missed the mark in other things—so much that the speculations of Greek philosophy have clouded Jewish and Christian thinking. From Xenophon to Plato, and from Plato to Philo and Augustine, Greek ideas have changed the anthropomorphic, human-looking God of the Hebrews into an incomprehensible intangible "substance" which no one can describe, whose nature is so abstract and whose presence so far removed from ours that, contrary to scripture, we *can't* know him, or it.

Jehovah Fulfills the Function of "Father" and "Son"

Jesus' referring to his "Father" in heaven in the four gospels agrees with Isaiah's hierarchy of father–son relationships that governs all levels of the ladder. But because the Servant–Tyrant Parallelism identifies the suffering Savior as the God of Israel, the King of Zion, we face another paradox that teaches us about the nature of God. Isaiah 53, which falls within this structure, describes the descent phase of the suffering Savior, while Isaiah 52, also within this structure, deals with his ascent as King of Zion when he displaces the king of Babylon. Jehovah's own "suffering" and "humiliation" thus don't stand alone but precede his "salvation" and greater "exaltation" as he ascends further.

Important questions arise when we consider this scenario. First, can we be sure that Jesus is the suffering Savior whom Isaiah identifies as his people's God? And if so why would Jehovah come to earth and take upon himself the form of a servant or vassal? Furthermore, if Jesus is the God of Israel then who is his "Father"? And finally, does Jehovah, who personifies salvation, himself need "salvation"? If so, from what? And isn't Israel's God, who made heaven and earth, already exalted? Why would he need further "exaltation"? We find answers to these questions in Isaiah's concept of a ladder to heaven, because the pattern acted out on ascending levels points us to what happens at the top.

First of all, let us see if Jesus' earthly ministry conforms with Isaiah's concept of a ladder to heaven. Perhaps such a comparison can tell us things we didn't know, things we couldn't very easily have known without Isaiah's literary patterns. People may speculate about what is true, preferring to believe one thing rather than another; hence today's proliferation of sects, affiliations, and denominations. Inspired writings nevertheless contain checks and balances by which we can test the truth of a teaching and weigh it against supporting evidence. An "idea of its time," moreover, must sometimes wait until God thins the veil enough for us to see. We may then discover that *God* is the missing link!

Let us return for a moment to the emperor–vassal paradigm that governs all relationships on the ladder. As King of Zion—as emperor/savior to his people—Jehovah is obliged to deliver those who keep his law and word from any mortal threat. In the "last days" that threat comes principally from the king of Assyria/Babylon, whose goal is to rule the world. Jehovah delivers his people by removing them from the path of destruction in an exodus and granting them permanent inheritances of land. Those who qualify for these blessings are the Zion/Jerusalem category and above. While some qualify for these blessings conditionally, others do so unconditionally, depending on their spiritual level.

The emperor–vassal model governs all divine–human relationships.

Jehovah is not obliged to deliver persons on the Jacob/Israel level, however, unless a proxy savior answers for their loyalties. In that case he will deliver them *for the sake of* the proxy savior, but only for a time. They themselves must enter into a covenant relationship with Jehovah and observe his law and word or they cannot live into the millennial age. As noted, Jehovah delivers persons on the Zion/Jerusalem level according to the terms of his covenant. However, he grants them lands of inheritance only provisionally, *for the sake of* the proxy saviors to whom they rightly belong. They inherit Promised Lands of their own when they attain the son/servant level and become priest-kings and queens.

Jehovah does all these things while performing the role of emperor/savior to his covenant people, mediating such salvation through persons on higher levels who fulfill ministering roles to those lower. And he does these things both in a general sense—as when mortal danger threatens during his people's lifetime—and in a particular sense, in the period immediately preceding his coming to earth. Then, as anciently, the emperor—the "Lord of Hosts"—musters his forces and arranges them in their ranks to meet the threat to his vassal/s. As Jude reminds us, Enoch predicted that "the Lord will come with ten thousands of his *holy ones*" to execute justice on all the ungodly (Jude 1:14–15; emphasis added).

The plot thickens when we regard death itself as the mortal threat. The blessing of physical protection enables God's people to live out their lives, aiding their ascent as they rise to life's challenges. But when death finally overtakes them they are still disadvantaged unless God redeems them physically by restoring them to life. In that case their descent into death, with its "suffering" and "humiliation," would constitute a prelude to ascent, with its "salvation" and "exaltation." Death would be no loss but a gain. The *physical* experience of death and resurrection would then typify the *spiritual* cycle of "ruin" and "rebirth" or descent into chaos and re-creation on a higher level (see Figure 119).

Figure 119 **Parallel Physical and Spiritual Cycles of Descent and Ascent**

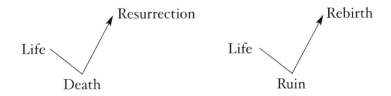

But let us assume God eliminates death for his people. How is he going to do that? In the case of the king of Assyria/Babylon and other tyrants, he mostly uses human agents to thwart the threats they pose to his people. But no human being is capable of eliminating death, not even when empowered by God. Persons in the seraph category may do miracles such as raising the dead, but they can't *abolish* death, which was a consequence of Adam's and Eve's transgression. Only God can do that. However, he can't do it contrary to justice; he works solely within the parameters of justice that he has established for his people. He follows the emperor–vassal model that governs all divine–human relationships.

To complicate things, in our fallen state we are all sometimes transgressors, which would perpetuate the curse of death. Only God, therefore, can eliminate death, not by waving a magic wand, which would destroy justice, but by taking our transgressions on himself—by paying the price of justice on our behalf. The only way he can do that, however, is to assume the role of a *vassal* to an emperor—to serve as a proxy savior who answers for the loyalties of his people. But that would require Israel's God to defer to *his* "Father," a higher God, so to speak, than himself. Also, because paying the price of justice on behalf of others constitutes a descent phase prior to ascent, that implies Jehovah, too, ascends.

Jesus' reference to his "Father" thus conforms with Isaiah's ladder to heaven, which links all spiritual levels in a hierarchy of father–son relationships (see Figure 120). It also agrees with the plurality of the name "God/Gods" (*ĕlōhîm*), and with the title El Elyon—the "Most High God"—whose "Son" Jesus is (Psalm 82:6; Luke 1:32). Jesus' earthly ministry thus constituted his descent phase as a proxy savior, while his ascension to his Father in heaven and coming in glory to reign on the earth are his ascent phase. Because God is a plurality, not only male and female but also Father and Son, Jesus' ascent implies heirship, the same as on lower levels, in which a son assumes the function of his father.

Figure 120   **A Hierarchy of Father–Son Relationships**

The "Most High God" as Father

Jehovah/Jesus as Son

Jehovah/Jesus as Father

Seraphs/Saviors as Sons

Seraphs/Saviors as Fathers

Sons/Servants as Sons

Sons/Servants as Fathers

Zion/Jerusalem as Sons

When Jesus calls himself the "Son of *Man*" while at the same time referring to his "Father" in heaven, the Most High God, he discounts the idea that he was born by a different process than the normal, except that his God was also his Father. Thus, John calls Jesus the "only begotten of the Father"—that is, in the flesh, on the earth, not originally (John 1:14). His mother Mary being "with child *of* the Holy Ghost" doesn't mean that the Holy Ghost was his father but that she conceived by "the power of the Most High God" while under the *influence* of the Holy Ghost (Matthew 1:18, 20; Luke 1:35). Lastly, just as the Most High God had literal "seed" or "offspring" so did Jesus himself (Isaiah 53:10).

Because offspring is the first and most important of all covenant blessings, for Jesus *not* to have had offspring would mean he was cursed. That is precisely the fate of the king of Babylon with whom the King of Zion (Jehovah/Jesus) is juxtaposed in the Servant–Tyrant Parallelism. The archtyrant ends up having no offspring while in the parallel verse the suffering Savior has offspring (Isaiah 14:21; 53:10). Such offspring is *proof* that he is innocent of the crimes for which he is put to death as otherwise no descendants would have survived. Although the suffering Savior serves as Father/emperor to his sons/vassals under the terms of the covenant, only *literal* offspring fulfills this first blessing.

Moreover, if Jesus is now in the "express image" of his Father, as Paul states, and if our destiny is "to be conformed to the image of his Son," then essential aspects of the human life cycle—birth, procreation, death, and resurrection—are also divine (Romans 8:29; Hebrews 1:3) (see Figure 121). Otherwise Jesus would not have been born as a babe—Jehovah would have manifested himself other than as a Man. Instead, Jehovah walked and talked with Abraham like a man because he *was* a Man, destined to be his people's Savior. He spoke with Moses "face to face" because he *had* a face. Isaiah saw him seated on a throne because Jehovah was a King of kings (Genesis 18; Exodus 33:11; Isaiah 6:1).

God doesn't do the kinds of things we do just to make himself more accessible to us. Rather, we grow into his image and likeness by doing the kinds of things *he* does. By serving as saviors in the pattern of Jehovah himself, we become like him. To the degree that we are "holy" and "valiant" as he is, we resemble him. Our highest role model for "loyalty" to God and "compliance" with his will is the Son's loyalty to the Most High God and compliance with his will in redeeming humanity from evil. Isaiah's ladder to heaven is thus not only a ministering model—it is primarily a pathway to divinity. Jesus' earthly ministry was a pure expression of Isaiah's paradigm of spiritual and physical ascent.

Figure 121   **Aspects of Humanity Inherent in Divinity**

Birth $\longrightarrow$ Procreation $\longrightarrow$ Death $\longrightarrow$ Resurrection

The New Testament's anticipation of Jesus' second coming similarly parallels Isaiah's endtime scenario, in which Jehovah comes to earth as *Salvation*. Jesus' name, Yeshua, which means "Salvation," concurs with Isaiah's personification of Jehovah as *salvation*: "You will call his name Jesus, for he will save his people from their sins" (Matthew 1:21); "O Jehovah, be favorable to us; we have waited for you. Be our *arm* from morning to morning, our *salvation* in troubled times" (Isaiah 33:2; emphasis added); "Jehovah has made proclamation to the end of the earth: Tell the Daughter of Zion, 'See, your *Salvation* comes, his reward with him, his work preceding him'" (Isaiah 62:11; emphasis added).

This same God—"Salvation"—saves his people from their sins: "You have burdened me with your sins, wearied me with your iniquities. But it is I myself, *for my own sake*, who blot out your offenses, remembering your sins no more" (Isaiah 43:24–25; emphasis added); "I have removed your offenses like a thick fog, your sins like a cloud of mist. Return to me; *I* have redeemed you" (Isaiah 44:22; emphasis added); "He was pierced for our transgressions, crushed because of our iniquities; the price of our peace he incurred, and with his wounds we are healed. We all like sheep had gone astray, each of us headed his own way; Jehovah brought together on him the iniquity of us all" (Isaiah 53:5–6).

Jehovah/Jesus thus fulfills the roles of both emperor and vassal—of "Father" *and* "Son"—in saving his people from their sins. Only by so doing can he redeem them from death. By freeing them from the effects of transgression, he frees them from the perpetual curse of death, from a fallen physical and spiritual state. On the one hand, he functions as emperor to his vassals, delivering them from death. On the other, he acts as his people's proxy savior, as a vassal *to* an emperor—the Most High God. According to the terms of emperor–vassal relationships, the father/emperor is obliged to deliver not only his loyal son/vassal but also the people of the vassal, all who give him their allegiance.

The Most High God Reverses the Curse of Death

The Most High God, then, must not only save his Son, Jehovah/Jesus, from death but also his Son's people, consistent with a vassal's proxy role. Once death had become a part of the human experience of descent and ascent, only a God—Jehovah—could abolish it by dying and rising from the dead. But how can a God who is the *source* of life—the giver of eternal life—himself die? However, we are talking about physical death, not the death of the spirit that lives on. In that respect, Jehovah's cycle of death and resurrection is the same as ours. His spirit leaves the body but returns to it again afterwards.

Moreover, how can anyone reverse physical death without first being physically dead?

Some people claim that Jesus' crying "My God, my God, why have you forsaken me?" when dying on the cross showed that his God had abandoned him. However, that ignores that Jesus rose from the dead. Jesus' words were the first line of David's prophecy of the sufferings of Israel's Messiah—Psalm 22. It predicts how Messiah would be mocked, smitten with pain and thirst, his hands and feet pierced, and his garments divided. It is a Jewish practice to this day to read just the first line of prayers, many of which are taken from psalms, when there isn't time to read the whole. The latter part of Psalm 22 tells how in the end his God hears the suffering Savior and vindicates him (Psalm 22:22–25).

Can one physically reverse his death without first being dead?

In the pattern of the Davidic Covenant, when the Savior/Son answers for the disloyalties of his people they too become eligible for rising from the dead. The Most High God, then, resurrects them also. God's endtime servant follows the same pattern: "By his *knowledge* [of the terms of the covenant], and by bearing their iniquities, shall my servant, the righteous one, vindicate many" (Isaiah 53:11; emphasis added). That is, he obtains their protection against the archtyrant—the false god *Sea* and *River*—thereby saving them from death. No wonder the Canaanite myth in which Baal conquers *Sea/River* and *Death* appealed to the Israelites! Human nature's desire was, and still is, to attain immortality.

The emperor–vassal model is thus itself evidence of the plurality of God. By using that model to define the relationship between God and his people, Moses, Isaiah, and other prophets made it central to their theology. In providing the pattern of a ladder to heaven, Isaiah points us to the nature of God himself.

What happens on lesser levels is a type of what happens at the top, and what happens at the top is an example for levels below. The picture we end up with is a beautiful tapestry of a celestial Family, with Father and Mother at the head of the family tree and their descendants stretched out in levels below them according to their "loyalty" to God and "compliance" with his will (see Figure 122).

Figure 122   **God—The Head of a Heavenly Family**

The Most High God—Father and Mother

The Most High's Son and Heir—the Savior-God

Seraphs/Saviors—Kings and Queens of God's People

Sons/Servants—"Sons" and "Daughters" in God's Image

Zion/Jerusalem—God's Covenant People Who Ascend

Other Children of God on the Earth—Candidates for Ascent

Paul's saying that we may become co-heirs with Jesus thus makes sense: "Because you are *sons*, God has sent the Spirit of his *Son* into your hearts, crying, 'Abba, *Father*.' So you are no longer a *servant*, but a *son*; and if a son, then an *heir* of God through Christ" (Galatians 4:6–7; emphasis added); "The Spirit testifies with our spirit that we are the *children* of God. And if children, then we are *heirs*—heirs of God and joint-heirs with Christ—if indeed we suffer with him in order that we may also be glorified with him" (Romans 8:16–17; emphasis added). Paul knew Isaiah's concept of sonship *to* God as heirship *of* God and that "suffering" and "humiliation" precede "salvation" and "exaltation."

From observing the cosmos we know God's creation has been in progress billions of years and that it will continue billions of years. And because creation is *cyclical* in nature we can't assume ours is the sole anomaly—that we are the only ones in this unending expansion who, on judgment day, come to a halt. In other words, after encouraging us to pass through the enthralling experience of ascent, after re-creating us again and again until we become like him, God would stop all further ascent for all eternity. That is to say, we wouldn't really become God's *heirs*; heaven would actually be a hell, a place of spiritual and physical "damnation" where any further ascent would be discontinued.

Persons on levels higher than Jacob/Israel who assume a state of mortality on this earth, including Jehovah, show the opposite—that ascent entails more than one lifetime. Just as no-one can become God's heir all at once, so no-one can claim it is impossible to advance beyond our present life, that this is our sole chance for glory or "exaltation." In fact, an essential feature of ascent is that those who have ascended before us are there to assist us and that we, as we ascend, assist those who follow after. If, as Isaiah teaches, we can become sons/heirs and daughters of God as he is the Son/Heir of the Most High God (see Figure 123), then any gospel teaching the contrary falls short of the truth.

Figure 123 **Ascent to Heaven as Heirship of God**

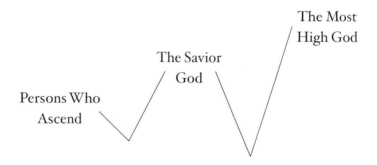

The counsel Jesus gives to "call no man your father *on the earth*, for One is your Father, who is in heaven," sets the highest standard for God's people to follow (Matthew 23:9; emphasis added). Jesus thus encourages us to live a higher law that accepts the Most High God as our Lord (emperor), just as Jesus does. In other words, he invites us to become sons (vassals) and heirs of the Most High God just as he is. That counsel is of the same order as Jesus' saying "Be perfect even as your Father who is in heaven is perfect" (Matthew 5:48). We achieve such perfection by ascending higher and higher until we are *one* with Jesus, who is one with the Father, which oneness defines the nature of God.

Still, the reality of life on earth is that few even live the lesser law let alone the higher law that Jesus and Isaiah reveal. To deliver us from mortal danger, or to merit divine intervention against forces too formidable, we will be served by, or serve as, proxy saviors—"fathers" and "lords"—though we may not address them as such. All who ascend, including "kings" and "queens," "foster fathers" and "nursing mothers," have a Father/Savior—Jehovah/Jesus—who points us to the Most High God, the Eternal Father. Thus, even covenantal terms such as "father" and "son" ultimately yield to familial ones, fulfilling what we always were by virtue of our birthright, and what we also may become.

Jehovah Serves as Both Savior and Sacrificial Victim

Still missing from this picture is the *type* of sacrifice in the past that prefigured the future. Animal sacrifice suited Jehovah's saving of humanity from the effects of transgression not only because no human type could fully portray Jehovah's proxy sacrifice but because animals are innocent. The closest human type of the Son's "loyalty" to his Father and "compliance" with his will—in being willing to die *voluntarily* as a human sacrifice—was Isaac, who was a grown man at the time. Abraham's obedience to God and Isaac's obedience to Abraham was all God required before he "arrested" Isaac's sacrifice, replacing him with a ram. That ram thus became a type of the Father's sacrifice of his Son.

This may help us better understand what animal sacrifice is about. The Passover Lamb, for example, substituted for Israel's firstborn sons during the final "plague" or covenant curse that came on the Egyptians. The death of Egypt's firstborn sons turned the key in getting Israel freed from bondage. The traditional "savior" role of firstborn sons in individual families meant that after their death the entire Egyptian nation was in danger of disintegrating. On the other hand, the Passover Lamb secured Israel's release from covenant curses, including bondage in Egypt and the plague of death. Like King Hezekiah, the lamb served a proxy role in obtaining God's deliverance from mortal danger.

No human type could fully portray Jehovah's proxy sacrifice.

The function of firstborn sons in individual families of the ancient Near East followed a pattern similar to that of vassal kings in emperor–vassal relationships. While a father's duty was to provide for and ensure the protection of his family, the firstborn son—his heir—took on that role when his father was unable (see Figure 124). Joseph in Egypt was the type of a firstborn son who served as a savior to his father's family by saving them from a seven-year famine when his father Jacob was old. But Joseph also became the type of a righteous son who replaced a sibling as heir of the birthright—thus assuming the role of firstborn—when Reuben, Jacob's first son, transgressed and fell from his place.

To comprehend *all* proxy roles it is important to understand the Passover Lamb. As a *type*, it foreshadowed what happens on the highest spiritual levels. First, the lamb stood in for Israel's firstborn sons who inherited the birthright in individual families. Second, the lamb was a yearling of the flock without blemish, symbolizing the prime condition—of "righteousness"—of the one who assumes a proxy role. Third, the lamb was slain by the shedding of blood, which blood, on the doorposts and lintels, caused the angel to "pass over" Israel's firstborn sons when administering the plague of death. The lamb symbolically paid the price of justice on their behalf so they could escape being slain.

Figure 124   **The Place of Firstborn within the Family**

Father

Firstborn

Family

The lamb's performing that proxy function resembles the role later assumed by Davidic kings such as Hezekiah. Although God didn't require Hezekiah to die by the shedding of blood, in other respects his role resembled the Passover Lamb's. In Hezekiah's day the angel dispensed the plague of death on the besieging Assyrians, while people inside the city were "passed over." Because God "arrested" Hezekiah's sacrifice—so that he didn't die like a Passover Lamb—we must look for a proxy role *higher* than Hezekiah's of which the Passover Lamb was a *type*. Because God didn't require a proxy savior to die, but rather delivered him from death, the only eligible role we find is God's own.

From these things we can conclude that Jehovah, when fulfilling the role of a proxy savior to deliver his people from death, would (1) be a firstborn son, as Isaac was to Abraham; (2) be an innocent person in the prime of life; (3) be slain by the shedding of blood; and (4) be a Davidic king. When Jesus said, "Search the scriptures, for . . . they testify of me" (John 5:39), he referred to more than messianic prophecies, many of which, in fact, predict the temporal roles of his endtime servant. Rather, the traditional function of firstborn sons, the sacrifice of unblemished beasts, and the role of ancient proxy saviors—all foreshadowed what Jehovah/Jesus would do in redeeming his people from their sins.

Messiah had to be a son of David because David set a precedent and was thus a *type* of a righteous king performing a proxy role on behalf of his people. God protected those loyal to David so long as David was loyal to God. As a "son" and "firstborn" of God, David served as a "father/savior" to his people (Psalms 2:6–7; 89:26–27). The only one who fulfilled *all* proxy roles, however, was Jehovah/Jesus (see Figure 125). As the Son and Firstborn of his Father, he was slain so that death might pass from all who accepted him as their Father/Savior. He was a Davidic king by virtue of his lineage and because all on or above the son/servant level serve as kings and priests to those to whom they minister.

Figure 125   **Jehovah as Proxy Savior—A Composite of Types**

Firstborn Son

Sacrificial Victim

Davidic King

Jehovah/Jesus as
Suffering Savior

Moses, too, was a king and a priest (Leviticus 8; Deuteronomy 33:4–5), his kingship spiritual, not political. He too fulfilled a proxy role on behalf of God's people, though not at their exodus from Egypt. As a historical precedent—and therefore as a *type*—the Passover Lamb foreshadowed that only God could deliver his people from death and, for that matter, from all covenant curses. Human proxies suffered in order to qualify God's people for deliverance from the effects of transgression. They had to be righteous and innocent themselves. But only Jehovah would be slain like a lamb so that curses could be *reversed*. In Israel's God every type of "deliverance" and "salvation" would be fulfilled.

Saviors on levels below Jehovah could become God's firstborn sons by adoption, as with David (Psalms 2:6–7; 89:26–27). By ascending the ladder they could become God's *heirs*, it being their birthright by virtue of divine lineage. The idea of a "firstborn" was thus something a son/vassal of God could grow into, just as anciently a righteous son grew into that role when he replaced a birthright son who had fallen. Jehovah's role as the Firstborn Son of the Most High God implied that above all he was his Father's heir. But his ascent to his Father's glory would follow his descent into death (see Figure 126). His "salvation" and "exaltation" would be equal to the requisite "suffering" and "humiliation."

Figure 126   **The Son's Descent to Death and Ascent to Glory**

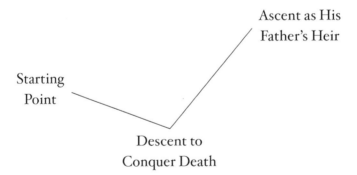

Isaiah saw his descent: "He was despised and disdained by men, a man of grief, accustomed to suffering. . . . Yet he bore our sufferings, endured our griefs, though we thought him stricken, smitten of God, and humbled. . . . He was harassed yet submissive, and opened not his mouth—like a *lamb* led to slaughter. . . . Who can apprize his generation that he was cut off from the land of the living for the crime of my people to whom the blow was due? . . . Jehovah willed to crush him, causing him suffering, that, if he made his life an *offering for guilt*, he might see his offspring and prolong his days, and that the purposes of Jehovah might prosper in his hand" (Isaiah 53:3–4, 7–8, 10; emphasis added).

The Passover Lamb, then, helps us perceive the price of justice Israel's God pays on behalf of his people by suffering death through the shedding of blood—blood typifying the *mortal* state he would assume. As a part of the Egyptian nation, God's people couldn't hope to escape death. By enslaving the Israelites and failing to free them, Pharaoh unwittingly brought covenant curses on the entire nation. That is because those who infringe on the rights of a vassal suffer the curses of the covenant the emperor makes with the vassal. The emperor—God—had made such a covenant with his vassals—Abraham, Isaac, and Jacob—his people's progenitors, promising to deliver them and their posterity.

The curse of bondage the Israelites suffered would nevertheless at first have been a consequence of their transgressions. But there came a time when the curse had served its purpose. The people had been chastened and their cries went up to God. Upon repenting, as shown by their observing the Passover according to God's word, they qualified for deliverance. Like a proxy savior, the Passover Lamb paid the price of justice on their behalf so that God could extend his mercy to them. Moreover, the Passover was to be celebrated throughout all their generations, not merely to memorialize their deliverance from death and bondage but to commemorate Jehovah's sacrifice that transcended time.

The Passover Lamb paid the price of justice on their behalf.

Messiah's death by the shedding of blood at Passover was a fulfillment of the ancient type. Jesus' *voluntary* descent into death coincided with his Father's obligation to deliver his righteous Son. Because the emperor was bound by the terms of the covenant to deliver a loyal vassal from a mortal threat, the only way he could do so now was to resurrect him. In effect, Jesus' resurrection from the dead—his overcoming the curse of death—confirmed his sacrifice as acceptable and completed the cycle of redemptive events. Additionally, the emperor was bound by the terms of the covenant to deliver not only a loyal vassal but also those who were his, for whom the vassal answered to the emperor.

Because humanity had inherited death through Adam's and Eve's transgression, the only way the Most High God could now deliver his Son's people from death was to resurrect them also. Jehovah/Jesus, as Father/Savior of the human family, thus ensured, through the sacrifice of his life and subsequent resurrection, that all would rise again to new life. But they would do so under the terms of God's covenant, according to God's laws of justice and mercy, each on the level he had attained—whether higher or lower—so long as they accepted Jehovah as their Father/Savior. Thus, even sinners could say "You, O Jehovah, are our Father; our Redeemer from Eternity is your name" (Isaiah 63:16).

Other sacrifices, like the Red Heifer, Peace Offering, and Scapegoat, nuance Jehovah's atonement for transgression (see Figure 127). The priestly practice in primitive societies of ritual purification may have served the purpose of hygiene but it also symbolized spiritual purification through Jehovah's sacrifice for sin. In effect, all proxy salvation lacks meaning except in the context of Jehovah's redemptive roles. While human proxies could merit *degrees* of salvation, Israel's God alone, as both priest and sacrifice, could truly "make atonement" for sin and overcome death for all time. Jesus' sacrifice was thus not only retroactive to the Passover but applied to all generations who inherited mortality.

Lastly, the Passover Lamb was the type of a hierarchical order that governs all salvation obtained on the highest levels. While the lamb fulfilled a proxy role on behalf of Israel's firstborn sons, preventing their perishing like Egypt's native firstborns, the role of Israel's firstborns, in turn, was that of saviors of their fathers' families. When Pharaoh saw the similar structure in his own society disintegrate (with himself at the head of his people or "family"), he changed his mind about not letting Israel go. Unlike true proxy saviors, however, the Passover Lamb and other animals were never *voluntary* sacrifices so far as the animal was concerned. That again shows animal sacrifices were only a type.

Figure 127   **Jehovah's Sacrifice for Transgression—**
A Composite of Types

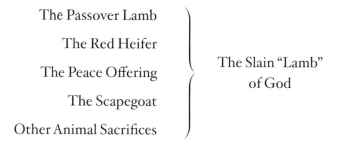

The Passover Lamb

The Red Heifer

The Peace Offering

The Scapegoat

Other Animal Sacrifices

The Slain "Lamb"
of God

In conclusion, the Passover Lamb, by standing in for Israel's firstborn sons, was a type of the Firstborn Son of the Most High God—the "Lamb" of God. Levels below Jehovah who become his "sons" and "firstborns" assume essentially the same role firstborn sons did anciently. Those ancestral heirs of the birthright, who sought the physical preservation of their families, were another type of proxy savior. A big difference between the two is that sons/servants and seraphs/saviors answer to God—their emperor—not just on behalf of their own families but on behalf of all to whom they minister (see Figure

128). The emperor delivers the people of a vassal, whether family or not, *for the sake of* the vassal.

Figure 128   **The Type of a Hierarchy of Proxy Functions**

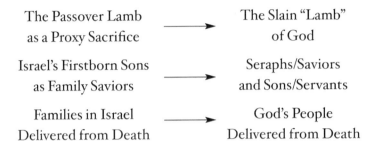

The Passover Lamb
as a Proxy Sacrifice
→
The Slain "Lamb"
of God

Israel's Firstborn Sons
as Family Saviors
→
Seraphs/Saviors
and Sons/Servants

Families in Israel
Delivered from Death
→
God's People
Delivered from Death

The Door Opens beyond Salvation to Exaltation

The roles we have discussed that Israel's God fulfills when redeeming humanity from evil—of Father and Son, Priest and Sacrifice, Savior and Firstborn—all fall in the category of "salvation," that being a gift from God which we receive on condition we "repent" of sins and "return" to him. Repentance, in turn, is the essence of living the *lesser law* that prepares us for "rebirth" as Zion/Jerusalem and redeems us from the Fall and its evil effects. When we attain that sinless and innocent state we are "saved"—in the sense that Isaiah and New Testament writers define "salvation." To that definition, however, Isaiah adds physical "deliverance" from mortal danger, particularly in the "last days."

Should we die in this sinless state, God will resurrect us on the Zion/Jerusalem level. But if we fall away and return to our sins, we must repeat the repentance process until, by living the lesser law, we can retain our state of innocence. As mentioned, an essential part of ascending to Zion/Jerusalem involves passing tests of "loyalty" to God and "compliance" with his will by keeping the terms of his covenant. God's law and word, not the commandments of men, are the requirements God has stipulated in order for us to receive "salvation." His blessings are free, but God requires us to do our part or he can't honor his obligation. It takes both parties to a covenant to make the relationship work.

Even so, getting that far is only the beginning of our spiritual journey. It gets us on the path to heaven but doesn't qualify us for the unconditional blessings God promises his elect. To inherit those blessings, we must live the *higher law* by keeping the terms of the individual covenant God makes with those who ascend. In other words, God's redemption of humanity, through which all may inherit "salvation," opens the door for some to go higher to "exaltation." Without that *foundation*—without God and people meeting the requirements for "salvation"—there can be no attaining "exaltation." In effect, with our salvation from sin God's redemptive role is finished and our own savior roles begin.

> It takes both parties to a covenant to make the relationship work.

As we pass through "ruin" and "rebirth," "suffering" and "salvation," and so forth cyclically as we ascend, God continues to deliver us from trials and evils. Only now more is required of us than before because the higher we ascend the more we resemble Jehovah/Jesus in our descent and ascent phases. On his path to "exaltation" Jesus said he did nothing but what he had seen the Father do (John 5:19). And he asks us to follow him and do the kinds of things he has done. As we do so, obtaining deliverance from covenant curses, we may sit on his throne as he sits on his Father's throne (Revelation 3:21). After fulfilling our earthly ministering roles, we may receive a "crown of glory" (1 Peter 5:4).

Paul informs us that "our present sufferings are not worth comparing with the glory that will be revealed in us," for God's creation "eagerly awaits the materialization of God's *sons*"

(Romans 8:18–19; emphasis added). From Isaiah's perspective, as we ascend the ladder we cyclically pass through "suffering" and "humiliation" until God re-creates us and we are born as his "sons" and "daughters." Just as Jesus suffered before he "entered his glory," so do we—going "from glory to glory" as we ascend—until we resemble him (Luke 24:26; 2 Corinthians 3:18). Inheriting these promises, we become "partakers of the divine nature" and "*heirs* of God" (Romans 8:17; 2 Peter 1:4; emphasis added).

New Testament parallels to Isaiah's theology of ascent to glory or "exaltation" show that while the Son of the Most High God, by serving as Father/Savior, *saves* his people from their sins, the Most High God *exalts* those who become "sons" of God in the image of his Son. That accords with Isaiah's ladder concept, on which higher levels minister to those lower but are themselves ministered to by ones above them (see Figure 129). The Son, however, leads us *to* the Father, as without the Son—without the ability he affords us to rise higher than Jacob/Israel—we can't know or have access to the Father. In short, on the highest levels of the ladder the Most High God, too, fulfills a role as our Father.

The New Testament or New *Covenant* is thus not a departure from the Old Testament but rather takes the old to another level. The new covenant was always God's invitation to Israel. At Mount Sinai, however, Israel turned it down, repudiating its higher law in favor of a lesser. That higher law pertains to a higher covenant, the terms of which prepare one for glory or "exaltation." Israel again gave it up when it rejected Jesus and when the early saints digressed from the purity of his precepts as they came under Greek and Roman influence. Israel will have a final chance to accept it in the "last days," when God's servant and his associates begin their ministry of preparing God's people to meet God.

Figure 129 **Ministering Roles on the Ladder to Heaven**

The Most High God
—Exaltation of Seraphs/Saviors, Sons/Servants

Jehovah, the King of Zion
—Spiritual Salvation of Zion/Jerusalem

Seraphs/Saviors
—Divine Intervention for Zion/Jerusalem

Sons/Servants
—Physical Deliverance of Jacob/Israel

In the light of the suffering Savior's identity as Israel's God, the King of Zion, as well as the opportunity all have to ascend to heaven, it may seem odd that Jesus could be condemned for claiming to be the Son of God (John 19:7). Likewise, the early Christian theology of salvation through Jesus Christ, and of glory with him as *heirs* of God, was considered such damnable doctrine by those in Isaiah's Babylon category that the most abominable persecutions were heaped on those who taught it. And yet, through the very afflictions the early saints suffered they realized their hope. Jesus himself, after a most painful and humiliating death at the hands of his accusers, inherited the glory of his Father.

The king of Babylon's aspiration in the Servant–Tyrant Parallelism to "ascend in the heavens and set my throne above the stars of God"—to become "like the Most High [God]"—was fulfilled in Jehovah/Jesus, Son of the Most High God (Isaiah 14:13–14). Analogical relationships of persons who appear in the Servant–Tyrant Parallelism show that the King of Zion would realize that goal, not the archtyrant. The latter's self-exaltation, in fact, as he attempts to rule the world, leads to his final humiliation. The Son's humiliation, meanwhile, leads to his final exaltation when he comes to reign as King. By following the Son in his ascent to glory, we may become sons of God in his *likeness*.

Jehovah Is Judge, Lawgiver, and King of His People

In spite of all God does for his children—preparing the way for them to be saved from sin and to attain a heavenly glory—not all accept the kindness he shows them. For them there is thus no "salvation" and no "exaltation"; they remain in their fallen state as though he hadn't redeemed them. Through their willful transgressions they repudiate the "suffering" and "humiliation" he has endured for their sake. God therefore deals with them as a divider, severing them from the rest of his children. As a just God, he must impose justice on those who reject his terms for mercy. That scenario acts itself out in full before Jehovah comes to earth as King of Zion, when he separates the righteous and the wicked:

"[He comes] to sift the nations in the sieve of falsehood; with an erring bridle on their jaws [he will try] the peoples. But for you there will be singing, as on the night when a festival commences, and rejoicing of heart, as when men march with flutes [drums and lyres] on their way to the mountain of Jehovah, to the Rock of Israel" (Isaiah 30:28–29); "See, all who are enraged at you will earn shame and disgrace; your adversaries will come to nought, and perish. Should you look for those who contend with you, you will not find them; whoever wars against you will be reduced to nothing. For I, Jehovah your God, hold you by the right hand and say to you, 'Have no fear; I will help you'" (Isaiah 41:11–13).

In the day of their deliverance, when their enemies suffer God's justice, those of Zion/Jerusalem proclaim Jehovah as their "Judge," "Lawgiver," and "King" (Isaiah 33:22). Of course, he was always those things, but now his people realize it through personal experience. They discern that God knows his children better than they know themselves. As they learn to exercise faith in him in their darkest hour, he comes through for them wonderfully in saving them from destruction. God judges them worthy of "deliverance," "rebirth," "inheritance," etc., and their enemies worthy of "punishment," "ruin," "disinheritance," etc., depending on whether or not they accept his acts of infinite love.

> God knows his children better than they know themselves.

In that endtime setting, when the going gets rough, many people show "disloyalty" to their Maker and come out in "rebellion" against him, not realizing that their "loyalty" to God and "compliance" with his will can release them from woes. They would rather "curse God and die" than live to enjoy the glorious new age. They can't bring themselves to take God at his word, to put it to the test and observe the result. They would sooner stand on their pride, confined like prisoners in their self-imposed cells, even at the cost of their salvation. Thus, they can never know the freeing effect of giving up their will for God's. They are to be pitied, the more so because God loved them as he did the rest.

Judicial, legislative, and executive functions of government merge in Jehovah's millennial reign. As Judge, Lawgiver, and King of his people, however, he doesn't ask that they accept him carte blanche. Israel's God *earns* the respect of his people by the things he performs on their behalf and by imposing on them the consequences of their actions. Because he suffers the depths of divine justice to pay for their transgressions, Jehovah is the highest qualified to act as his people's Judge. Because he keeps the terms of the covenant to the limit in order to redeem them, he is competent to be their Lawgiver. And because he serves as their Savior and Exemplar, it is his right to reign as King (see Figure 130).

Figure 130   **Jehovah's Attributes as His People's Ruler**

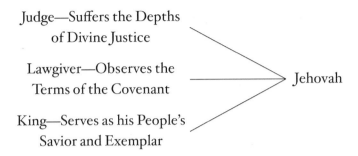

Judge—Suffers the Depths
of Divine Justice

Lawgiver—Observes the
Terms of the Covenant → Jehovah

King—Serves as his People's
Savior and Exemplar

In God's Day of Judgment no one will be able to say "You have no idea what I had to deal with," or "You put me through this while you sat aloof on your heavenly throne," or "I had to sin to survive," and so forth. Israel's God paid the ultimate price to save his people, suffering the pains of all persons everywhere so that they might not suffer under the law of justice if they would repent. He knows firsthand about enduring sorrows and afflictions. Being a just Judge, Jehovah cannot judge under the law of mercy those who refuse to repent. His sacrifice on their behalf is in vain if they still cling to their sins. Their road of return begins with letting go of evil and acknowledging Jehovah as their Savior.

In his role of Lawgiver—when imparting the law of his covenant—Jehovah doesn't resemble the often abusive enforcers of human law in the world at large. He simply says to his creatures "These are the terms under which you will find eternal happiness and everlasting joy." He leaves it to us whether we observe them or not. As Maker of the universe, he reveals its unchangeable laws, including his relationship to us. While he shows us the way to heaven, himself guiding us, lighting our path, and helping us follow, he doesn't stop us from going after the evil one, the Lawbreaker, who is quite happy to lead us down a tortuous road to hell, robbing us of the most precious gift of all—eternal life.

God has to enforce "punishment" on those who transgress, no less than he grants "deliverance" to those who don't. Where strict justice is the rule—because mercy can't apply—persons who persist in wrongdoing must themselves pay the price of their transgressions, enduring "suffering" for all their sins. But even then, after a full consciousness of guilt sears their souls, they still can't obtain "salvation" unless they choose, at some point, to repent. That is the only way out of their predicament. No escape from their plight occurs until they accept Jehovah as their Savior. With that initial act of "loyalty" and "compliance" their return journey begins, including the prospect of ascent to heaven.

Death, too, is an opportunity for spiritual growth.

As his people's King—who decides matters of life and death and governs the affairs of his kingdom—Jehovah is more than equal to the task. Because he knows all about death, dying, and suffering, his permitting death to be a part of the human experience can't be something cruel or vindictive. If we imagine it so, it may be because our faith in God is weak. God sees the big picture and how even an "untimely death" may, in fact, be timely. By now, we have learned that not all "suffering," including death, is a "punishment." Death, too, is an opportunity for spiritual growth, for the dead and living alike—for those dealing with the loss of a loved one who has now begun a new phase of life.

Just as our spiritual lives don't begin on the earth, so our physical lives don't end here. Except in cases of regression beyond the "point of no return," what we acquire in any phase of growth continues with us wherever we go. There may be a time when we can't use every faculty and ability, as in the interval between death and resurrection when our spirits experience other challenges. But being a righteous ruler, God makes provision for us all to enjoy the fruits of ascent. When our trials are over, God "replenishes Zion." Isaiah's words ring true: "Your faithfulness in time [of trial] will prove to be a strength, your wisdom and *knowledge* your salvation" (Isaiah 33:5–6; emphasis added).

Jehovah Provides a Pattern for Life after Death

Because the emperor is bound by the terms of the covenant to deliver only those who are loyal to his vassal, their savior, those who deny Jehovah their Savior merit no deliverance of *any* kind. Unlike the conditions for "salvation," which involve keeping his law and word, people would at least have to acknowledge Jehovah as their Savior in order to be resurrected. While some who pass into the next life may take their time doing so, persons in the Perdition category never do. Of these, therefore, Isaiah says "They are dead, to live no more [or 'not to be brought back to life'], spirits who will not resurrect; you have appointed them to destruction, wiping out all recollection of them" (Isaiah 26:14).

Because God gives his children their agency to choose between good and evil, those who deny God can't escape the curse of death, neither physical nor spiritual death. After passing the "point of no return" in their descent down the ladder, such persons are totally unwilling or unable to make a course correction. Their physical death—when their bodies disintegrate into "dust"—forms the type of their spiritual death in the Pit of Dissolution. Like physical matter, spiritual "matter" can't be destroyed but can be recycled. For them, therefore, not only God's redemption but their creation itself was a waste. The rest of humanity, however, in due time comes forth in the resurrection from the dead.

Types of rising from the dead include Elijah's raising the widow's son and Elisha's raising the son of a woman who had been barren (1 Kings 17:17–22; 2 Kings 4:17–35). Although neither was resurrection in a real sense, each foreshadowed what would itself set a precedent—Jesus' resurrection from the dead. But Jesus' resurrection wasn't just a type—it was the precursor of the physical "rebirth" of the whole mass of humanity. It was God's answer to people's experience of mortality, to aging, dying, and disintegrating into "dust." Jesus' victory over the grave was the signal event of all time, giving hope to billions that they too would live again in the flesh in the flower of their youth.

> Jesus' victory over the grave was the signal event of all time.

While the resurrection of God's people could begin with Jesus' atonement for transgression, death could now also be abolished. Just as death came into the world with Adam's and Eve's transgression in the Garden of Eden, so Jesus' atonement removed the consequences of transgression for the Zion/Jerusalem category and above. God's covenant thus paved the way for his people to banish death itself: by doing away with transgression they could avert covenant curses, and by averting curses death could disappear. God's people, therefore, could achieve immortality *while living on the earth*. The "translated" state Enoch, Elijah, and John attained could become the common lot of humanity.

Because God's law is eternal, it applies equally in this life and the next, except that mortality is the best medium for ascent—for us to repent and return. By confessing Israel's God as their Savior, even those on lower levels can at last be resurrected from the dead, though in a "resurrection of damnation" (John 5:29). God answers for their disloyalties in delivering them from death, which curse was a consequence of Adam's and Eve's transgression, not their own (see Figure

131). But God can't save them from their own sins and their consequences so long as they refuse to repent. Those choose evil, therefore, continue to incur "ruin," "punishment," "suffering," "humiliation," and "disinheritance."

The dynamics of life after death thus operate on similar principles as life here and now. But the change in circumstances requires that those on the Babylon level ascend to Jacob/Israel if they would be resurrected. As noted, in this life the Jacob/Israel category and ones lower ultimately disappear. In the next life, the Babylon category, too, disappears, as accepting Jehovah as one's Savior pertains to the *Jacob/Israel* level. One must at least become a believer and express that minimal degree of loyalty toward him to take advantage of his atonement for transgression. Thus, Jehovah says "To me every knee will bow and every tongue confess [allegiance]"—if not in this life then in the next (Isaiah 45:23).

Figure 131   **Resurrection of Repentant and**
Unrepentant Persons

Zion/Jerusalem—With Residual Effects of Iniquities

Jacob/Israel—With Residual Effects of Sins and Iniquities

Babylon—A Category Pending Resurrection

Like everyone else, those of Babylon who pass into the next life arrive there on the level they were on in this life. Only there they find themselves in the company of their own kind—with others on their level. They remain in that disagreeable society until they recognize that repentance is their only way out. The hell they chose for themselves, with all who live there used to oppressing one another, remains their home until at last they acknowledge Jehovah and turn their lives around. Only then can God commence removing the consequences of their transgressions and lift the curse of a broken law. Then, perhaps, they may still salvage what is left of their lives and ask God to re-create them.

Their wickedness in time has a bearing in eternity.

Because spiritual ascent is an unchanging principle, even people of Zion/Jerusalem who pass into the next life find themselves in a *provisional* category. When Jehovah says "As the new heavens and the new earth which I make will endure before me . . . so will your offspring and name endure" (Isaiah 66:22), he is describing a son/servant category or higher with whom God makes an unconditional covenant. Because ultimately the earth itself ascends to the son/servant level—that being a chief purpose of its creation—the Zion/Jerusalem category must ascend with it or, in the end, go someplace else. The earth's physical transformation keeps pace with the spiritual ascent of its inhabitants.

On that same eternal principle, people of Zion/Jerusalem who pass into the next life may yet ascend from a conditional to an unconditional state of blessedness. By accepting a new set of terms each time we ascend—by embracing a higher law pertaining to a higher covenant—we may eventually rise to still loftier levels. However, there remains the possibility that we may never catch up with peers who have ascended more rapidly than us. Because "time" on lower levels moves much slower than on higher ones, those who ascend advance faster than those who delay ascending. That disparity resembles the rapid orbits of celestial bodies nearer the center of a galaxy relative to ones on the outskirts.

People in the Zion/Jerusalem category—the first level of blessedness—nevertheless receive resurrection *and* "salvation," which involve forgiveness of sins and deliverance from evil. Persons in the son/servant category, on the other hand—

the second level of blessedness—experience resurrection, "salvation," *and* "exaltation." God makes unconditional his individual covenants with them and blesses them with "everlasting inheritances" of thrones and dominions. Lastly, seraphs/saviors—who attain the third level of blessedness—differ from sons/servants in the degree of their "exaltation" (see Figure 132). Like Enoch, Elijah, and John, they may also overcome death in this life if they choose.

Figure 132   **Different States of Existence in the Next Life**

Seraphs/Saviors—Resurrection, "Salvation," Higher "Exaltation"

Sons/Servants—Resurrection, "Salvation," "Exaltation"

Zion/Jerusalem—Resurrection, "Salvation"

Jacob/Israel—Resurrection, No "Salvation"

Babylon—Category Vacated after "Punishment"

Perdition—Spiritual Death in the Pit of Dissolution

Thus, heaven isn't one big place in which all are thrown together who "get through the gate." Rather, the same spiritual levels that exist in this life, or that existed before it, exist there too. Because order and organization characterize the kingdom of God, those in the highest heavens minister to ones less high. How we live our lives on the earth determines which level or "mansion" we inhabit in heaven. What we sow, we reap; as we do to others, so it is done to us. Jesus showed the way in all things that are necessary for us to inherit "eternal life" or "eternal *lives*" (Hebrew *ḥayê ʿôlām*). Everything about Jesus' life exemplified what Isaiah teaches about salvation from sin and ascent to glory.

Those who complete their journey, far beyond the Zion/Jerusalem level, will always call Jehovah their Judge, Lawgiver, and King. He continues to fulfill these functions to all who ascend. Just as his "humiliation" was their humiliation—when they followed his model of descent before ascent—so his "exaltation" is their exaltation, for which glory they praise him for all eternity. In effect, the God of justice we so often observe in the Old Testament is the same God of mercy we find in the New Testament. Persons who ascend comprehend the interplay of justice and mercy on their path to "exaltation." They also realize that the final drama of human history depends on them for its happy ending.

Jehovah Comes in Glory to Reign on the Earth

When Israel's God implements his reign on the earth, "He will not judge by what his eyes see, nor establish proof by what his ears hear. He will judge the poor with *righteousness*, and with equity arbitrate for the lowly in the land; he will smite the earth with the *rod* of his *mouth* and with the *breath* of his *lips* slay the wicked" (Isaiah 11:3–4; emphasis added). That statement has several possible applications: (1) Jehovah will judge his people righteously; (2) he will judge his people through the agency of his servant, who personifies *righteousness*, who is his *rod* and *mouth*, *breath* and *lips*; and (3) he will destroy the wicked with the aid of the archtyrant, who is his other *rod* and *mouth*, *breath* and *lips*.

All meanings apply. Many people confuse Jehovah/Jesus' coming to the earth *in person* with events that occur at his coming. But Isaiah shows that the "day" of Jehovah's coming covers all related events, including the archtyrant's cleansing of the earth and the preparatory work by God's servant and his associates among God's people. The servant's role is to "proclaim liberty to the captives and the opening of the eyes to the bound, to herald the year of Jehovah's favor and *the day of vengeance* of our God" (Isaiah 61:1–2; emphasis added).

The archtyrant's role is to "cause destruction throughout the earth . . . to make the earth a desolation, that sinners may be annihilated from it" (Isaiah 13:5, 9).

Jehovah's coming is not just one event but many.

The archtyrant personifies God's *fire*, *sword*, and *anger* in the following passage: "See, Jehovah comes with *fire*, his chariots like a whirlwind, to retaliate in furious *anger*, to rebuke with conflagrations of *fire*. For with *fire* and with the *sword* will Jehovah execute judgment on all flesh, and those slain by Jehovah will be many" (Isaiah 66:15–16; emphasis added). The archtyrant's wiping out the wicked from the face of the earth is a necessary prelude to Jehovah's coming: "Have you not heard how I ordained this thing long ago, how in days of old I planned it? Now I have brought it to pass. You were destined to demolish defended cities, [turning them] into heaps of rubble" (Isaiah 37:26).

Jehovah's coming means destruction for some and deliverance for others: "From the West men will fear the name of Jehovah, from the rising of the sun his glory. For he will come [upon them] like a hostile *torrent* impelled by the Spirit of Jehovah. But he will come as Redeemer to Zion, to those of Jacob who repent of transgression" (Isaiah 59:19–20; emphasis added); "Behold, Jehovah Omnipotent coming from afar! His *wrath* is kindled, heavy is his *grievance*; his *lips* flow with *indignation*, his *tongue* is like a devouring *fire*" (Isaiah 30:27; emphasis added); "Tell the daughter of Zion, 'See, your *Salvation* comes, his reward with him, his work preceding him'" (Isaiah 62:11; emphasis added).

These and many such prophecies of Isaiah have both a literal and figurative meaning. Isaiah may say one thing on the surface when we read his words literally, but he reveals further details when we catch the figurative implications of his words.

Jehovah's coming, therefore, is not just one event but many. On the one hand, Jehovah cleanses the earth with the aid of the archtyrant—his *fire* and *sword*, *anger* and *wrath*, *grievance* and *indignation*. On the other hand, Jehovah's servant—his *arm* of *righteousness*, *rod* of power, *mouth* and *lips*—prepares those who repent and return to meet God. Lastly, Jehovah comes as *Salvation* to commence his millennial reign of peace on the earth (see Figure 133).

Figure 133   **Jehovah's Coming to the Earth—**
                    A Composite Event

The Archtyrant Cleanses
the Earth

The Servant Prepares   Jehovah's Coming
People to Meet God

Jehovah Comes to Reign
as Salvation

Isaiah nuances Jesus' prediction that his coming would be as a "thief" in the night (Matthew 24:43–44). Isaiah portrays the king of Assyria/Babylon as just such a thief, one who robs a wicked world of its wealth: "I will commission him against a godless nation, appoint him over the people [deserving] of my vengeance, to pillage for plunder, to spoliate for spoil" (Isaiah 10:6). The archtyrant boasts of plundering the world of its riches: "I have done away with the borders of nations, I have ravaged their reserves, I have vastly reduced the inhabitants. I have impounded the wealth of peoples like a nest, and I have gathered up the whole world as one gathers abandoned eggs" (Isaiah 10:13–14).

A type of Jehovah's coming in person was his descent on Mount Sinai: "O that you would rend the heavens and descend, the mountains melting at your presence, as when fire is lit for boiling water, which bubbles over from the heat, to make yourself known to your adversaries, the nations trembling at your presence—As when you performed awesome things unexpected by us: your descent [of old], when the mountains quaked before you!" (Isaiah 64:1–3). As before, God's cloud of glory protects his people from the elements and from their enemies: "Over the whole site of Mount Zion, and over its solemn assembly, Jehovah will form a cloud by day and a mist glowing with fire by night" (Isaiah 4:5).

A type of Jehovah's coming was his descent on Mount Sinai.

All rejoice as Jehovah comes: "O Jehovah, you are my God; I will extol you by praising your name. For with perfect faithfulness you have performed wonders, things planned of old. . . . You were a refuge for the poor, a shelter for the needy in distress, a covert from the downpour and shade from the heat. When the blasts of tyrants beat down like torrents against a wall, or like scorching heat in the desert, you quelled the onslaughts of the heathen: as burning heat by the shade of a cloud, you subdued the power of tyrants. . . . In that day you will say, 'This is our God, whom we expected would save us. This is Jehovah for whom we have waited; let us joyfully celebrate his salvation!'" (Isaiah 25:1, 4, 9).

At his coming, persons on the seraph level see Israel's God in his glory and view the earth from above: "Your eyes will behold the King in his glory and view the expanse of the earth. . . . The insolent people are not to be seen, a nation of incomprehensible speech, whose babbling tongue was unintelligible. Behold Zion, the city of our solemn assemblies; let your eyes rest upon Jerusalem, the abode of peace, an immovable tent, whose stakes will never be uprooted, nor any of its cords severed. . . . May Jehovah cause us to dwell there, a country of rivers and broad streams. . . . None who reside there will say, 'I am ill'; the people who inhabit it will be forgiven their iniquity" (Isaiah 33:17, 19–21, 24).

Jehovah's coming—the Second Coming of Jesus Christ—will be a composite of every former coming of Israel's God, whether to individuals or to his people as a whole. He will descend on Mount Zion and manifest his power as on Mount Sinai, but he will personally converse with his elect as he did with Abraham, Isaac, and Jacob, with Moses and Elijah, with Isaiah and others. Those who experience these divine encounters will know his love for people everywhere. As his grace diffuses through the earth, down the ladder to the least creature, it will inspire many to serve him. Jehovah's peaceable rule and his glorious presence will transform the earth into the wondrous Paradise foretold of old.

Postscript: Paul's saying that the "things of God" can be understood only through the "Spirit of God" (when God's Spirit dwells in us) puts at a disadvantage almost the entire world. How many people, or rather how few, possess that Spirit today. Just as one can't serve two masters, so one can't enjoy the companionship of both the Holy Ghost and what we might call the "unholy ghost." That ungodly spirit, which pervades the lowest levels, constantly assails us through the media, advertising, modern music, and popular culture.

Another disadvantage is that few of us have any grounding in the Old Testament, many having heard only childhood stories of Bible characters whose lives inspired us to "be good." In fact, Jews are more acquainted with the Talmud, Christians with the New Testament, and Moslems with the Kor'an than with the foundation on which these build. Yet, without that foundation it is impossible to "put it all together." We build tall superstructures on foundations that won't support us when the storms of the "last days" start raging.

Considering that our lives consist of just a few years spent in our community—in our part of the country, in our nation, on this continent, on this planet, in this universe, in our galaxy, in our cosmos—we, from that perspective, may not seem very significant. But it is precisely for us that all this exists. If we would exercise the same curiosity in studying the scriptures as we do our immediate environment, we would see that the more we explore what God is trying to tell us, the more rewarding are the things we discover.

If, for a moment, we could borrow God's perspective and see how our lives fit into *his* scheme of things, it would open our minds to the limitless potentialities he has created for us. But God may not let us see things like that right now, the same as he doesn't take away our struggles of just getting through life. That would be too easy; it would spoil the whole reason why we are here. Out of love for us, he lets us gather our own intelligence as we wade through this world's "virtual reality," guided by whichever spirit we choose.

If we wish to make God the foundation of our lives, then ought we not to accept him at his *entire* word, including the Old Testament, not just the bits and pieces we like? When Israel's God and his forerunner arrive on the scene, will we be ready to receive *more* of what God has to say when we haven't accepted all he has already given us? If how much "mass" we accumulate during our earthly sojourn is going to have an eternal impact, then where do we want to end up? Do we want to be an asteroid, a moon, a planet, or a star?

9

ASCENDING
THE LADDER TO HEAVEN

Ascent to heaven occurs through keeping the terms of God's covenant—by observing his law and word. Sacred architecture parallels three spiritual levels people may attain in this life. Phases of spiritual ascent parallel phases of physical development. Man-made traditions prevent us from ascending to heaven. Pure religion aids our entering into God's presence.

Ascending a ladder to heaven may seem like a fantasy but it represents life's highest reality. It is the reason we were born on this earth—a divine design of such sweeping scope it lifts our spirits to the loftiest realms of possibility yet answers the lowest aspirations of even the least creature. The prophet Isaiah, who sets forth this otherworldly system of ministering and being ministered to, surpasses all other prophetic writers in presenting a theology whose ultimate goal is to ascend to God and be like him. Yet, sadly, Isaiah is also the prophet who has come under the fiercest attack, from both dissenters in his own day and academics in ours who have attempted to explain his message away.

A problem people have with Isaiah's writings is their almost overwhelming magnitude—both their sheer volume (sixty-six chapters) and their awesome poignancy. These writings combine the most eloquent phraseology of language with the most profound concepts and ideas. Isaiah ranges the whole field of human expression, from cutting, unrelenting satire to elevated and sublime sentiment; from no-holds-barred scolding to tender appeals to remember God; from telling it like it is to hiding the meaning in allegory. No wonder scholars have felt impelled to dissect the Book of Isaiah into many pieces so they can view them individually and try to grapple with and make sense of everything.

Scholars have struggled with the book's three distinct historical settings—preexilic, exilic, and postexilic—that is, Israel before, during, and after its exile from the Promised Land. In the light of literary structures that span the length and breadth of the book, however, these three settings form a linear structure modeled on the ancient Egyptian narrative pattern of Trouble at Home, Exile Abroad, and Happy Homecoming. In that pattern, the hero of the story finds his life in danger in his homeland and is forced to flee abroad among a strange people. There, he grows to maturity and learns who he is. At that point, he desires to return home, is welcomed back, and is appointed to high office.

Like the Prodigal Son, God's people come to themselves.

Isaiah adapts this pattern for his own prophetic purpose: when God's people turn to evil, God removes them from the Promised Land and disperses them among the nations of the world. The experience of exile is a just "punishment"—a consequence of wickedness—but also a chance to "grow up." Like the Prodigal Son, when God's people come to themselves and realize who they are, God welcomes them back; he appoints them as kings and priests—as his vassals—ruling over "everlasting inheritances" in his kingdom. A type of such a "descent before ascent" was Jacob, ancestor of the nation of Israel, who fled to Haran to escape the wrath of Esau, but who returned in glory to the Promised Land.

This threefold structure coincides with a pervading nationalism in the first part of the book, universalism in the second part, and individualism in the third part. In other words, Israel *as a nation* rejects God (Isaiah 1–39); Israel in exile becomes a *universal* entity (Isaiah 40–54); and *individuals* among those in exile respond to the endtime mission of God's servant and return home to the Promised Land (Isaiah 55–66). These repentant persons renew their allegiance to God and form the new nation of his people that survives into the millennial age— Zion/Jerusalem. Their return "pilgrimage" to the place Zion or Jerusalem in the new exodus is a physical manifestation of their spiritual "ascent."

Another linear structure that Isaiah uses adapts the themes of Threat, War, Victory, and Feast from the Baal myth in Ugaritic literature. Isaiah transforms these into the prophetic themes of Apostasy, Judgment, Restoration, and Salvation. That four-part structure similarly spans the Book of Isaiah but appears also in mini-cycles in its first few chapters. It reflects the cycle of events in Israel's history as a whole as well as in the lives of individuals. Lastly, three tests of loyalty God's people must pass are patterned after Mesopotamian themes. They and other structures, including Isaiah's Seven-Part Structure, show that the Book of Isaiah is a *single* composition, the work of one author (see Figure 134).

Another question scholars raise is Isaiah's naming of Cyrus, the Persian king who lived over a century and a half *after* Isaiah.

How could Isaiah have known of him that far in advance? That portion of the book, scholars conclude, could not have been written by Isaiah. And so they divide his writings into parts they believe were written at different times by different authors. But Isaiah's use of the name "Cyrus" isn't purely historical but follows his pattern of naming persons who set *precedents* and who therefore serves as *types* of the "last days." Isaiah's Seven-Part Structure combines the type of Cyrus with those of Moses, David, and others to form *composites* of types of God's endtime servant.

Figure 134   **Isaiah's Multiple Literary Structures**

Trouble at Home, Exile Abroad,
    Happy Homecoming

Apostasy, Judgment, Restoration,
    Salvation

Three Tests of Loyalty of   The Work of
    God's People   One Author

Isaiah's Seven-Part Structure

The Servant–Tyrant Parallelism

Other Linear and Synchronous
    Structures

I believe scholars' problem is whether Isaiah has actually seen the future, not whether he names anyone. You can account for differences in writing style—as, for instance, between Isaiah's early oracles, which were spoken, and his later discourses, which were written—by the fact that later in his life he ascended to the seraph level and had a vision of the end from the beginning. He then "retired" as a speaking prophet but continued to write. The central question at issue is one's belief system: do we really believe in God and prophets? Intellectual pride, on the other hand, can't admit that someone could know more than what the current scholarly position allows and which it jealously guards.

Those who love the truth will search until they find it.

In fact, there exist many ways we can interpret the writings of Isaiah. He seems to have included something for everyone, something adapted for every spiritual category of people. Many love Isaiah's poetic style and read his words mainly for that. Others are content to enjoy Handel's *Messiah* or hear a sermon citing Isaiah's messianic prophecies. Some consider Isaiah's writings as they do ancient myth—fascinating but not necessarily relevant to our day. Yes, there is plenty for people to overlook and explain away. But there is also much on which the believer can build. Isaiah's literary talents challenge us to rise to the occasion—they make us either come to terms with hard truths or deny them.

More than anything, Isaiah's teachings have the power to change lives, to awaken souls to an awareness of their infinite worth. Those who love the truth will search until they find it, but those who hate it will defend their turf at all costs even if it means denying the Word of God. Isaiah's writings can blind those who are closed-minded and enlighten those whose minds are open. Some, on reading Isaiah, will say, "So what?" while others will esteem his words as invaluable, as the words of eternal life. When we are out of harmony with God we turn away from the very light to which those who love God gravitate. Isaiah's writings have that effect on people, separating the righteous from the wicked.

All Prophecies of the "Last Days" Are Fulfilled

Assuming we understood the essence of Isaiah's message, wouldn't we want to know where we might fit into his picture of endtime events? Isaiah's use of ancient history as an allegory of the "last days" helps us realize how realistic those events will be. What happened in the past affected real people who belonged to real nations, just as the future will affect us. Isaiah's drawing on past events *selectively*—by painting only a partial panorama of former events—allows him to accurately describe two time frames. Although history repeats itself, it never does so exactly but involves new players who participate in new versions of old events. Still, the new events will be as real as in the past.

By giving us a preview of things now rapidly approaching, Isaiah does us a service. Wouldn't we rather take part in what we know something about than be caught unawares in a rash of happenings, blown about like a reed in the wind? In character with his seraph status—having seen far into the future to the end of time—Isaiah wrote for the purpose of helping God's people not simply to avoid calamity but to participate in God's redemption of humanity. When we see events occurring in our day that resemble Isaiah's scenario, therefore, we can take comfort in the fact that we know beforehand what they are leading up to. We can look past the evil, knowing that the good will win in the end.

Isaiah must have known that by revealing the nature of Israel's God and his atonement it would cost him his life. "The Ascension of Isaiah" describes his enemies putting him to death by sawing him in half—just as in our day scholars have cut up his writings into parts. Alluding to published books, Isaiah says "All tables [or 'tablets/books'] are filled with vomit" (Isaiah 28:8). Half-digested truths are served up to eat! Of our time as well as his own, therefore, Isaiah says "Bind up the testimony; seal the law among my disciples! I will wait for Jehovah, who hides his face from the house of Jacob, and expect him" (Isaiah 8:16–17). Few would learn life's purpose while many would unwittingly perish.

Not just Isaiah but all ancient prophets looked forward to the time when wickedness would be done away and righteousness reign. Men of God prophesied of the "last days" in particular, predicting the key events that precede the millennial age (see Figure 135). Isaiah captured the *totality* of these portentous events, preserving a balance between their positive and negative aspects. There isn't a hint of fantasy in what he foretells of the future, yet he is without equal in portraying God's glorious promises to his elect. Isaiah makes the point that God's blessings follow his people's wading through tribulations. He thus lets us know that tribulations have a purpose; they are not an end in themselves.

Figure 135   **An Endtime Fulfillment of Diverse Prophecies**

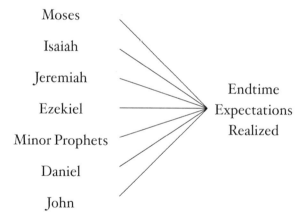

Just as the "last days" have been a focal point of all prophecy, so their divinely inspired predictions will all be fulfilled. At the end of the world God's people realize every dream and vision that has been revealed of God. There was never a time before it, nor may there be one after it, that will see God's plan so completely accomplished. In one brief historic interval all history comes together, concluding a key phase in humanity's climb upward, rewarding the faith of many but shattering the hopes of multitudes. Jehovah will remove wickedness from the world, leaving only righteousness to reside in its place. He will reign among us, his presence gracing the earth, never to separate from us again.

As an integral part of this endtime scenario, the archtyrant will mastermind the unimaginable, causing chaos on such a scale as to change of face of the earth. Even God will seem to lend him support as he performs his will in erasing evil. When the iniquity of the world's inhabitants is "full"—when their dysfunctions become so deep-rooted that the rising generation has no hope of healing—then God will permit the Antichrist to make an end of them. After people have received the preaching of the "good news" as if it were bad news, after they have tortured and murdered its messengers, they will come face to face with the Destroyer. The "last days" of their lives will be their worst-case scenario.

The king of Assyria/Babylon's destructive impact on the world, although immense, will pale in significance next to the restorative effect of God's servant and his seraph-associates. God will turn on the lights for those who repent of wrongdoing by imbuing with power thousands of his "holy" and "valiant" ones. As they perform their labors on the model of Jesus, Moses, and Elijah, they meet with comparable results. The brilliant dawn of the millennial age that follows the dark night of the most horrific nightmare will seem like a joyful awakening from sleep. Old things will be done away and everything become new. People will lay aside their corruptible mortal garment for one of immortal beauty.

Ascending the Ladder Is a Step-by-Step Process

Just as we grow up physically, so we must grow up spiritually to reach our full stature. If we ascend only partway up the ladder, it is as though we die in our youth, never to realize living life to the fullest. Of course, we will always have growing pains, awkward stages, and changes in vital functions; those are a normal part of our development as we grow into our role of co-creators with God. We will also experience spiritual injuries from knowingly or unknowingly transgressing God's law. Yet there is a way to be healed, even without leaving scars. But when spiritual atrophy sets in, when men lose their will and give up the fight, then their light goes out and the gloomy grave beckons them enter.

Four physical phases we pass through—childhood, adolescence, adulthood, and mature age—parallel four spiritual phases of ascent, namely Jacob/Israel, Zion/Jerusalem, sons/servants, and seraphs/saviors (see Figure 136). Children play, adolescents learn, adults raise families, and the aged contribute to the security of their posterity. One can't simply skip from one stage to the next but must complete each in turn. As we round out one phase we are prepared to proceed to the next. Some, however, continue through life content just to play, to act adolescent, to abandon the family, or to squander their inheritance. These make life harder for the rest, but they also provide greater opportunities for growth.

Figure 136   **Parallel Physical and Spiritual
Phases of Development**

Childhood ⟶	Jacob/Israel
Adolescence ⟶	Zion/Jerusalem
Adulthood ⟶	Sons/Servants
Mature Age ⟶	Seraphs/Saviors

Jacob/Israel resembles childhood because our spiritual attributes are still embryonic and undeveloped. Childish interests and youthful fancies occupy our thoughts and determine our behavior, overshadowing our understanding of life. We depend on adults for our knowledge of the outside world, accepting implicitly their authority and seniority. Zion/Jerusalem resembles adolescence because it is the soul's first awakening to an awareness of its power to act independent of others, to take responsibility for its own actions and decisions. Learning may be largely by trial and error as we begin to experiment with good and evil. The peer group grows in importance for gaining a sense of self-identity.

Sons/servants compare with adults who take independence to the next level by getting married and raising children of their own. Their commitment to each other and to their offspring is complete. Their lives assume the added dimension of service as they minister unselfishly to one another. Seraphs/saviors are like those of advanced age, whose wealth and experience serve the younger generation that appeals to them for help. Their wisdom and counsel lend balance and stability to the extended family. The inheritance they leave behind forms an assurance of future security. These phases of development reinforce the idea that what is physical is a type of what is spiritual—both follow the same pattern.

Wherever we now find ourselves on the ladder, that is our best chance for ascent. In that, we may trust our Maker who put us there. Just as we can't tell which came first, the chicken or the egg, so we can't pinpoint the origins of life, only where we are here and now. Our challenge is to cheerfully accept the hand life has dealt us, to make the most of this fleeting moment in time. From what we know of God's loving dealings with his children, we may assume that our circumstances in life are the most suited for our growth or we wouldn't be here. Wishing things were otherwise diverts our attention from the task at hand, from the opportunity we have to improve our condition and that of others.

Our circumstances in life are the most suited for our growth.

The many examples of ascent we find in the Bible can encourage us in our own attempts to do the same. Persons whom Isaiah names, such as Abraham, Moses, Hezekiah, or himself, act as types of the future, but they are also heroes and saints who did what we all can do. They aren't people to put on a pedestal but real-life examples we can follow. Their blessings can be our blessings and their everlasting happiness ours too. Israel's God shows his love for us not only in the gift of himself, in atoning for our sins, but also in the lives of all who serve him by serving his people. The Elijah who ascended to heaven wasn't always imbued with divine power. God blessed him as he wants to bless each of us.

Concerns about our rank in God's kingdom, in society, or in a church, synagogue, or mosque are meaningless when we realize that we advance spiritually only as fast as God re-creates us. As everyone runs his or her own race, envy of each other is in vain. Those who ascend will likely always be ahead of those who haven't yet ascended, but they will be behind others who have ascended ahead of them. Just as today we are the sum total of our prior experience, both in this life and previous to it, so tomorrow, by the grace of God, we will be what we chose to be. Positions we hold may assist our ascent, but they can also lead to descent, depending on whom we serve—God or ourselves.

The Hopi tribe of Native Americans teaches that if we advance as far as we possibly can in this life, then we won't have to wade through three more worlds after this one to get to where we are going. In Isaiah's context of a ladder to heaven, that means if we ascend from our starting point, Jacob/Israel, to the level of seraphim (three levels), we will arrive at the highest goal God has set for us on this earth—the third level of blessedness (see Figure 137). As noted, the kabbalist model of the Tree of Life similarly proposes that God created us four levels below his own. By ascending three levels, therefore, we reach the level next to God's. On the two highest, God manifests himself to us directly.

By calling each rung on the ladder by a different name, Isaiah teaches that each time we ascend we assume a new identity—like Abram's change of name to Abraham and Jacob's to Israel. The meanings of the names Abraham ("Father of Many Nations") and Israel ("Ruling with God") suggest that a new name implies a new appointment from God to fulfill a particular *role*. The names God gives aren't arbitrary but reflect a function or office. They express what its recipient does on that level in order to ascend to the next. Descriptive names Isaiah uses, such as "watchmen" for seraphs, similarly convey that idea. Isaiah's name ("Jehovah Will Save") expresses his mission of heralding Salvation.

Figure 137   **Three Possible Levels of Ascent in This Life**

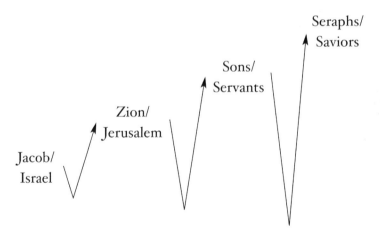

Just as a child has little idea of what it is to be an adult—until he or she *becomes* an adult and does the things adults do—so we have only a shallow idea of what it means to be a "son" or "daughter" of God until we meet his requirements and he re-creates us as such. When the Israelites declared at Mount Sinai "We will do and we will hear" (*na'ǎseh wĕnišmā'*), they expressed that spiritual principle—with the doing comes the understanding (Exodus 24:7). In other words, it isn't realistic to expect that we can know what it means to ascend a level on the ladder until we have actually kept the terms of God's covenant on that level. Only after we *live* God's law and word do we fully learn their intent.

A guiding principle the Israelites recognized was faith in God. By exercising faith—by being willing to put God's terms to the test—they were able to ascend the ladder. Noah's faith led him to build an ark when no rain had yet fallen on the earth. David's faith caused him to declare that God would deliver Goliath into his hand. Elijah's faith prompted him to proclaim a contest with the prophets of Baal to prove who was God. Esther's faith caused her to call a fast and come in to the king to plead for her people. Each act of faith—through which these persons passed tests of "loyalty" to God and "compliance" with his will—crowned multiple acts of faith by one who kept God's law and word.

The Tabernacle Is a Type of Ladder to Heaven

Architectural models of a ladder to heaven, such as the Tabernacle in the wilderness and the temple in Jerusalem, illustrate ascent. Three enclosures, one inside the other, established boundaries within which persons eligible could enter (see Figure 138). The temple's outer court paralleled Jacob/Israel, the inner court, Zion/Jerusalem, and the "sanctuary," sons/servants. A "Holy of Holies" housed the Ark of the Covenant, on which cherubim—the equivalent of seraphim—surrounded Jehovah's throne. From the Ark, Jehovah spoke with Moses—who was himself on the seraph level—face to face. Priests entered the sanctuary, Levites the inner court, and the people of Israel the outer court.

Jehovah chose the Levites to fulfill the "savior" role of firstborn sons when they rallied to his side following Israel's worship of the Golden Calf (Exodus 32:26–29). Their lives were "consecrated" to God in place of the firstborn sons of his people to "make atonement" for Israel and to perform the service of the tabernacle (Numbers 3:5–13; 8:5–19). But God didn't intend that to be permanent—it was an interim arrangement until his people lived up to *their* divine calling. No office, however sacred, has significance of itself, only as it serves God's people and the one who fulfills it. King Solomon, for example, replaced the Levite, Abiathar, with a non-Levite, Zadok, to officiate as priest (1 Kings 2:35).

Figure 138   **Architectural Model of a Ladder to Heaven**

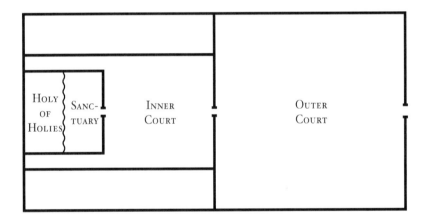

As with animal sacrifice, one could get so involved with the ritual of the sanctuary as to forget what it symbolized. Ritual then became an end in itself, with unhappy results. Fire consumed Nadab and Abihu, the sons of Aaron, when their office as priests became more important than their service on behalf of God's people (Leviticus 10:1–3). By the end of the Second Temple Period, it wasn't uncommon for a high priest to die in Jehovah's presence in the Holy of Holies while making atonement for the people. The priest's spiritual level didn't match his ecclesiastical calling—as if one could see God and live without ascending the ladder, or "make atonement" after rejecting the Lamb of God.

The curtain hanging before the Ark of the Covenant symbolized the "gate of heaven." Through that veil, a person physically entered God's presence. In his vision of the ladder to heaven, Jacob saw God at the gate, not to keep him out but to invite him in. As with Jacob, father of the people of Israel, so with his descendants—all who make themselves eligible, not only Moses. As the seventy elders discovered on the Mount, no earthly curtain, inside or outside the tabernacle, could keep those who ascend from seeing God. The purpose of a ladder is to lead to the top. In emperor–vassal relationships, the emperor's sons/ vassals entered his presence at set times to renew their covenants with the emperor.

> The purpose of a ladder to heaven is to lead to the top.

From another perspective, therefore, ascending the ladder to "heaven" doesn't mean only entering heaven itself but rather God's presence, whether in this life or the next. Those who qualify for that privilege here qualify for it there. Ultimately, because God re-creates the earth as it ascends the ladder to keep pace with its occupants, the earth itself becomes "heaven." Jehovah's coming to reign on the earth in the millennial age, and the earth's regeneration to a new Paradise, commence that process. Even then, however, only sons/servants and levels higher see God. Although God's people "will inherit the earth forever" and "[their] eyes see the Master," only upper categories do so (Isaiah 30:20; 60:21).

At the moment Jesus died the veil of the temple rent in two, from top to bottom, in an earthquake (Matthew 27:50–51). His atonement for transgression opened the door for all who are eligible to enter God's presence, not just those officiating. His plan of redemption provided equal opportunity for everyone to pass through the veil. Just as Israel's God performed the roles of emperor and vassal to redeem his people from death, so he served as priest and firstborn to make atonement for the human family, and as a proxy sacrifice to pay the price of justice for all. Isaiah sums it up: "O Jehovah, you have brought about our peace; even all that we have accomplished you have done for us" (Isaiah 26:12).

The Great Pyramid of Gizeh provides another architectural model of ascending levels (see Figure 139). If we accept the pivot point where one goes either up or down a passage as the equivalent of Jacob/Israel, then the pyramid's lowest chamber corresponds with Babylon. Called the "Chamber of Chaos," that upside-down room lies below ground level. A bottomless fissure extending under that chamber corresponds with Perdition. But if one ascends at the pivot point, then the first room one comes to is the "Queen's Chamber," beautifully lined with white limestone. Well above ground level and symbolizing purity, it corresponds with Zion/Jerusalem, those whom God has forgiven their sins.

Not stopping there but continuing on, one enters a lofty gallery leading upward, resembling a "Hall of Fame." That gallery reflects the attributes of holiness and valor of those who ascend to the son/servant level, who model themselves on the Holy and Valiant One of Israel. Just before the end of that passage one encounters a great step that must be climbed before the floor levels out leading to the "King's Chamber." The stonework in and around this majestic room is of granite. The great step corresponds with a final test a candidate must pass before he ascends to the son/servant level. In King Hezekiah's case that test coincided with the dual trial of his illness and the Assyrian siege of Jerusalem.

At the top of the great step one comes to an antechamber that is entered by passing through a small, low passage and then a "veil," also of stone, symbolizing the sacredness of that space and the humility of the one who enters. The antechamber is situated directly above the Chamber of Chaos that lies below ground level, signifying the candidate's overcoming the powers of chaos. Having risen above the evils of Babylon—its worldliness, injustices, lust, lies, pride, and ambition—one is now ready to enter into the presence of God. A final low passage suggests obeisance before God, the King, as one emerges into his chamber. Turning right, one sees an open sarcophagus, representing the risen Lord.

Figure 139   **The Great Pyramid of Gizeh**

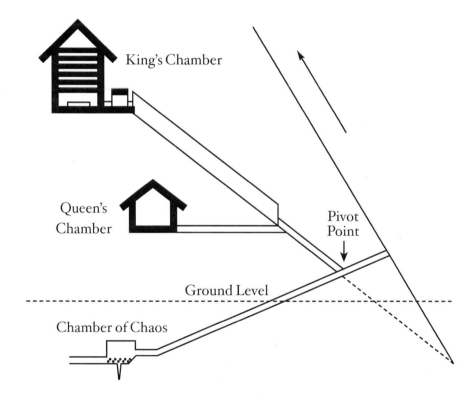

That is one way we can understand the Great Pyramid's architecture. Others see it as a timeline that foretells the end of the world from the beginning. The pyramid's passages and chambers, however, parallel Isaiah's ladder to heaven and its requirements for ascent. Of course, God uses any means he chooses to reveal truth, ancient or modern, Israelite or non-Israelite, religious or secular. No one has a monopoly on truth, and he invites *all* to return to him. A person sees God at the son/servant level no matter what nationality he belongs to. In Egyptian ascension texts one is led into the presence of the king by those who minister about his throne—the equivalent of Isaiah's seraphim (Isaiah 6:1–6).

Additional architectural models exist that symbolize a ladder to heaven. Threads of truth survive from ancient times in legend and tradition, some written down, others by word of mouth; some in their purity, others corrupted. Most reliable are diverse sources that substantiate each other, such as a theology of ascent in prophetic literature *and* in sacred architecture, though they may overturn the popular notions of our day. We can recognize the truth of something by its liberating effect on the human spirit. God's Spirit testifies to us that it is true. Lesser truths, especially when accepted as the *only* truths, lead to spiritual bondage and intellectual poverty, to outward posturing and inward emptiness.

Human Traditions Impact the Worship of God

I am sure we would rather learn all we can before passing into the next life, and would rather help others ascend than unwittingly oppose them. Anger and rage, Isaiah teaches, are a sign of those who spurn God's law and are "a law unto themselves." God says "Those who gather into mobs are not of me" (Isaiah 54:15). To assume that killing others in God's name lands their souls in Paradise, or that those not of their faith will go to Hell because they don't believe as they do, marks the lowest spiritual levels. Such a Hell and such a Paradise are myth, a moldering relic remaining from a dark age. A God of love can never be partial in judgment, but men grow callous when puffed up in pride.

The fact that God has given humanity its agency to *choose*, and has made that, above all other considerations, an inherent part of his plan in saving and exalting his children, means that he expects us to permit others the same privilege. Consequently, persons or institutions that destroy or diminish people's freedom to act within the righteous rule of law are in opposition to God. Their rationale for justifying themselves, whether political or religious, is clearly *antichrist*, though they may believe "they do God a service" by denying others the rights they appropriate to themselves. In his Day of Judgment, God will expose as false the authority they claim in support of their unrighteous dominion.

Isaiah's ladder to heaven puts every soul on an equal footing.

Those who condemn others for what are not transgressions are themselves transgressors. Isaiah's ladder cuts across false assumptions and puts every soul on an equal footing. Its step-by-step process is not Isaiah's innovation but God's. Could God have devised a nobler plan for his children to attain eternal happiness? Could they appreciate the joys of heaven without passing through sorrows on earth? Could they know good from evil without having experience with both? Surely, descent before ascent on a ladder to heaven is a perfect paradigm for living "happily ever after." God waits for his people at the top, sending helpers all the way down. He himself came down to pave their path to the top.

A prominent seat in the synagogue won't ensure our salvation—living God's law will. Honoring him with our lips or "paying penance" won't gain us a place at God's right hand, but whether his word has a place in our hearts—whether we "know" him and he "knows" us. God's measure of righteousness is not how many beads we count but how willing we are to serve others. With God, repenting of wrongs counts more than defending a religious doctrine: "Wash yourselves clean: remove your wicked deeds from before my eyes; cease to do evil. Learn to do good: demand justice, stand up for the oppressed; plead the cause of the fatherless, appeal on behalf of the widow" (Isaiah 1:16–17).

Traditional Christianity has deviated from the teachings of Jesus no less than traditional Judaism has from the Law of Moses. While pious people in these religions live God's precepts the best they know how—forming the backbone of their sects— their institutions have no power to take one through heaven's gate. What person practicing modern Judaism has ascended to see God as the elders of Israel did with Moses on the mount? Who, by observing the current code of Christianity, has seen Jesus transfigured, has seen Israel's God in his glory, as did Jesus' three disciples? If what is missing from this scenario isn't restored, things will go on as they are and Jehovah/Jesus cannot come.

God *must* intervene if things are to change. From the patterns of the past we know it requires one like Moses to again open the heavens. Then, people will discern much of modern religion for what it is—a substitution of man-made precepts for divine ones, making God's word ineffectual: "My Lord says, 'Because these people approach me with the mouth and pay me homage with their lips, while their heart remains far from me—their piety toward me consisting of commandments of men learned by rote—therefore it is that I will again astound these people with wonder upon wonder, rendering void the knowledge of their sages, the intelligence of their wise men insignificant'" (Isaiah 29:13–14).

God has stipulated that we should not add to or take away from his Word: "Do not add to the word that I command you, nor take away from it, but keep the commandments of

Jehovah your God which I have given you" (Deuteronomy 4:2; 12:32). John practically repeated Moses' warning, applying it to the prophecy *he* received (Revelation 22:18–19). Instances of adding to and taking away from God's law and word in religious observance are too numerous to mention. They make "busy work" for those who *add*; they create a spiritual vacuum for those who *take away*. The source of the problem is a deference to man and his ideas instead of to God, turning children of God into pious pawns.

God must intervene if conditions are going to change.

Religious practices can thus *prevent* us from keeping the terms of God's covenant. By teaching manmade precepts as the Word of God, clerics may lend an aura of holiness to what is profane. Such are "lighters of fires, who illuminate with mere sparks" (Isaiah 50:11). God's servant and his associates, therefore, must "open eyes that are blind," must "herald salvation" anew (Isaiah 42:7; 52:7). Their teaching pure religion will make Jehovah's coming possible. In a spiritual desert they will "prepare the way of Jehovah." In a doctrinal wilderness they will "pave a straight highway for our God," declaring "Behold your God!" empowering many to "ascend as on eagles' wings" (Isaiah 40:3, 9, 31).

In the light of Isaiah's Seven-Part Structure and other literary devices, Isaiah's writings are a key witness of the New Testament teachings of "salvation" from sin and "exaltation" to glory, as noted. But they also reconcile Judaism and Christianity in their purest forms. As both religions originated with the same God, there *has* to be a point where they fully interface, where the Old and New Testaments are in full agreement. Isaiah is such a meeting point and he shows where they concur (see Figure 140). There may be things each faith has not known about the other, or about itself, but that only means there is more to learn. If the "proof is in the pudding," then we are at liberty to put Isaiah to the test.

Figure 140   **A Point of Origin of Judaism and Christianity**

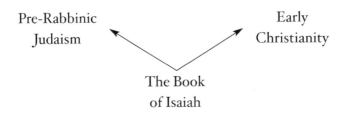

For Christians to deny the prophecies of the Old Testament differs little from Jews denying the teachings of Jesus. *Both* are the Word of God. Though one may reject the man Jesus, who matches Isaiah's profile of Israel's God, his teachings are still "good news." Though we may relegate Isaiah to antiquity, his writings are still "good news" and relevant to today. From both we learn that the tests people faced anciently will recur at the end of the world. In that case, could a similar situation occur as happened in the past? Could God's people today reject the higher law by turning popular religion into another Golden Calf? Could one who "comes in the name of the Lord" again be put to death?

True religion isn't a display like the Golden Calf. It is unpretentiously performed at home, in the work place, and in acts of kindness done in secret. So, too, true worship isn't just an emotional exercise but "compliance" with God's law and word. No one worships God so well as he or she who, with unwavering "loyalty" to God, ascends the ladder all the way to heaven. Such souls, God receives into his presence to dwell with him and with sibling celestial beings in everlasting joy. As we discard man-made precepts and traditions and follow divine directives, God will again perform the miracles he did of old. The pure religion God founded for humanity's happiness unfailingly fulfills its purpose:

"Then will your light break through like the dawn, and your healing will speedily appear; your righteousness will go before you, and the glory of Jehovah will be your rearguard. Then, should you call, Jehovah will respond; should you cry, he will say, 'I am here.' Indeed, if you will banish servitude from among you, and the pointing finger and offensive speech, if you will give of your own to the hungry and satisfy the needs of the oppressed, then will your light dawn amid darkness and your twilight become as the noonday. Jehovah will direct you continually; he will satisfy your needs in the dearth and bring vigor to your limbs. And you will become like a well-watered garden" (Isaiah 58:8–11).

Pure Religion Answers Life's Tough Questions

A person who allows God's law and word to operate in his life cannot help but grow into an awareness of the purpose of life. As you ascend the ladder it becomes evident how all aspects of human nature, good and evil, interrelate. Your outlook changes to where you can contemplate the whole panorama of experience and comprehend that all of it, in fact, is good, that even the bad can lead to good when we see it through God's eyes. Such a person will know that because God is good, absolute evil cannot exist—that God didn't create or sponsor it, but that good and evil are only manifestations of his blessing or curse. Where curses occur, they serve primarily to persuade us to repent and return.

Jesus followed his own rule when he said "Resist not evil!" in submitting himself to unrighteous judgment. He turned the evil that people imposed on him to good by atoning for humanity's transgressions and reversing the curse of death. Those on the highest levels follow him by drinking from the bitter cup of divine justice. Whether a curse that afflicts you is a consequence of your own or another's transgressions, the only way to get rid of it is to take ownership of it and see it through to the end. Proxy saviors, who, on behalf of others, seek God's intervention or deliverance from mortal danger, follow God's pattern of making amends for the misdeeds of those for whom they intercede.

We should remember, however, that people under a curse such as famine, pestilence, bondage, and invasion have at some point brought such retribution on themselves by their own transgressions, often over generations of breaking God's law. Yet, the prophets remind us that God is kind and long-suffering, that the curses of the covenant, although a consequence of wickedness, can be reversed by righteousness. But we must accept words like "righteousness" and "wickedness" by God's definition of these terms, not the world's, which regards as acceptable what to God is detestable. In short, reversing a curse requires special circumstances, mostly involving a proxy savior's intercession.

Because God is good, absolute evil cannot exist.

We often hear the protests of indigenous peoples who have been trodden underfoot by foreign invaders. Ethnic groups of Native Americans, for example, have ardently demanded redress. But when Europeans first came to Central America, thousands of human sacrifices were routinely offered on pyramid temples, desecrating sites of worship that were possibly once sacred. North American tribes were locked in perpetual feuds, committing atrocity after atrocity without consideration of their common humanity. Still, the curse of God that pursues a people can, in the end, turn into a blessing—God can reverse it. Then, if their oppressors persist in their persecutions, the curse could overtake *them*.

How will God reverse covenant curses in the "last days"? Isaiah predicts that kings and queens of the Gentiles will minister as foster fathers and nursing mothers and intercede with God on behalf of his people in their lost and alienated state. When "ruin," "punishment," "suffering," "humiliation," and "disinheritance" finally influence his people to put away their wickedness, to return to their roots and rediscover the God of their fathers, then God appoints his sons/servants and seraphs/saviors to minister his law and word to them so they may again enjoy the blessings of the covenant. Pure religion, therefore, not politics, brings "rebirth," "deliverance," "salvation," "exaltation," and "inheritance."

Isaiah's endtime scenario is marked by a proliferation of false teachers and rejection of the true: "Their heart ponders impiety: how to practice hypocrisy and preach perverse things concerning Jehovah, leaving the hungry soul empty, depriving the thirsty [soul] of drink" (Isaiah 32:6); "[They] say to the seers, 'See not!' and to those with visions, 'Predict not what is right for us; flatter us: foresee a farce!'" (Isaiah 30:10). False prophets, against whom Jesus warned, take it upon themselves to speak and act in God's name (Isaiah 9:15; 28:7). God's answer it to "call" and "appoint" his servant and his associates to restore his pure law and word so that he may bless his people (Isaiah 42:1–7; 62:6–9).

Many people ask how God could have let millions of Jews, Gypsies, and Slavs perish in the Nazi Holocaust. One might additionally ask whether Moses didn't predict these things when he enumerated the blessings and curses of God's covenant (Deuteronomy 28). Before the Babylonians destroyed Jerusalem and its temple, Jeremiah confronted God's people with having "changed gods," violating the terms of the covenant. Still, in both cases God brought good out of evil. Jews learned to appreciate what they had lost. The Holocaust dispelled much of the enmity that existed between Jew and Gentile, softening the feelings of Christians enough for world leaders to approve a Jewish state in Palestine.

A purely political mandate doesn't guarantee permanence.

A purely political mandate, however, doesn't guarantee permanence in a Promised Land. For the descendants of Abraham, Isaac, and Jacob to inherit the land of their fathers in Moses' day, God required that they *themselves* keep his law and word. As God hasn't changed, that is still the case. The Jews repossessing Palestine after an absence of two thousand years was an answer to the prayers and righteous lives of generations of the three tribes of Israel who principally comprised the kingdom of Judah—Judah, Benjamin, and Levi. But because permanence is possible only by observing the terms of God's covenant, that leaves an important element in God's formula for peace still to be accounted for.

As we learn the lessons God and history teach us, we can start reversing the world's curses by turning our own "ruin" into "rebirth," "punishment" into "deliverance," "suffering" into "salvation," etc., by living God's law. We can influence and inspire those around us by ministering to them physically and spiritually. We can watch for the signs of the times that alert us to the prophesied new versions of old events, signaling God's opening of the heavens. The ascent of many in that day will cause the enmity between Christian, Jew, and Moslem to dissipate like the dews of Hermon. The battle for the birthright will turn in a more fruitful direction as all seek to serve God by serving one another.

If our earth was born out of the debris of a mighty star that exploded as a nova or supernova—thereby giving life to its offspring—and if, as Isaiah teaches, those who ascend become stars, members of a celestial family, then our destiny is to assist in the earth's ongoing creation by raising its vibration to the

level from which it came (see Figure 141). To do so, we must
live a higher law. The mighty star or stars that gave us birth
had themselves gone through such a transformation. Jesus had
attained "glory" with the Most High God "before the world was
[made]" (John 17:5). His star—a nova or supernova?—wasn't the
only one the wise men saw when he was born, though it was
his star.

Figure 141   **The Earth's Journey to Exaltation**

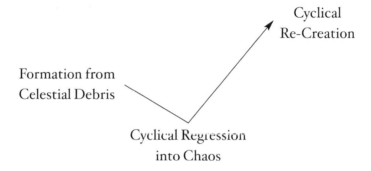

All the good we do in the world, therefore, forms an
essential part of God's plan to redeem this earth from its fallen
state, to raise it to its primordial frequency by our spiritual
and physical struggles. Toward that goal, every creature has a
role to play. God foreordained that, together with himself, we
would create a new world out of chaos, by our blood, sweat,
and tears making it an everlasting "inheritance" for ourselves
and our descendants. The new heavens and new earth God
has destined us to inherit—where there is no more need of
the sun to give light—testify of the earth's attaining that
exaltation (Isaiah 60:19–20; 66:22). Its transformation into a
new Paradise is the exciting first step.

The very destiny of the earth, of God's covenant people, and
of us as individuals is thus linked within an organic process in
which all who ascend the ladder ultimately meet in a heaven on

earth, a place where God resides and where all know him. The earth's rite of passage—as God re-creates it and it ascends from one phase to the next—is inextricably linked to and dependent on the personal rites of passage of its inhabitants as they individually live the higher law of God and he re-creates them in his image and likeness. When a sufficient number fulfills its divine destiny as sons and daughters of God, God makes the earth itself a "celestial" environment from which they may ascend higher still.

Reaching Out in Love Is the Vehicle for Ascent

Individually speaking, a percentage of God's children appear ruined, punished, suffering, etc., from birth or from sustaining misfortune early in life. Of a man born blind, whom Jesus healed, his disciples asked "Who has sinned, this man or his parents?" Jesus answered "Neither . . . but that the works of God might be manifest in him." The disciples understood the curse to be a result of transgression, though it didn't originate in the immediate family. Jesus took ownership of the curse and reversed it. In that instance the man who had been blind saw, but those who saw were blinded (John 9:1–3, 39). Even as the blind man was reborn, delivered, saved, and so forth, so his accusers met the opposite fate.

> Although all have the same chance to ascend, not all do so alike.

But what would have happened if Jesus had not healed the man? He would have continued like countless other souls born with disabilities, cast upon the mercies of their fellow human beings. To all appearances their "descent before ascent" would take an entire lifetime without a choice in the matter. But that would be drawing a conclusion about something of which we know very little. Rather, Isaiah's model of a ladder to heaven, which is based on the principle of our agency to *choose*, suggests that such "unfortunate souls" would most likely have consented to the nature of their descent before assuming life in this mortal state. Although all have the same chance to ascend, not all do so alike.

In other words, such are special spirits indeed, who have accepted physical "ruin," "punishment," "suffering," "humiliation," and "disinheritance" as their whole lot in life. Only in the next life—at their resurrection—may they experience "rebirth," "deliverance," "salvation," "exaltation," and "inheritance," physically speaking (see Figure 142). Their spiritual descent before ascent would still happen cyclically, *aided* by their physical disability, depending on how they handled their hardships while actually experiencing them. Some have greater difficulty dealing with limitations than others. Conversely, a few, like Helen Keller, who became both blind and deaf, excel in turning misfortune on its head.

Figure 142   **Mortality Itself as Descent before Ascent**

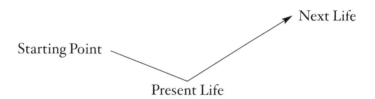

Helen Keller attributed her astounding success to Anne Sullivan, who, as a little girl, had lived like a caged animal in a Boston mental institution. Doctors had given her up as a "hopeless case" and ignored her. Sullivan, in turn, was aided by an aging nurse who went outside her line of duty in loving and befriending the girl. Instead of living and dying in her dark cell, Anne Sullivan rose above her "insanity" and assisted others at the institution to deal with their disabilities. In the light of Isaiah's ladder to heaven, that story is a classic example of ministering and being ministered to of fairytale proportions. Thousands of souls received hope and new help on account of Helen Keller's accomplishments.

But what do we suppose would have happened if that one individual had not gone out of her way to minister to another? What a travesty is happening today as parents of handicapped children hand them over to indifferent institutions! In many cases, not only do they pass up their own opportunity to ascend by ministering to a child who needs a larger measure of parental love than the rest, they may cause the child to abort its rebirth, being so abandoned. God arranges special circumstances for us to ascend, which, if we ignore, may not come around in life a second time. How great, then, will be our regret when we face our eternal future, knowing we neglected its best prospect for happiness!

Of course, that scenario repeats itself in many less serious instances. If only we could recognize our challenges as an opportunity for rising higher, that such descent can mean ascent when we truly accept our circumstances. Reaching out in love—unconditional love—is the epitome of keeping God's law and word on every level of the ladder. The inverse is also true: "If you love me, keep my commandments," and, "If a man loves me, he will keep my words" (John 14:15, 23). As Isaiah notes, "It is the will of Jehovah that . . . [his people] magnify the law and become illustrious." Says God, "So is the word that leaves my mouth. . . it achieves the purpose for which I sent it" (Isaiah 42:21; 55:11).

Reaching out in love is keeping God's law and word.

We don't need to focus on the saddest cases of suffering to realize that our entire mortal experience is a descent that can lead to ascent, for everyone, not just those most disadvantaged. When God cast Adam and Eve out of the Garden of Eden for transgressing his word and *cursed* the ground "for their sake," he gave them and their descendants the chance to rise higher by passing through trials, using such hardships to further their advancement. Still, they had more than mortality to deal with. How high we ascend is determined by how we conduct our lives. Knowing that God is our partner throughout our earthly experience, however, makes our lives tolerable if not always pleasurable.

God seeks after his people at all times and in all places in their adversity, even when they forsake him. God's servants also reach out to them, though people may reject them too. If God and his holy ones, who serve as our role models, take love to the limit, should not his people likewise love God with all their heart, might, mind, and strength, and their neighbor as themselves? By giving us these two great commandments, God is saying that nothing short of that will achieve his goal for us; nothing less works if we want to experience "salvation" *and* "exaltation." There is no other way to ascend to heaven. We may imagine an easier path, even preach it to one another, but it will not take us there.

To the degree that we reach up to God in love, he ministers down to us, his children, inspiring us with his Spirit and sending his servants into our lives. Heaven and earth meet when we receive those whom God "calls" and "appoints" to minister in his name. As we respond positively to God's love, we learn how to serve others more effectively. Our confidence increases the more we live the truth and participate in the synergy of God's *oneness*. Being "partakers of the divine nature" may become a reality here on earth. When God re-creates us as his sons and daughters and fills us with his holy Spirit, that is when people acknowledge "Surely God is in you; no other gods exist" (Isaiah 45:14).

Covenant Keeping Is a Key to Spiritual Ascent

What do all ascending levels of the ladder have in common? Making and keeping covenants with God. God interacts with his servants and people through covenant relationships. If we want to succeed with God, therefore, we must do things his way. He has determined beforehand the terms or laws of the covenant that aid our ascent. He has also excluded other formulas for climbing the ladder, even if they differ only a little from his own. In short, there is just one path into God's presence—his path. His covenants with his people benefit all who keep them. He is the benefactor and we are the recipients of his blessings. By keeping our commitments we rise above our current level to a higher one.

A covenant agreement is the best arrangement in divine–human and human–human relationships because it defines the nature of the relationship so that everyone knows where he or she stands. Once the parties to a covenant accept its terms, it is binding on all. Those who keep the terms of the covenant profit from the relationship, while those who break them forfeit its blessings. As God never breaks a covenant he makes, it isn't God but we who suffer from violating its terms. Civilization itself is evidence of the stability and prosperity of a society that honors its covenants, political or religious, and of the instability and impoverishment of an anarchical one. It is a measure of any society today.

There is one path into God's presence—his path.

Israel's history illustrates both ends of the covenant spectrum—its best blessings and worst curse—with the blessings of the covenant destined to win in the end. But let us suppose you were God and had a plan to save and exalt your children. How would you implement it? Would you commence covenant communities all over the world and then hope all goes well, trusting they wouldn't envy and compete with each other, each claiming God favored it above the rest? Or would you start with one man—Abraham—and make a covenant with him and his descendants, trusting he would pass on his divine heritage to them, himself being an example of the benefits of such a relationship with God?

After Abraham had passed tests of loyalty, and God was about to save Lot out of Sodom for Abraham's sake, God said "Abraham will surely become a great and mighty nation, and all nations on the earth will be blessed because of him. . . . For I know him, that he will charge his children and his household after him to keep the way of Jehovah by doing what is right and just, so that Jehovah may bring upon Abraham what he has promised him" (Genesis 18:18–19; 19:29). Abraham's example to his posterity would be the type of Israel's example to the nations of the world. God's intent was that the nations would see his people's prosperity and come into the covenant God had made (see Figure 143).

Figure 143   **God's Telescoping Plan of Salvation for the World**

Abraham ⟶ Israel ⟶ Nations of the World

Israel became "illustrious" in the days of Moses and Joshua, and David and Solomon, winning converts to God's covenant. Even in times of national decline, however, *individuals* could still climb the ladder by living God's law, just as Elijah did. In person-to-person relationships such as marriage, if one spouse breaks the covenant, causing the other to suffer the consequence, the first's faithfulness to its terms may still enable him or her to ascend. What counts with God is whether his people demonstrate "loyalty" to him and to each other. In Ezekiel's day, God declared a curse on Jews who broke a covenant they had made with Nebuchadnezzar, king of Babylon—their enemy! (Ezekiel 17:11–21).

Some covenants cannot aid ascent. A vow of celibacy made before God, for example, while it may serve the preaching of God's word today as in Paul's day, prevents ascent beyond a certain point. Given the choice, one can't ascend without a spouse to the son/servant level. In such cases God may mercifully release the covenanter from a vow made in ignorance that didn't conform to God's pattern of ascent. But God still requires him or her to undertake the annulment with discretion; it *was* a sacred vow. Symptomatic of modern society's descent to the Babylon level is covenant breaking. The casual cancellation of marriage vows, for example, has become almost as common as covenant making.

Because we no longer revere the sanctity of the marriage covenant, the foundation of civilization that is built on divine law has begun to disintegrate. How we relate to our spouse and offspring is a reliable indicator of how we relate to God. Do we regard them as sacred, our top priority? Or do we betray them, withholding our love and tender devotion? As the family is a microcosm of our relationship with the rest of humanity—for good or evil, for blessing or curse—the home is where we most show our "loyalty" to God, where we visibly display our "compliance" with his will (see Figure 144). God provides a pattern of covenant love for his wife, the Woman Zion, and for us his errant children.

In contrast to the iniquity we generate by breaking covenants, and the sorrows we heap on the rising generation, through *keeping* God's covenants we free ourselves from dysfunctions and bring renewed happiness. Our "compliance" leads to levels of blessedness of which those who go back on their "loyalty" have no notion. When we pass every test, and our covenant becomes unconditional, God blesses us and our descendants through endless ages as he did Abraham. We can thus be a power for incalculable good just as we can for untold evil. We can make ourselves God's enemy or make God our best friend. God can lift us up to where he lives or hurl us to hell to dwell with fellow felons.

Figure 144   **The Family as a Microcosm of Covenant Love**

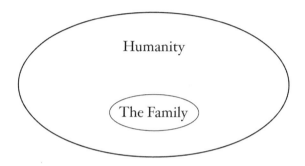

What sets the believer apart are supplications to God. God laments that his people don't talk to him: "You do not call upon me, O Jacob; you have grown weary of me, O Israel" (Isaiah 43:22). On the other hand, many who *do* importune God haven't repented of evil: "When you spread forth your hands, I will conceal my eyes from you; though you pray at length, I will not hear—your hands are filled with blood" (Isaiah 1:15). But Isaiah declares "Inquire of Jehovah while he is present; call upon him while he is near. Let the wicked forsake their ways and sinful men their thoughts. Let them return to Jehovah, and he will have mercy on them; to our God, who graciously pardons" (Isaiah 55:6–7).

All who are loyal and compliant God accepts, Israelite or proselyte: "The foreigners who adhere to Jehovah to serve him, who love the name of Jehovah, that they may be his servants—all who keep the Sabbath without profaning it, holding fast to my covenant—these will I bring to my holy mountain and gladden in my house of prayer. Their offerings and sacrifices will be accepted on my altar, for my house will be known as a

355

house of prayer for all nations" (Isaiah 56:6–7); "I will make with them an everlasting covenant: their offspring will be renowned among the nations, their posterity in the midst of the peoples" (Isaiah 61:8–9). God blesses all who serve him as he blessed his servants of old.

Covenant keeping with God is the sole guarantee we have of overcoming curses. Although humans are a compound of godly and ungodly, with tendencies to do evil equal to those of doing good, God has determined that we need never yield to evil but can continually cleave to good. God proves all who covenant with him in his own way and in his own time, and we mustn't downplay the test when it comes. There is surety in "holding fast to [God's] covenant," as God gives the victory to those who do. The joy of the saints—all who overcome evil—will in large measure consist of their common covenant bond, knowing that all who set foot through heaven's gate have fought the same fight.

Postscript: The end of a book and I have written only a poor apology of what Isaiah's ladder is about. Getting through the gate is such a personal journey I wonder if people will catch on? What an irony that religious codependency can *prevent* us from knowing God. Although God sends his servants to minister to us, and we honor them, in the end we answer to God not to them, much less to lower levels and those whom God hasn't sent. Having partaken of a poisoned apple, many live in a spiritually altered state. As Tevia asked of popular practice in *Fiddler on the Roof*, "Tradition, tradition. . . . But how did this tradition get started?" How indeed?

When ascending to heaven, finding your direction is crucial or you could end up in the wrong place. God has factored that hazard into our quest or ascent would be easy. He counsels us "Ask and you will receive. Seek and you will find. Knock and it will be opened to you." How else can a person approach God, having no idea what God is like? He or she buys into a creed that advocates one thing only to find out years later that the truth lies somewhere else. God knows that sorting out the true God from the flawed versions of him can be a big obstacle in taking one's first steps up the ladder, not to mention course corrections along the way.

People honest about themselves, who endeavor to make peace with God—who pass Isaiah's "third test of loyalty"—may thus wade through darkness in the short term but shine in the long term. Like a star that forms when matter collapses and caves in on itself, they may go through times of intense compression, but when fusion finally begins all is bright. They are their own proof of God. If this book renews our optimism about the divine purpose of life, if we draw nearer to God from reading it, then my reason for writing it will have been served. May we say "Thank God" for our lot in life, but of sin and transgression, "Enough already."